T0392903

Interrelationships Between Sport and the Arts

This multidisciplinary collection examines different dimensions of the interrelationships between sport and the arts. It is a consequence of the Fields of Vision initiative that challenges their typical separation into distinct realms. Whether at school or in the highest realms of public life people struggle to reconcile the two; they lack the necessary conceptual vocabulary. Worse, there are entrenched positions characterised by mutual suspicion, distrust and denigration. In contrast, the contributors to this book challenge the creativity/competition binary and highlight the potential for collaboration in theoretical discourse, policy, education and professional practice. In doing so, the authors draw strength from the Olympian ethos of the Greeks and the vision of the founder of the modern Olympic movement, Pierre de Coubertin. The book seeks to 'problematise, interrogate and provoke'. The papers shed new light on sport and the arts as representations of cultural identity and embodying processes of social change.

This book is a significant new contribution to understanding both sports and the arts, not just in their separate contexts, but also in amalgam. It represents a valuable resource for researchers and advanced students of Sports, Visual Art, Literature, History, Sociology, Social Theory and Cultural Studies. It was originally published as a special issue of *Sport in Society*.

Jonathan Long is an emeritus professor with the Institute for Sport, Physical Activity and Leisure at Leeds Beckett University, UK. For over 40 years he has been researching the role that the many aspects of leisure have within society. His work has an emphasis on social justice and social change.

Doug Sandle is a visiting research fellow, Institute for Sport, Physical Activity and Leisure, Leeds Beckett University, UK. He was the instigator of the Fields of Vision initiative that led to a programme of events that over a decade explored the relationship between the arts and sport.

Sport in the Global Society: Contemporary Perspectives

Series Editor: **Boria Majumdar**, *University of Central Lancashire, UK*

The social, cultural (including media) and political study of sport is an expanding area of scholarship and related research. While this area has been well served by the *Sport in the Global Society* series, the surge in quality scholarship over the last few years has necessitated the creation of *Sport in the Global Society: Contemporary Perspectives*. The series will publish the work of leading scholars in fields as diverse as sociology, cultural studies, media studies, gender studies, cultural geography and history, political science and political economy. If the social and cultural study of sport is to receive the scholarly attention and readership it warrants, a cross-disciplinary series dedicated to taking sport beyond the narrow confines of physical education and sport science academic domains is necessary. *Sport in the Global Society: Contemporary Perspectives* will answer this need.

Sport, Outdoor Life and the Nordic World
Edited by Nils Asle Bergsgard, Solfrid Bratland-Sanda, Richard Giulianotti and Jan Ove Tangen

The Ultras
A Global Football Fan Phenomenon
Edited by Mark Doidge and Martin Lieser

The 1935 Australian Cricket Tour of India
Breaking Down Social and Racial Barriers
Megan Ponsford

The Potential of Community Sport for Social Inclusion
Exploring Cases Across the Globe
Edited by Hebe Schaillée, Reinhard Haudenhuyse and Lieve Bradt

The Professionalization of Action Sports
The Changing Roles of Athletes, Industry and Media
Edited by Guillaume Dumont and Holly Thorpe

Interrelationships Between Sport and the Arts
Edited by Jonathan Long and Doug Sandle

For more information about this series, please visit:
www.routledge.com/Sport-in-the-Global-Society--Contemporary-Perspectives/book-series/SGSC

Interrelationships Between Sport and the Arts

Edited by
Jonathan Long and Doug Sandle

Routledge
Taylor & Francis Group

LONDON AND NEW YORK

First published 2023
by Routledge
4 Park Square, Milton Park, Abingdon, Oxon OX14 4RN

and by Routledge
605 Third Avenue, New York, NY 10158

Routledge is an imprint of the Taylor & Francis Group, an informa business

British Library Cataloguing in Publication Data
A catalogue record for this book is available from the British Library

ISBN13: 978-1-032-35038-7 (hbk)
ISBN13: 978-1-032-35040-0 (pbk)
ISBN13: 978-1-003-32497-3 (ebk)

DOI: 10.4324/9781003324973

Typeset in Minion Pro
by Newgen Publishing UK

Publisher's Note
The publisher accepts responsibility for any inconsistencies that may have arisen during the conversion of this book from journal articles to book chapters, namely the inclusion of journal terminology.

Disclaimer
Every effort has been made to contact copyright holders for their permission to reprint material in this book. The publishers would be grateful to hear from any copyright holder who is not here acknowledged and will undertake to rectify any errors or omissions in future editions of this book.

Contents

Citation Information

The chapters in this book were originally published in the journal *Sport in Society*, volume 22, issue 5 (2019). When citing this material, please use the original page numbering for each article, as follows:

For any permission-related enquiries please visit:
www.tandfonline.com/page/help/permissions

Notes on Contributors

Stephen Carl Arch, Department of English, Michigan State University, East Lansing, MI, USA.

Franco Bianchini, Culture, Place and Policy Institute, University of Hull, Hull, UK.

D. Chatziefstathiou, School of Human and Life Sciences, Canterbury Christ Church University, Canterbury, UK.

Lynn Froggett, Psychosocial Welfare, University of Central Lancashire, Preston, UK.

E. Iliopoulou, Department of Economic and Regional Development, Panteion University, Athens, Greece.

Jonathan Long, Emeritus Professor, Institute for Sport, Physical Activity and Leisure, Leeds Beckett University, Leeds, UK.

M. Magkou, Institute of Leisure Studies, University of Deusto, Bilbao, Spain.

Stephen Mumford, Deputy Head of Department/Curriculum Officer, Department of Philosophy, Durham University, Durham, UK.

Mike O'Mahony, History of Art Department, University of Bristol, Bristol, UK.

Cătălin Parfene, Ecole des Hautes Etudes en Sciences Sociales, Paris, France.

Doug Sandle, is a visiting research fellow, Institute for Sport, Physical Activity and Leisure, Leeds Beckett University, Leeds, UK.

Christopher B. Stride, IWP, SUMS, University of Sheffield, Sheffield, UK.

Matti Tainio, Faculty of Art and Design, University of Lapland, Rovaniemi, Finland.

Kai Syng Tan, Social, Genetic and Developmental Psychiatry (SGDP), Institute of Psychiatry, Psychology and Neuroscience, King's College London, London, UK.

Layne Vandenberg, Yenching Academy, Peking University, Beijing, China.

Investigating the interrelationships between sport and the arts

Jonathan Long and Doug Sandle

The fields of vision sport/arts initiative

This volume is one of the outputs arising from the *Fields of Vision* initiative. Previously there have been a number of seminars around the UK, a conference and subsequent publication of papers (Sandle et al. 2013), a manifesto,[1] several exhibitions, a film screening and even a revue.

Fields of Vision started because its founders identified their shared interest in both sport and the arts even though they are thought of so separately in the fields of education, philosophy, research, policy and provision and people excelling in one are not expected to excel, or even show interest, in the other. Transgressive exceptions are remarkable because they are exceptions. One of the first goals for *Fields of Vision* was to locate other transgressors and bring together practitioners and policy-makers in dialogue with scholars and researchers to create a shared understanding of the benefits of co-operation. The resultant network examined the potential economic, social and cultural benefits from bringing together sport and the arts, and has sought to foster interdisciplinary work by scholars and researchers and collaborations with practitioners and policy-makers. Now, of course, sport and the arts, like other leisure and social practices, may be used to exercise social control. Both worlds are social constructions contributing to hegemonic relationships. For example, Doyle (2009, 4) observes:

> It is tempting to think that Art and Sport sleep in separate beds … we tend to imagine these worlds as separate spheres, in which sport is fully masculine, and art is coded socially as effeminate.

However, we contend that at the very least they represent sites of resistance as well as repression.

We started from the proposition that there are links between the arts and sport which can help to increase participation in each and promote cultural citizenship. Some social groups with lower income and educational levels are often put off by the air of exclusivity and high 'cultural capital' requirements of traditional arts activities. Equally, it seemed plausible that the arts could play a role in changing the sporting experience and widening audiences for sport by communicating alternative messages about what sport is. We also wanted to explore the collaborations between sport and the arts which can stimulate cultural experimentation and take a fresh look at the aesthetics of sport, as well as look at the potential benefits to physical and mental well-being of greater collaboration, which might address problems generated by modern lifestyles.

Different worlds coming together

The cover of the earlier collection of papers (Sandle et al. 2013) features an artwork by Jason Minsky, who, in 2007, was artist in residence to Leeds Rugby and Headingley Carnegie Stadium, home of the rugby league team, Leeds Rhinos, the rugby union team Yorkshire Carnegie and also Yorkshire Cricket. Using a variety of media and processes he endeavoured to capture the life of a stadium that hosts three different sports on its adjacent international standard rugby and cricket pitches, and the presence of a double sided stand. For example, his large photomontage diptych, 'Over the Garden Fence' features both close-up and distant views of a perplexed captain of Leeds Rhinos (the rugby league team) standing on the rugby pitch, rubbing his head and holding up a cricket ball. The other panel shows the captain of the Yorkshire County Cricket team standing on the adjoining cricket pitch bemusedly holding a rugby ball. He thereby evokes childhood memories of back street games and 'please can we have our ball back'. More importantly in the current context, in highlighting the unique nature of the stadium he draws attention to the uncomprehending distance between sports separated by a matter of a few yards, in just the same way as we are confused by the lack of understanding between the realms of sport and the arts despite their being part of the same government ministry (see Long and Bianchini in this volume). Taking a more international perspective, Jahn (2006, 17) suspects that at least since the 1990s, the relationship between the two has been one of 'mutual scepticism or lack of interest'.

The screening presented by *Fields of Vision* was the film of David Storey's book, *This Sporting Life*. Although he straddled the worlds of sport and the arts (playing rugby league for Leeds Reserves while studying at the prestigious Slade School of Fine Art in London), Storey reflected on how uncomfortable this was: 'being perceived as an effete art student made the dressing room a very uncomfortable place for me' and 'at the Slade meanwhile I was seen as bit of an oaf' (Collins 2013, 53). There are of course others prepared to engage with both sport and the arts. For example, at one of the Fields of Vision exhibitions (ceramic sculptures by artist Mandy Long, which explored physicality and human movement in sport), the running coach of Olympic medal holders the Brownlee Brothers observed: 'Excellent – every sports stadium should have an art gallery'.

While there are contemporary artists following the example of the ancient Greeks in producing art work in response to sport, and some major sporting events such as the Great North Run that celebrates running with an accompanying arts programme, these are inspiring exceptions. However, as contemporary artists increasingly use a diverse range of media, such as video, performance and installation, opportunities exist not just to represent and celebrate sport but for critique and issue-based work that questions and interrogates aspects of sport practice and its culture. Perhaps too, the greatest opportunity for synthesis lies with new arts practices (like poetry slams and graffiti) and sports (like skateboarding or free running). The papers in this volume not only highlight the potential for greater collaboration and interdisciplinarity between the arts and sport in theoretical discourse, social and cultural policy, education and professional practice, but also present opportunities giving some optimism for the future.

The papers

Within the complex context of historical debates on the aesthetic nature of sport and its relationship to art (e.g. Best 1974, [1985] 1988; Whiting and Masterson 1974) and extending his own work, such as on spectator's engagement with sport (Mumford 2011), *Stephen Mumford* argues here that sport cannot be an art as such and that the two are fundamentally distinctive. However, he argues for 'the special nature of the sporting aesthetic' and that while the aim in sport is to compete, rather than the production of aesthetic value, competition in sport is at least part of the explanation of its aesthetics. He establishes three features of sport: competition, indeterminism and emergent holism in relation to team sports. These lead to sport's distinctive aesthetic. One of his points is that the distinctiveness of sport and the arts resides in their being subject to different historically evolving institutional processes. While sport may not be 'art', nonetheless it does have 'a special and distinctive aesthetic role, providing an experience for the viewer that cannot be found elsewhere'.

Jonathan Long and *Franco Bianchini* demonstrate and bemoan the separation between sport and art in their respective UK and England strategies and identify a paucity of 'intercultural mediators'. They consider this somewhat counterproductive given the similar social remit given to the arts and to sport with regard to health and well-being, education, employment, countering crime, cohesion and inclusion. Fortunately, despite the separation at the national level, they see more hope in what is happening at the local. Having offered their critique of existing strategies, they then identify the potential that is not being fully realized and suggest policies that might help to secure that.

Bringing art and sport together has the potential to extend audiences for both and lead to positive outcomes for promotion, community programmes, public relations and funding. However, *Lynn Froggett* is looking for more. The evaluation her team conducted of the *imove* component of the Cultural Olympiad identified different forms of project that combined sport and the arts, from those that are simply 'additive' to others that are 'interactive' (combining to produce something novel) and 'transformative' (professionals dependent on participants to develop completely new cultural forms). In light of this, Froggett considers the potential for 'transcending dualities of mind/body and art/sport' in the creation of 'third space' in the search for a new language with which to discuss the relationship (akin to the emergence of sci-art).

Stephen Arch challenges the Cartesian dualism of a mind–body split, certainly insofar as it relates to sport as an embodied practice. Using literary narratives about sport to explore embodied subjectivity and their representation of the sporting self he reveals how the self is transformed through athletic training and competition. The literary skills of the authors allow them to do more than simply describe sporting experience, and come closer to the felt/lived experience through inclination, repetition and habit that achieves deep physical, emotional and psychic transformation. This serves to create an aesthetic appreciation of the beauty of sport for participant and spectator alike.

Recognizing the coincidence of the emergence of modern sport and photography, *Mike O'Mahony* examines how they came together despite the technological limitations of the medium in its early years. He shows how the visual vocabularies that were deployed generated new visual conventions. In part because of the technological limitations 'artistry and artifice' were used to produce fine examples of sports photography. Although initially limited to traditional forms of portraiture and posed shots intended to represent sporting action, the composite technique was used to compensate for the inability to capture the movement central to the practice of sport.

Rather than photographs, *Chris Stride and Layne Vandenberg* analyse the way sporting statues represent values. In this case, it is how footballing statues in China uphold cultural and political values such as the primacy of hard work, learning and saving face in defeat. At the same time, they are required to support China's efforts to integrate itself into global football and win the right to host (and win) the FIFA World Cup. The tension between the popularity of football locally and the lack of success of the national team has produced statues that represent anonymous figures and tackling scenes rather than celebrating individual stars.

Running is one of the sports that has aroused the interest of those writing about aesthetics (Martin 2007). Here, *Kai Syng Tan* and *Matti Tainio* both draw upon running to discuss socio-cultural aspects of sport and human movement. In her paper, *Tan* provides an account of the RUN! RUN! RUN! Biennial programme as an interdisciplinary discourse, using creative methodology, metaphor and arts practice. Discussing the wider cultural and social questions raised by the programme, her paper challenges existing assumptions in the arts about sport and highlights the sociocultural context of running and its use as political act of defiance. Individual experiential aspects of running are used alongside examples from the RUN! RUN! RUN! programme to argue for a closer understanding and synergy between arts and running. Tan concludes by asserting that 'works of art that have continued to intrigue are not those that provide the answers, but those that problematise, interrogate, and provoke'.

Tainio maintains that aesthetic aspects of sport are neglected and marginalized compared with physical aspects of human movement that can be measured and quantified statistically. Acknowledging the historical context of such a bias he argues that this hegemony can nonetheless be challenged and modified by newer sports practices and social trends. His argument is that sport and its 'corporeal openness, enjoyment and creativity' are part of an aesthetic experience that can produce positive life effects and have an obvious social impact on what is referred to as 'post-sport practices'. He concludes that the aesthetics of physical movement widens our understanding of contemporary culture, which if embraced would result in a more inclusive physical culture involving a wider range of activities and experiences.

In a very different literary project from Arch, *Cătălin Parfene* considers the opus of the Romanian writer, Camil Petrescu, who used his literary skills to advance the cause of securing an ethnically pure national football team as part of the construction of the culture of the new Romania between the two world wars. Regarded in Romania as the founder of the modern novel, Petrescu argued persistently for Romanianization of the national football team by removing the representatives of ethnic minorities (mainly Hungarian and German) even if this meant the team losing its matches. In case readers need reminding, like the statues considered by Stride and Vandenberg, this crusade against foreigners highlights the political ramifications of both arts and sports.

Using the example of *Urban Dig* in Athens, *Dikaia Chatziefstathiou, Eirini Iliopoulou* and *Matina Magkou* assess the contribution of the kind of local initiative referred to by Long and Bianchini. *Urban Dig* uses sport and the arts together to facilitate community development.

At the same time it serves to illustrate one of Froggett's themes, with the authors arguing that 'sports and art can compose a common cultural language' and that this represents a tool for communities to 'co-create urban space'. The project offers an illustration of how these sports-art representations and practices can be used in participatory-planning in re-imagining the production of space.

Coda

The full title of the journal, *Sport in Society: Cultures, Commerce, Media, Politics*, demonstrates how suitable a location it is for this collection of papers. Just as the members of the Fields of Vision network itself, the contributors to this collection come from a broad range of disciplinary backgrounds: aesthetics, community development, cultural studies, history, international relations, leisure studies, literature, sociology, philosophy, policy analysis and psychology. Like the works of art that Tan prizes, we believe that these papers 'problematise, interrogate, and provoke'. They shed new light on sport and the arts as representations of cultural identity embodying processes of social change. Despite the conceptual distance that has been put between these two social constructions it is clear, as demonstrated by these papers, that there are initiatives that show how these barriers between sports and arts can be hurdled. That kind of appreciation is not just the preserve of scholars writing in academic journals. A visitor to one of the Fields of Vision exhibitions commented:

> Inspirational: It's a celebration of movement and physical expression. Sport should not purely be about the outcome. How we physically interact with our environment is such an integral part of who we are. We must never take that for granted. Thank you

Note

1. To read this common declaration of principles and practice and find out about becoming a signatory, please go to the Fields of Vison web site: https://artsinsport.wordpress.com/a-manifesto-for-the-arts-and-sport-together/.

Disclosure statement

No potential conflict of interest was reported by the authors.

References

Best, D. 1974. "The Aesthetic in Sport." *The British Journal of Aesthetics* 14: 197–213. doi:10.1093/bjaesthetics/14.3.197

Best, D. (1985) 1988. "Sport is Not Art." In *Philosophic Inquiry in Sport*, edited by W. Morgan and K. Meier, 527–539. Champaign, IL: Human Kinetics.

Collins, T. 2013. "Sex Class and the Critique in Lindsay Anderson's This Sporting Life." In *Fields of Vision: The Arts in Sport*, edited by D. Sandle, J. Long, J. Parry, and K. Spracklen, 53–61. Eastbourne: Leisure Studies Association.

Doyle, J. 2009. "Art Versus Sport: Managing Desire and the Queer Sport Spectacle." *X-TRA Contemporary Art Quarterly* 11 (4): 4–17.

Jahn, A., ed. 2006. *Body Power, Power Play: Views on Sports in Contemporary Art*. Stuttgart: Hatje Cantz.

Martin, C. 2007. "John Dewey and The Beautiful Stride – Running as Aesthetic Experience." In *Running & Philosophy –A Marathon for the Mind*, edited by M. W. Austin, 171–179. Malden USA, Oxford UK and Carlton Australia: Blackwell Publishing.

Mumford, S. 2011. *Watching Sport: Aesthetics, Ethics and Emotions*. London: Routledge.

Sandle, D., J. Long, J. Parry, and K. Spracklen, eds. 2013. *Fields of Vision: The Arts in Sport*. Eastbourne: Leisure Studies Association.

Whiting, H., and D. Masterson, eds. 1974. *Readings in the Aesthetics of Sport*. London: Lepus.

The aesthetics of sport and the arts: competing and complementary

Stephen Mumford

ABSTRACT

Sport has a distinctive aesthetic that derives from its ontological basis in competition, indeterminism and emergence. The aim in sport is to compete, rather than the production of aesthetic value. An effective way to secure the latter, however, is pursuit of the former: competition in sport is at least part of the explanation of its aesthetics. The dramatic spectacle of sport, on the other hand, can also be explained by the metaphysical indeterminism that it must assume. If sporting outcomes were either deterministic or entirely indeterministic, sport would have no interest for us. Instead, outcomes are produced by actions that dispose towards certain outcomes without necessitating them. Finally, emergence is productive of aesthetic values especially in team sports, where the whole can be substantially more than (or less than) the abilities of the individual players. These three features, taken together, account for the special nature of the sporting aesthetic.

The peculiarity of the sporting aesthetic

The connection between sport and art is a complex one, as is evident from the lively literature that was once generated on the topic (see Aspin 1974; Best 1974, 1978, [1985] 1988; Cooper 1978; Elliott 1974; Gaskin and Masterson 1974; Reid 1970). There is plenty of art about sport, and there are many examples of competitions involving art, but a more vexed question concerns whether sport is or ever could itself be art. It is less controversial that aesthetic values are to be found in sport (Gumbrecht 2006) but even here we should acknowledge the peculiar nature of such aesthetics and their complex connections with the sports that produce them. This will be the topic of the present paper.

The aesthetics of sport, it will be argued, stem from the particularities of what I will call the metaphysical basis of sport, understanding metaphysics in a broad sense. I am not offering a complete survey of what this basis of sport is. I will largely, though not entirely, neglect the topic of causation, for instance, even though it could be argued that it is the most significant metaphysical concept in sport (Mumford 2015b). Instead, I will concentrate on three features of sport that explain some of its distinctive aesthetics. The point is to show how and why sport is capable of producing the special kinds of aesthetic values that it does.

Again, the paper cannot be complete even on this more limited topic; but by illustrating three distinctive features of sport the main claim will be supported. The approach throughout will be that of analytic philosophy.

The three features in sport, that I claim explain some aspect of its distinctive aesthetics, are:

- Competition
- Indeterminism
- Emergent holism, in relation to team sports

I will consider each of these in turn.

Competition

The clichés that sport is art and that some of its greatest players are artists are refuted through a consideration of the role of competition and, in particular, the goal of winning (see Mumford 2011, ch. 5). The point of sport is to win and its goals are entirely lusory (from ludos = game playing). For example, nothing really hinges on jumping over a very high bar. No life is directly saved, nor is any natural disaster averted. And if it were so vital to get to the other side of the bar, it would be much easier to walk under it. Nor does it really matter that a football is forced into the net or a golf ball into a small hole. These 'accomplishments' matter only within a context of game playing and in compliance with a set of constitutive rules, for instance, that the golf ball go into the hole by being struck with a club or putter rather than being placed into it by hand. It is the game – the competitive game – that gives these outcomes the meaning that they have. It can, thus, be said that ceasing to hold a lusory attitude to such goals is to cease playing the sport and to commence some other activity. For example, if in football one stops trying to win the game, by outscoring the opposition, and instead begins juggling the ball, then one is not really playing football anymore but doing something else, such as trying to impress or entertain.

It follows from this that even though sport produces beauty and other aesthetic values quite frequently, if one's primary aim in participating is to produce aesthetic values, then one is not truly playing sport: perhaps one would instead be making art, or attempting to do so (bearing in mind that what makes something art is not simply that it produces aesthetic value, as we shall see). Thus, when sport is being played – in pursuit of the lusory goals – then any aesthetic that is produced is incidental; that is, it is non-essential to the activity *qua* sport.

There is of course a class of sports that seem to present an obvious counterexample to this claim. Some sports have aesthetic values as an explicit aim, such as ice dance, gymnastics, diving and synchronized swimming. Aren't these cases where the aesthetic is the primary goal? But a little further consideration reveals that we do not have to reverse our original judgement. In such examples, the competitors aim to present the aesthetic virtues of the relevant sport to the judges in order to win. They remain *competitors*, even though the competition is a competition to produce aesthetic value. What count as the aesthetic virtues of the sport is, of course, defined and codified such that there is a degree of clarity over what the athlete must produce in order to be a winner. And it is apparent that the aim of winning is the primary goal if one considers the following: what happens if such a sport revises its norms of aesthetic value? Perhaps a particular move, which is considered to produce aesthetic value, is suddenly prohibited in the codification. It would then almost certainly be the case that every serious competitor would cease employing that move in their routine. Indeed, continuation of its use would suggest that winning was no longer that athlete's goal. The athlete would then have stopped competing in that sport and, again, have decided to produce beauty instead as an alternate activity. Hence, the case of the 'aesthetic sports' does not change our original judgement that competition is in every case the aim of sport.

This judgement might seem to denigrate the role of aesthetics in sport: it must always be secondary, where it is produced, we say. But the relationship between sport and its aesthetics is complex. This is because a class of aesthetic values are such that they tend to be produced in the pursuit of the lusory goals of sport. In simpler terms, competition has a tendency to create aesthetic value. I admit that I am saying very little on the ontology of aesthetics: what exactly is the nature of aesthetic value and the manner in which it exists, whether it is 'real' or subjective, and so on. But this is mainly because the points I am making hold no matter which of the accounts of aesthetic value are adopted and it is thus not pertinent to enter those debates here. What matters is that it is in pursuit of the lusory goals that such values are produced. Arguably, the competitive aspect of sport contributes most to its aesthetic dimension. When athletes try their hardest, run their fastest, jump their highest, take a shot with most care and control, this is when the aesthetics of human movement are at their greatest. And the point yields something of a paradox of the sporting aesthetic: it is produced most when the aim is not to produce it.

Let us compare two runners. One is barely trained, taking a run in an attempt to regain long-gone fitness, has received no coaching to develop an efficient running style and, indeed, with increasing tiredness starts to flail around with a lack of control and gets slower and slower until the run stops. The other aims to beat all competitors, runs with efficiency, grace and style, paces the effort to finish strongly, has a well-developed musculature because of a prolonged sporting career and training regime, and completes the same distance in a fraction of the time of the other runner. Now, again staying clearer of some bigger ontological questions on the nature of aesthetics, it is without doubt the second kind of runner who produces the higher aesthetic value and the greater aesthetic experience for the viewer. Similarly, we are attracted by power, speed, extension, control, elegance, technique and so on: all the physical features that also tend towards sporting success in competitive contexts. Hence, by not pursuing sporting aesthetics but, rather, sporting success, one is more likely to produce those aesthetic features in any case, which is why we can think of this relationship as somewhat paradoxical.

The mystery of this connection between the competitive nature of sport and the aesthetic values it tends to produce is dispelled when one considers that there are other cases where something is gained primarily in pursuing something else. For example, striving to be happy is not itself very successful in making one happy. If one simply wants to be happy, but with little idea of how such happiness is to be achieved, one is likely to end up without it. Instead, someone might want a big family or a successful career, or to write a novel, to be loved and so on, and in attaining those goals also finds that they are happy. Similarly, your aim could be to save the planet from environmental disaster rather than saving money on your fuel bills. But if you reduce your energy consumption in order to save the planet, this will most likely tend towards reducing your energy bills nevertheless.

What is true of sport might be true of a number of other practices. Competition occurs not just in sport but also in games, in careers and, of course, there can be art competitions such as the Turner Prize and the Booker Prize for fiction. It could be that, in appropriate circumstances, competition is connected with increased aesthetic value. But there are other cases of competition that seem to have no connection whatsoever with aesthetic value and might even lessen it. The economic competition for resources could, for instance, have an aesthetically detrimental effect on the environment or landscape. I have no general theory to offer that distinguishes aesthetic-enhancing competitive practices from those that are neutral or detrimental. For my argument, I need only the claim that, in the case of sport, competition can tend towards the aesthetic. The word 'tendency' is vital, however. A tendency is stronger than a pure contingency but might be less than a necessity. Smoking tends towards cancer, for example, meaning that smokers are thought to have a higher chance of cancer, ceteris paribus, than non-smokers. But it is not necessitated that any particular smoker gets cancer (Mumford and Anjum 2011, ch. 8). Similarly, the competitive nature of sport tends towards its aesthetic enhancement; but there could easily be some cases where it doesn't. There are many instances of two marathon runners deliberately crossing the line together without competing to do so first. And although the competitive aspect of sport has been suspended in these cases, they might yet provide beautiful moments.

Indeterminism

The second metaphysical feature of sport I consider, that is productive of a part of its aesthetics, is indeterminism. It may seem surprising that there is a link between indeterminism and aesthetics but one can indeed be found. One has to acknowledge, however, a distinctive aesthetic feature of sport, which itself is controversial, namely its dramatic aspect. It is here that the topic of causation is also relevant but I will not be considering it in any philosophical detail.

We need first to understand the distinction between determinism and indeterminism if we are to grasp how it bears on the sporting aesthetic. Determinism is best understood as the view that there is only one possible future (as, e.g. Van Inwagen 1983, 2) and that this is/was true at any point in history. Indeterminism would then be most simply understood as the negation of that, though we will see that the term indeterminism could be used to describe many different sorts of situations. There are also a variety of different reasons why determinism would be the case. Some might say that the current total state of the universe together with the laws of nature fix all future states of the universe. Another way of looking at determinism is the view that every event has a cause and a cause always necessitates its effect. A further view, which doesn't need causation at all, would be just that the whole history of the universe is predetermined, set in stone, and no one can do anything to change it.

It is notable that neither determinism nor indeterminism – as the latter is typically understood – fits well with the idea of sport. If we apply the idea of determinism to sport, it would entail that there is only one possible winner of any particular contest. There can only be one result, presumably no matter how much, or how little, the contestants try. Sport then loses its point for the competitors and its interest for the spectators. Consider, for instance, how we feel if we ever hear that a game has been 'fixed' or, worse, if we knew in advance that it was fixed. It would lose all sporting interest to us immediately (though it might be interesting from other perspectives, e.g. a criminal one). Although it also includes slightly different issues, consider also how watching a sporting contest that has already occurred, even without knowing the result, seems to lack some of the excitement of watching a contest that is live and where the outcome is still to be decided (Fisher 2005). These cases seem to show us that we want to watch sport where the result is genuinely up for grabs, rather than the contestants playing out what is already decided. And then why distinguish the case of a fixed match, in which the result has been agreed in advance, and a match that is fixed by the laws of nature to permit only one possible outcome?

While it makes no sense for sport to be premised on determinism, then, things seem hardly better if indeterminism is the case. Suppose that the outcome of a sporting contest is decided by some random element, akin to the toss of a coin. Would that be of comfort to either the participants or the spectators who were concerned about the necessity of sporting outcomes? If the results are a matter of pure chance, then we seem in hardly any better position. Coin tossing would not make a good spectacle. The problem would be that the players would have no control over the outcomes, hence no say in what they are. Why then train in advance? Why have a strategy or tactics? One couldn't have a legitimate strategy in coin tossing. It is supposed to be a game of pure chance in which you are not allowed to influence the outcome. And, then, why would it be of any interest at all to watch such a game of chance? Indeed, games of chance might be some fun to play, if there are stakes involved, but they would be of very limited interest to watch. We want to see sporting participants negotiate their ways through a series of challenges, using skill, strength, dexterity and experience to conquer them. There is some aesthetic appeal in seeing such problem-solving and this can only occur if the sportsmen and women have influence over the outcomes.

If we had a stark choice between determinism and this randomized version of indeterminism, then it seems there is no place for meaningful sport. Fortunately, there is a version of indeterminism that allows us what we need. Furthermore, we can see that it provides a metaphysical basis for a key aesthetic feature of sport. This is a form of indeterminism that, while it denies that everything is necessitated, it also denies that sporting outcomes are purely random matters. Both those options deny the athletes any control – because both deny there is any alternative to the actual outcomes that the athlete is able to bring about. Instead, the solution is in terms of tendencies once more: the better athlete tends to beat the weaker because they have a power to do so (Mumford and Anjum 2014). Training hard so that you have the requisite sporting skills increases your likelihood of success, though this will in almost every case be a matter comparative to the other contestants. Tendencies can reveal themselves in frequencies of outcomes, though, again, they don't have to. They only tend to do so. If a stronger team plays a weaker team 10 times, then, you would expect the stronger team to win most contests (and we will avoid saying that the team that wins most is the stronger simply in virtue of that fact, for this would make skill and aptitude redundant in explaining why one team tended to beat the other). But in any single contest, the weaker team has a chance. It is still worth them turning up and trying their best; and it remains an interesting spectacle for us to watch such a contest. Even over 10 games, the weaker team has a chance – a slimmer chance – of winning the majority: but it is a chance that will tend towards zero (without reaching it) as the number of contests increases.

Adoption of a metaphysics of tendencies allows one to deny the necessitation of outcomes that follows from determinism but without lurching to a world of pure chance. Indeterminism is true, strictly speaking, even if just one event is not wholly determined. In rejecting determinism, then, one need not accept the extreme version of indeterminism in which randomness rules all. Instead, we can have a view of sport, as in causal action generally, in which the players have influence over outcomes and can attempt to sway them in their favour, even though they do not have absolute control. They can certainly be causally responsible for the outcomes they produce but where producing an outcome does not require guaranteeing it. And it is this form of indeterminism, I argue, that is responsible for what we call drama in sport, where I take dramatic value to be a sub-category of aesthetic value.

To make this claim more persuasive, I will illustrate it with a couple of examples and then offer some justification for a dramatic interpretation of sport.

My first example comes from football. Assume that a shot is taken, coming away from the player's boot in a general direction that she cannot control exactly but which is as best as she can do under the game circumstances to get it on target but away from the goalkeeper. It hits the crossbar and lands down on the line. Will it have backspin and come back out; or it will it have forward spin and bounce into the goal? If it genuinely could go either way, then it is exciting and dramatic to watch. A lot can hinge on such fine margins, which can make a big difference to the result of the contest. If it goes in, we certainly hold the scorer responsible. We assign her the credit: for although the shot was close to being a miss – had there been just a little less forward spin – she exercised her footballing skill in making the shot, she deliberately kicked it in the right sort of direction, and so on. So even though she was unlikely to have the requisite control to repeat the same shot exactly as it was, she was exercising her skill and she did succeed in projecting the ball in a direction where it had a tendency to go into the goal. But sporting situations are often hypersensitive, where the slightest difference in initial conditions can make a huge difference in outcome. Had the boot contacted the ball in some very slightly different way, that it was impossible for the player to control to such a level of detail, backspin might well have taken the ball away from the goal. Anyone wanting a real-life example of such a fine margin making all the difference need only consider Geoff Hurst's famous (or infamous) second goal in the 1966 World Cup Final. He hit the ball in the direction of the goal. It struck the bar and fell very close to the line. It was not within Hurst's complete control, when the ball left his boot, that it would bounce over the line after it hit the crossbar. It was probably not within his control, even, that it would hit the bar and bounce down. We can be confident that he was not aiming to score-off-the-bar, rather than directly. But what drama it produced when he did so.

The second example is a golfer who makes a putt towards the hole. For a real-life example, consider one of Tiger Woods' best putts, at the 16th hole of the 2005 US Masters. The shot was taken from the outer edge of the green with the ball resting against the cut of the rough. Woods planned to hit the ball uphill onto the green above the hole and then let it change direction and roll back down towards the hole. The shot was executed exactly as planned but with the ball having only just enough momentum to reach the hole. Indeed, it teetered on the brink of the hole for what seemed like a whole second before it finally dropped in. It would be implausible to say that Woods had total control over this exact ending. Were he to attempt the same shot all day, every day, for the rest of his life, it is unlikely that he could repeat the same dramatic finish, with the ball pausing on the cusp. Nevertheless, we are right to credit him with the successful shot. A golfer does his or her best to play a skilled shot with the best possible chance of falling in the hole. But there is no guarantee of outcome. Suppose it's a great shot. But still a gust of wind could divert it just at the wrong time, a blade of grass could spring up at the last second and change its course very slightly, or a squirrel could run across the ball's path and steal it. None of these matters are within the golfer's control. But if they don't happen, and the ball goes in, we are certainly right to give the golfer praise, and the trophy, even though he or she could not control everything that might have prevented the victory. That's how sport should be. But the more skilled a golfer is, the stronger a tendency his or her shots will have to go in the hole.

This indeterminism, and the uncertainty it leaves, contributes to the aesthetic of sport. We can be witness to a striving for – a tending towards – an outcome that is not guaranteed by the sportsperson's actions. Hence there is drama: the result is always up for grabs, fortunes can change rapidly on the basis of little things, anything can happen, even though some events are more likely than others. But it means that sport is oftentimes surprising, and thus, capable of filling us with a sense of wonder. Even where the outcome is not a surprise, there can still be the dramatic satisfaction of an uncertainty that resolves into a deserved victory, rewarding superior skill and strength.

Again there can be a comparison between this feature of sport, producing its particular aesthetic, and some similar cases in recognized arts. Improvised performance in jazz contains, for the audience and musicians, a thrill of uncertainty that hopefully gets resolved when, through skill and experience, the players are able to take the music through a journey to reach a satisfactory conclusion. Or consider the seemingly random drips of a Jackson Pollock painting. Pollock knew pretty well where he wanted the drips to fall but the technique allowed only a degree of control. Things could easily have gone wrong. But there was pleasure to be had when the painting was satisfactorily 'resolved' by those uncertainties resulting in an effective and powerful work of art.

Before leaving this topic of indeterminism as the basis of sporting drama, it should be acknowledged that the credentials of sport to qualify as real drama have been challenged. Elsewhere I have defended the claim that the drama in sport is real enough so I will not repeat all the points here (Mumford 2011, ch. 6). Briefly, David Best alleged that the cases of sport and drama are not analogous. For instance: 'It is the character of the athlete which is shown in sport, whereas in drama it is the character not of the actor but of the person he or she is portraying' (Best [1985] 1988, 536). However, the two cases are not so dissimilar. The sportsman or woman, indeed, seems to adopt a role when playing sport; for instance, he or she could be aggressive in a game against an opponent who is also a personal friend. And just as they might bring something of their own personality to the sporting role they play, so could an actor on the stage or screen. Indeed, this is a valid reason for a choice of casting: what the actor will bring to the part. The actor adopts a role for the entertainment of our dramatic sensibilities, and the same can be understood of the men and women of professional sport. Spectator sports are not just about winning and losing but also attracting paying customers to watch them: and they will do so if there is a serious prospect of drama being played out.

Emergence

The topic of emergence has been a thorny one in philosophy for some time. Its relation to sport has been rarely discussed but it seems highly relevant to team sports and, I will argue, is the ground of another feature of sport's aesthetics. Although emergence seems most pertinent to team sports it may not be exclusively so. It is certainly easier, however, to explain the idea first in terms of teams.

The philosophical notion of emergence concerns certain types of case where properties of wholes are not found among their parts. We have to be careful how we articulate this, though. Two right-angled triangles can form a whole that is a square, if they are aligned in a particular way. The whole is square but the two parts that form it are not squares. However, if this were to count as emergence, it would make it too ubiquitous and the case is best thought of as mere composition with an arrangement. Similarly, a whole might weigh 10 kg though none of its parts do. The weight of the whole is simply the addition or aggregate of the weights of the parts. For the concept of emergence to be useful, it should not apply to too many things. Nor should it apply to too few. We want a philosophical concept that applies to the sorts of things that we think ought to count as emergent, while also allowing that a precise, regimented concept could rule some things not to be emergent that pre-theoretically we thought were. This is how philosophy often works.

A duly serviceable notion of emergence has been offered by Anjum and Mumford (2017) and which can be applied to team sports. This is called the causal-transformative model. It says that emergence is where a whole has a property or power that is not found among the component parts, nor in their mere aggregation, and that this higher level property is a result of the causal interaction of the parts, leading to their change. This might sound complicated but it is simple once one has a few examples.

First, a non-sporting case. Water has a power to put out fires but none of its constituents do. Hydrogen and oxygen would both fuel fires. So how can the whole have this property that none of its constituents have? The answer seems to be that the parts of a water molecule – two hydrogen atoms and one oxygen atom – causally affect each other when they bond. The vacant spaces in the outer shells of electrons are completed by the binding; and given that many of the chemical properties of things are explained by their outer shells of electrons, it is not mysterious that in changing the constituents through the binding process the whole does not simply inherit the properties that the parts had before they were bound.

Now let us consider a sporting example. Some teams can be greater or better than the sum of the abilities of the individual players that make them up – were those players to be considered in isolation – while some can be worse. A good team plays as a whole, instead of as a collection of individuals. They become a unit that, if it is functioning well, affects the individual constituents and makes them better players. They become transformed through their participation in the whole (Mumford 2015a). A good team can function like a single entity in which the individual is subsumed, and this creates a high-level aesthetic that is available for the spectator's appreciation. When Nottingham Forest became twice-European Champions of football with a team of previously unsuccessful players, it was seen in these terms. This counts as emergence on the causal-transformative view. The negative case would also count, where participation in a whole makes players worse and it is a bad team, though this will be unlikely to produce any positive aesthetic value.

Can emergence really be the basis of an aesthetic judgement? It might seem odd to suggest that we appreciate emergent phenomena aesthetically. But there are plausible cases in the arts for comparison. Consider a jazz quartet. If one listens to the individual musicians play their parts individually, perhaps as they rehearse, then it can certainly be interesting and appreciated. But now let us put all four players together. As a whole, they play a piece of music, which has a pleasing unity to it. Let us take it that in a situation of playing together, the musicians affect each other positively. As sometimes happens, they coax the best performances out of each other, feeding off the energy of live performance and not wanting to let the others down, maybe even competing, in a sense, to be the best among them. This can certainly produce in us an additional aesthetic appreciation: not just because of the music sounding complete but also from hearing that it is such a fine improvisation as a result of the mutually enhancing effects of the musicians' collaboration. There can be something special about such a collective effort, particularly if one feels that the performance has a unique quality. This is the sort of thing that sends a tingle down the spine. And what is said of a collective musical performance can clearly apply to a cast of actors on the stage or screen: they too might bring the best out of each other and deliver a performance that is in some sense greater than the sum of the parts. We can appreciate not just the play but also that it was a fine delivery, performed well because the cast operated as a mutually improving whole.

The application to team sports is too obvious to labour as all the points discussed above can apply to any team sport. Seeing that a team is a well-honed machine, improving each individual's performance, is a special moment in sport: both for the spectators and, no doubt, the players. It is such performances that go down in sporting history. The team seems to be the *unit*: as if an entity in its own right, capable of performing collective actions. An organic unity in action can be wondrous. *The team* scores the goal and wins. It can be almost as if the players have lost their individual identities, which have been subsumed into the greater whole.

Although emergence has a clear application to team sports, we should probably not rule it out in relation to individual sports either. Some cases in which it could plausibly apply are where a coach and athlete work well together, bringing out the best in each other, resulting in the best possible individual performance for the athlete; or where stiff competition means that the opponents each unintentionally coax the best performance out of the other. The story of emergence is probably more complicated to tell in individual sports but it is worth remembering that an athletic performance, even in solo sports, is typically the result of a collaborative effort. The final performance can still be thought of as one part of a greater whole: the entire process that got the athlete to the starting line in well-prepared condition.

Common aesthetics

While there are some particularities of sporting aesthetics, as described here, this is not to say that the aesthetics of sport are entirely distinct from those of art or from naturally occurring aesthetic properties such as those found in sunsets. There are also similarities, as we have seen. We look at both art and sport for aesthetic value within the categories of drama, grace, economy, symmetry, emotional and intellectual engagement, beauty, and so on. Indeed, sport and art might then have much in common, which is doubtless why sport is so commonly spoken of as if it is art. I will not follow that line, not because I see art and sport as having conflicting essences, though. On this question, a non-essentialist institutional theory of both art and sport seems more plausible. Sport, like art, is a status bestowed upon certain forms of practice by a set of historically evolving institutions. And there is little doubt that the institutions of the art world and the sporting world are almost entirely distinct. This might seem in conflict with my earlier claim that winning was the primary goal of sport. Perhaps one might be tempted to say that, in contrast, aesthetic value is the primary goal of art and this shows sport and art to have distinct essences. But a clear contrast with art could not be made on this basis. After all, it is not only sports in which the purpose is to win, which we find also in games, in gambling and in quizzes. Furthermore, it is clear that there are now many instances of art that do not have the realization of aesthetic value as their primary goal: indeed, as no goal at all. This has been the case since at least Duchamp's fountain was deemed art.

The separation of art and sport is, then, unlikely to be found in philosophical analysis. It is a matter of culture and social practices. The more interesting philosophical issues concern the specific detail of the aesthetics of the practice. The references to art, within the context of a discussion of sport, are thus more significant insofar as they support the credentials of the identified values to be specifically aesthetic values. We could find similar values within more paradigmatic artistic practices, and this supports the claim that these are aesthetic matters. For, even if aesthetics are not the aim of all art, it is clear that they have been closely aligned with a lot of art as it did traditionally have a function of exploring the aesthetic, even if it now does so less.

There remains a question of whether the aesthetics within sport form a unique combination that is not found in any non-sporting practice. The analysis in this paper suggests that this might be so. Embodiment is of course a vital ingredient for the aesthetic appreciation of many sports. There is an aesthetic admiration of the human form in sport, especially in gymnastics, for instance. But the same might be said of dance. There is also admiration of skill and dexterity in sport but it is far from clear that this is a specifically aesthetic concern. In focusing on the three metaphysical features of sport – competition, indeterminism, and emergence – I have been able to show the grounds of a set of aesthetic values that, taken together, do seem to form a distinctive set. While admiration of the human form is common to both dance and sport, then, if we add the competitive, indeterministic and emergent elements, then we start to get something that looks unique. If that is the case, it supports the view that sport plays a special and distinctive aesthetic role, providing an experience for the viewer that cannot be found elsewhere.

Disclosure statement

No potential conflict of interest was reported by the author.

References

Anjum, R., and S. Mumford. 2017. "Emergence and Demergence." In *Philosophical and Scientific Perspectives on Downward Causation*, edited by M. Paoletti and F. Orilia, 92–109. London: Routledge.

Aspin, D. 1974. "Sport and the Concept of "The Aesthetic"." In *Readings in the Aesthetics of Sport*, edited by H. Whiting and D. Masterson, 117–137. London: Lepus.

Best, D. 1974. "The Aesthetic in Sport." *The British Journal of Aesthetics* 14: 197–213. doi:10.1093/bjaesthetics/14.3.197

Best, D. 1978. *Philosophy and Human Movement*. London: George Allen and Unwin.

Best, D. (1985) 1988. "Sport is Not Art." In *Philosophic Inquiry in Sport*, edited by W. Morgan and K. Meier, 527–539. Champaign, IL: Human Kinetics.

Cooper, W. 1978. "Do Sports Have an Aesthetic Aspect?." *Journal of the Philosophy of Sport* 5: 51–55. doi:10.1080/00948705.1978.10654140.

Elliott, R. 1974. "Aesthetics and Sport." In *Readings in the Aesthetics of Sport*, edited by H. Whiting and D. Masterson, 107–116. London: Lepus.

Gaskin, G., and D. Masterson. 1974. "The Work of Art in Sport." In *Readings in the Aesthetics of Sport*, edited by H. Whiting and D. Masterson, 139–160. London: Lepus.

Fisher, A. 2005. "Watching Sport—But Who Is Watching?" *Journal of the Philosophy of Sport* 32: 184–94.

Gumbrecht, H. 2006. *In Praise of Athletic Beauty*. Cambridge, MA: Belknap Press.

Mumford, S. 2011. *Watching Sport: Aesthetics*. Ethics and Emotions, London: Routledge.

Mumford, S. 2015a. "In Praise of Teamwork." *Journal of the Philosophy of Sport* 42: 51–5. doi:10.1080/00948705.2014.961158

Mumford, S. 2015b. "Metaphysics of Sport." In *Routledge Handbook of Philosophy of Sport*, edited by M. McNamee and W. Morgan, 274–284. London: Routledge.

Mumford, S., and R. Anjum. 2011. *Getting Causes from Powers*. Oxford: Oxford University Press. doi:10.1093/acprof:oso/9780199695614.001.0001.

Mumford, S., and R. Anjum. 2014. "The Tendential Theory of Sporting Prowess." *Journal of the Philosophy of Sport* 41: 399–412. doi:10.1080/00948705.2014.911097.

Reid, L. 1970. "Sport, the Aesthetic and Art." *British Journal of Educational Studies* 18: 245–258. doi:10.1080/00071005.1970.9973287.

Van Inwagen, P. 1983. *An Essay on Free Will*. Oxford: Oxford University Press.

New directions in the arts and sport? Critiquing national strategies

Jonathan Long ⓘ and Franco Bianchini

ABSTRACT

Taking as its starting point the Fields of Vision initiative's interest in promoting the potential benefits of bringing sports and arts closer together, this paper reviews how national (English) policy addresses that challenge. Four key strategic documents (the Government's Sport Strategy and its Culture White Paper as well as the strategies of Arts Council England and Sport England) are examined. That is supplemented by the views of significant individuals from this interface, including the research network funded by the Arts and Humanities Research Council (AHRC). Noting the similar social remit ascribed to sport and the arts by the government, shortcomings in the current strategies are identified as barriers to integration. 'Play' and 'movement' are briefly discussed as integrating concepts alongside our assessment of the potential of the arts/sport nexus, in areas including aesthetic innovation, promoting health and wellbeing, and encouraging wider participation and engagement. Having challenged existing national policies the paper suggests possible future directions.

Introduction

It has been argued that being part of the same government ministry (Department for Digital, Culture, Media and Sport – DCMS) is an opportunity to exploit the many potential inter-relationships between sport and the arts (e.g. Long et al. 2013). Indeed, the Culture and Sport Evidence (CASE) research programme commissioned by DCMS to establish the social value and wellbeing generated by cultural and sport activities (see for example, Fujiwara, Kudrna, and Dolan 2014a, 2014b; Taylor et al. 2015) might have been taken to reflect that belief. As shown by this paper, both policy areas have been set similar social challenges. Yet opportunities to maximize interactions between the two are commonly spurned despite Arts Council England (ACE) and Sport England (SE) now sharing the same London office block. Perhaps that is not surprising given the essential differences between the arts and sport identified by Mumford (this issue). Policy-makers seem to be reassured by assigning things to discrete boxes.

Sport is commonly perceived as focusing on competition and physical skills, while the arts are seen as fundamentally about representations of the world, and telling stories. There are in the UK deep-rooted cultural attitudes that polarize differences between the two realms. Arguably, the division between sport and the arts is as deep as that between the sciences and the humanities discussed in 1959 by CP Snow in his polemic, *The Two Cultures*. However, we prefer to take our lead from writers like CLR James (2005; originally 1963) who challenges the dismissive scorn cultural elites often direct at sport, arguing that sport feeds 'the need to satisfy the visual artistic sense' (276/7). He mounts an eloquent case for the art of cricket in particular.

Through the commercial paradigms applied to both sport and the arts in the context of the decline of the welfare state and of public funding, the two spheres of activity are increasingly in competition for people's leisure time and spending as well as for private sector sponsorship and advertising revenue. In some cases, the two policy areas are also in competition for public funding (see, for example, the funding pressures on the arts sector created by the need to fund the London 2012 Olympic and Paralympic Games). Yet at the same time, the 2012–2016 Cultural Olympiad gave fresh impetus to the arts/sport inter-section, as with the imove project in Yorkshire and the Humber (Froggett, this issue). We argue that treating sport and the arts as separate worlds neglects the potential that lies in exploiting the reactions that might be fired by bringing these two fields together.

From time to time sport and the arts have been drawn closer together in government thinking and consequent policy, though this has typically been in response to hardship and stress. For example, the Quality of Life Experiments (DoE 1977a) of the 1970s followed the oil crisis and the three-day week. Teams were deployed in four deprived areas (Dumbarton, Sunderland, Clwyd and Stoke-on-Trent) using cultural animateurs to combat deprivation by stimulating arts, sport and leisure activities generally. The authors of the resultant report noted that 'it was apparent that people do not necessarily see leisure needs and activities as divided between the "arts" on the one hand and "sports" on the other' (DoE 1977a, ix). However, despite documented success (DoE 1977b), the 'experiments' did not lead to comprehensive policy. Some two decades later the New Labour government's concern with social exclusion led to the establishment of a series of Policy Action Teams (PATs) to consider what policy instruments might promote social inclusion, by bringing together the actions and resources of different ministries. One of them, PAT 10 (1999), addressed the contribution of the arts and sport to social inclusion, and as such might have set a marker for the current interest in their ability to deliver social benefits. However, the subsequent implementation of the strategy tended to maintain the separation between the two fields (DCMS 2001).

Such 'moments' notwithstanding the arts and sport policy communities seem to have different ways of seeing (RIP John Berger), both the world and their particular purpose. Matters are not made easier by both being relatively low status public services with limited resources. There has been under-investment in DCMS generally, reflecting its lack of seniority as a government ministry. At local government level, these areas of discretionary activity are vulnerable at times of cuts in public spending ('austerity'). Fewer local authorities now have specialist unified leisure departments that might make more integrated provision (personal communication with Local Government Association, 29/8/17). Despite that, the examples of integration of arts and sport are generally to be found at local level. They can be viewed, for example, in the Cultural Olympiads from Athens 2004 onwards

(Froggett et al. 2013) and in Le Grand Depart, organized by Welcome to Yorkshire for the Tour de France in 2014. These have featured associated cultural programmes of arts-based events. Likewise, in the private sector there are some professional sports clubs that have demonstrated a commitment to the arts, with artist-in-residence programmes; in the case of Middlesbrough FC this has been running since the early 1990s.

Our recent investigations have examined where current public policy in England positions the Fields of Vision (FoV)[1] interest in the potential of the relationships between sports and arts. Having identified key points emerging from policy statements we consider the similar social remit the government ascribes to sport and arts, and suggest shortcomings of the current positions. We then turn our attention to future directions, in terms of both the initiatives proposed in government strategies and of our own assessment.

In addition to examining four key national strategy documents, we sought the views of significant individuals at the sport–arts interface, drawn on the discussions of the research network (FoV) funded by AHRC to explore this agenda, and set that within the context of academic literature.

National strategies for sport, the arts and 'Culture'

In December 2015, the government produced its *Sporting Future* strategy (HM Government 2015). This was quickly followed by the *Culture White Paper* in March 2016. It is strange that the government apparently does not see sport as part of 'culture'; it does include libraries, museums and heritage in its (implied) definition of culture, but not sport. Long and Strange (2009) have previously commented on the absence of sport from the collective mental map forming the cultural policy discourse. They note that in their interviews, apart from respondents with a specific sporting role, the role of sport in the city or its contribution to its cultural life was rarely considered. Those who 'did talk about sport did so in ways that highlighted its absence from debate' (69). This exclusion is not always the case; for example, the important Council of Europe study of cultural policy in European towns certainly included sport (Mennell 1976). Even Mumford (this issue), in arguing the distinctness of sport and the arts does not suggest that sport should not be considered part of culture.

Like the Westminster government, we are somewhat constrained in our mission because, while the UK Government might publish its strategy for sport and its Culture White Paper, sport and the arts are responsibilities devolved to the separate administrations in Scotland, Wales and Northern Ireland. We therefore examine here Sport England's strategy, *Towards an Active Nation*, published in May 2016 as a response to the government strategy, and the Arts Council England (ACE) strategy document *Great Art and Culture for Everyone (2010–2020)*, that was updated in 2013.

> The arts are part of our national identity … The arts are also good for us. They teach our children how to rise to a challenge, nurturing the character and discipline that will help them get on in life … [They are] good for our economy … use the arts to strengthen community cohesion and give our young people new skills for life and work. Above all, the arts are fun. Learning artistic skills can lead to a lifetime of enjoyment … dreams and ambitions you have for success, the lifelong friendships you make, all these things remind us of the unique way in which the arts can excite and inspire us all … So at the heart of this strategy are three ideas that can help us make the most of this unique power of the arts in our national life. First, we will be much bolder in harnessing the potential of the arts for social good. We will change arts funding so it is no longer merely about people taking part, but rather how the arts can have a

meaningful and measurable impact on improving people's lives… By harnessing the power of the arts for the good of our whole society, by investing in developing the talent of future stars … we can … make our country stronger for generations to come.

Most people researching in the area would not have been surprised to read the above text in the introduction to the *Culture White Paper* by the then prime minister, David Cameron. Except that is not what it is. It is Cameron's introduction to the government's sport strategy with 'the arts' swapped for 'sport'. Elsewhere there are of course differences, most notably in relation to international competition (especially the Olympics with just a few months to go to Rio 2016); investment in school sport and developing talent; and 'integrity'. On the other hand, despite the strategy being about an active nation, the attention given to elite success (the second of those themes) could certainly fit the arts.

The White Paper says that culture (meaning the arts and heritage):

- should be available to everyone
- can enhance the country's international standing
- has important social benefits in terms of health, education and community cohesion
- has beneficial effects on both physical and mental health with positive physiological and psychological changes in clinical outcomes, decreasing the amount of time spent in hospital and improving mental health
- can increase the likelihood of a young person going on to further and higher education
- can contribute to social relationships and/or make communities feel safer and stronger
- improves social mobility and has a huge impact on life chances … can open doors to careers
- can play a role in tackling crime
- brings huge benefits by providing better quality of life and wellbeing within local communities
- contributes to urban regeneration.

There is clearly a considerable commonality of discourse being applied to sport and the arts. To aid the analysis word counts were conducted for each of the policy statements identified above and word clouds produced using N-vivo (Figures 1–4). These excluded commonly occurring words not deemed to be significant in the current context.

Great Art and Culture for Everyone

Figure 1 represents the word cloud for the first of the strategy documents under consideration, which was produced by Arts Council England (ACE) for 2010–2020, as revised in 2013. Museums and libraries are prominent, no doubt in an attempt to secure the new arrangement whereby responsibility for them had been transferred to ACE. Not surprisingly, artists and excellence also feature prominently and there is much attention to structure and procedures: 'organizations', 'support', 'sector', 'investment', 'development'. An emphasis on the public is reflected in 'people', 'everyone' and 'engagement'. However, this shows the difficulty of dealing with individual words in this kind of approach. 'People' appear as workforce, consumers, creators; just as 'work' covers framework/our work as well as artists' works. From our perspective it is concerning that the document contains no mention of sport at all, though there are some references to the Cultural Olympiad as a showcase for the arts.

Figure 1. Great Art and Culture for Everyone – Word Cloud.

The Culture White Paper

The comparable word cloud for the White Paper (presented to Parliament in March 2016) similarly has a strong organizational theme, with such terms as 'funds', 'sectors', 'government', 'organizations', 'support', 'nations' and 'investment' being prominent (Figure 2). 'Heritage', 'museums', 'theatres', 'collections', 'galleries' and 'creative' all feature strongly. But this word cloud also demonstrates the need for caution in interpretation. Here, rather than referring to artworks, the appearance of 'works' tends to be about what works in terms of 'benefits', 'impacts', 'community', 'educational', 'data' and 'measures'.

Apart from the name of the Department in the headers, the only references to sport are incidental. First, sport appears alongside art when presenting findings from a British Council survey of 'factors making this country attractive', and data on volunteering from the Taking Part Survey. Second, sport and art are mentioned together in an observation that 'Ofsted inspectors take account of pupils' cultural development' (21). Later, in commending the North East Culture Partnership, DCMS notes that those contributing to the development of its *Case for Culture* included local sporting interests (34). Perhaps DCMS could take a leaf out of their book.

Figure 2. The Culture White Paper – Word Cloud.

Government strategy for sport

Published under the title of '*Sporting Future: A new strategy for an active nation*' in December 2015, the government's strategy for sport insisted that while sports bodies were expected to increase participation, numbers alone were insufficient and greater attention needed to be given to resultant social outcomes. The message was that this necessitated wider involvement among groups known to have lower levels of participation. This in itself was hardly new having been the tenor of a much earlier strategy, *Sport in the Community: The next ten years* (Sports Council 1982) and having re-surfaced from time to time in the interim.

The document contains only two mentions of the arts. The first in a section on local government: 'we want to encourage this type of partnership thinking at local level, including where local need or specific projects create natural synergies with the arts and heritage sectors' (14). That is followed by talk of directing Lottery funding at local level to bids 'when they are led by a strong coalition of [unspecified] local bodies'. The second mention of the arts occurs in a section on financial sustainability, which talks of copying the Arts Impact Fund, a partnership between ACE, Bank of America Merrill Lynch, NESTA & the Esmee Fairbairn Foundation. It commits the government to supporting 'the establishment of a Social Impact Fund for investment into sport, pooling public, philanthropic and commercial capital' and also to 'look at ways of enabling local communities to invest into their local sports facilities using models like community shares and crowdfunding' (56).

The word cloud in Figure 3 can be seen to reflect the concern with getting new people physically active. However, there is a tension throughout the document because, although the government is trying to set the strategy for the UK, responsibility for sport is devolved to the constituent home nations.

Figure 3. Sporting Future – Word Cloud.

Sport England strategy 2016–2021

The only reference to the arts in *Towards an Active Nation* (Sport England 2016, 21) observes:

> Sport England will fund wider forms of walking for leisure and dance than we do today by investing in what is most appealing to our target audiences, and will deliver on the outcomes. We will not displace existing funding (e.g. from Arts Council England) and will not intervene where there is already a strong commercial offer.

The central aim is again clear (and reflected in Figure 4): supporting new people to get physically active. To that end 'need', 'development', 'engagement' and 'community' are also prominent in Figure 4, and the document makes repeated use of 'customers'. Part of the rationale is to address the government's health agenda. Hence, the significance of those who are currently inactive, as the government's strategy maintains that 'the biggest gains and the best value for public investment is found in addressing people who are least active' (HM Government 2015, 19).[2]

Commonalities

So given the, for us, disappointingly little reference to the arts in the sport strategies and sports in the arts and 'culture' strategies, is it possible to identify things in common?

'Activity' comes top for both sport documents; the nearest equivalent for the arts strategy is 'engagement' (also featuring strongly in both sport documents) but that is well down the

Figure 4. Sport England: Towards an Active Nation – Word Cloud.

list. Activity is associated with 'people', which comes next for the sport documents but is again less prominent for the arts document, where it is supplemented by 'everyone' and 'community'.

Both the Sport Strategy and the Culture White Paper incorporate quotes from ministers in related departments in an understandable attempt to get 'buy-in'. In all the documents talk of partners and partnerships abounds. This might seem no more than common sense, especially as we advocate better integration of sport and the arts, but there is some concern that it might reflect organizations divesting themselves of responsibility. It can be no surprise that, particularly after the international financial crisis that started in the late 2000s and the subsequent government-imposed austerity measures, all the documents repeatedly return to questions of funding and investment. This accompanies an organizational theme addressing internal structure and dependence on other bodies. However, those envisaged relationships do not transcend the arts/sport divide.

Talk of 'development' is significant in all four documents, in terms of developing both skills and the overall economy. However, 'needs' are much more evident in the sport documents, where 'local' appears in relation to needs and opportunities. The theme of health and wellbeing is also given more attention in the sport documents than in the arts one, whereas education is apparently seen as being more significant for the arts.

The counts reflected in the word clouds can only take our analysis so far. We now shift our attention to 'social outcomes' (HM Government 2015, 8) or, in David Cameron's words, 'the impact on improving people's lives' (HM Government 2015, 6). So we now examine Cameron's challenge to sport to be 'no longer merely about how many people take part, but rather how sport can have a meaningful and measurable impact on improving people's lives… focus on the social good'. Given the fact that the *Culture White Paper* makes similar protestations, we examine arts policy in the same light.

Social benefit

On her appointment as Secretary of State at DCMS in July 2016, Karen Bradley commented: 'The civil society work is an exciting addition to DCMS and fits perfectly with the department's mission to enrich lives'.[3] This appears to reaffirm the view that 'art for art's sake' or 'sport for sport's sake' is no longer sufficient, in and of itself, to warrant public funding. In the strategy documents this is addressed in terms of: getting more people involved; enhancing wellbeing; educational contributions; and cohesion/inclusion.

Engagement and participation

The White Paper opens with a quote from Cameron (then Prime Minister): 'If you believe in publicly-funded arts and culture as I passionately do, then you must also believe in equality of access, attracting all, and welcoming all'. The ACE strategy is called *Great Art and Culture for Everyone*; the sport policy documents too aim to encourage those not currently participating to get involved. Jennie Price (Sport England's CEO) observes: 'We want everyone in England regardless of age, background or level of ability to feel able to engage in sport and physical activity … the balance of our investment needs to shift from people who would do this anyway to encouraging inactive people to become active' (Sport England 2016, 10).

Whereas the arts documents are oriented to consumption by audiences, sport is viewed in terms of more direct involvement, whether as physical engagement, volunteering or coaching (though in *Sporting Future* there is also attention to major events). All documents emphasize the importance of appealing to those not currently engaged and targeting funding to that end. For example, Sport England asserts that major grants will require applicants to involve 'a certain proportion' of inactive people. More generally, there is a commitment to at least 25 per cent spending on the inactive. Partly with that search for new participants in mind, the government strategy for Sport places greater emphasis on young people (5–14) and schools, though it then gives that less coverage than major sporting events. Moreover, school sport initiatives struggle in the face of the funding cuts required by austerity policies (Parnell, Spracklen, and Millward 2017). Such cuts damaged school sport and other opportunities for young people's engagement in sport (Phillpots 2013). Despite some new investment, the crisis in youth engagement in sport was exacerbated by the end of the Healthy Pupils Capital Programme and of the School Sport Partnerships, and by the removal of School Sport Co-ordinators.

In the ACE document, there is a recognition of the need to increase diversity, not just of practitioners and audiences/spectators, but of volunteers and workforce too.

> We need to make entry routes into employment, and opportunities for people to further their careers, fairer and more accessible to all. This is as true for the leadership and governance of the sector as it is for those entering the workforce. (ACE 2013, 34)

In the Culture White Paper (2016, 24) add: 'We will work with Arts Council England to understand the barriers that prevent people from particularly under-represented groups becoming professionals in the arts'.

The answer for arts policy-makers to the issues of alienation and lack of engagement is mainly to get people to 'understand', whereas sport policy-makers seem to be beginning to realize that to engage the disinterested the offering may need to change, to become more fun and informal, and less competitive (Sport England 2016).

Health and wellbeing

These strategic documents for both sport and the arts unproblematically assert the respective contributions to physical and mental wellbeing, and therefore to cost saving through less demand on the health budget (though ACE offers no more than a brief acknowledgement of the wonder of the arts). For example, the White Paper protests the contribution, expresses a desire to know more and promises to work with ACE, the Heritage Lottery Fund and Public Health England, though not Sport England, to secure these gains. Whereas in the past the arts might have emphasized the psychological and sport the physical, there is now a growing emphasis on sport's contribution to mental wellbeing. The Cultural Commissioning Programme[4] notwithstanding, sport seems to have advanced further in demonstrating the case and establishing joint initiatives with the health sector. Sport England has a clearer idea than the arts of what they will do, e.g.:

> We will create a new, dedicated fund of £120 million to tackle inactivity over the next four years, building on the insight we gained from our Get Healthy Get Active pilots… at least 25 per cent spending on the inactive … work with Public Health England on creating suitable messages … programme of work with leading health charities to engage those with long term conditions (19). … Many councils have taken the opportunity to integrate physical activity into public health policy as part of a wider shift from a system that treats ill-health to one that promotes wellbeing (13).

Education, skills and talent

This theme receives much attention across the documents in terms of children's education, of the development of artistic talent or sporting ability, and of enhancing employment skills. In relation to the arts, there is a fundamental belief that (young) people have to be educated to appreciate the arts and that arts education enhances education generally. In the White Paper (19) Nicky Morgan, then Secretary of State for Education, goes so far as to assert that 'access to cultural education is a matter of social justice'. Participation in sport too is presumed to improve rather than detract from educational performance. The *Culture White Paper* seems to have picked up on the idea in sport of talent development pathways, particularly for the workforce (otherwise ACE wants to make sure the 'right' talent is encouraged to develop). In a rapidly changing environment both arts and sports need their workforce to acquire new technical, business and soft skills, though with no suggestion that there may be any overlap between the two workforces. In *Towards an Active Nation* (37), Sport England envisages working with CIMSPA[5] to support the professionalization of the sector's workforce to create a framework of skills, establish career development pathways and provide sector staff with quality CPD to retain the most talented.

Community cohesion and social inclusion

The government's *Sporting Future* insists that 'sport can help build stronger communities by bringing people together, often from different backgrounds, to make them feel better about where they live, improve community links and cohesion and build social capital' (75). Caroline Dinenage, then Minister for Women, Equalities and Family Justice, argued that 'sport has huge potential to break down barriers. It can bring people of all ages, backgrounds and cultures together, acting as a powerful social glue' (70). Undoubtedly it can, but it also has the potential to divide (e.g. Wagg 2002). Despite the prime minister's aspirations, the *White Paper* contains nothing more than three assertions (e.g. 'cultural participation can contribute to social relationships, community cohesion, and/or make communities feel safer and stronger' (15). There is nothing at all in the ACE strategy on this theme.

Sport England still seems happier talking about 'community development' rather than cohesion or inclusion, even though it supposes that what is entailed in such activities is involving current non-participants in sport, rather than community development *per se*. Thus, responsibility for inclusion is acknowledged in terms of equality of opportunity to develop talent. Volunteering, which Sport England is keen to encourage, is promoted to build social inclusion and community cohesion. 'We know that people who volunteer in sport, for example, are more likely to feel they belong in their area and people who take part in sport are likely to enjoy stronger social links with other people' (75).

Future initiatives

The White Paper makes a number of promises regarding interesting initiatives for the arts alone, insisting for example that the national arts and heritage Lottery funders will be brought together to deliver a 'Great Place' scheme (now running), which will support 'local communities' (studiously avoiding local authorities) that 'want to put culture at the heart of their local vision, supporting jobs, economic growth, education, health and wellbeing' (9). Not only would it be easy to incorporate sport, the case for added value would be considerable. The next suggestion, to launch Heritage Action Zones, is reminiscent of the 10 Sport Action Zones (2001–6) that were set up to help combat low levels of participation in sport in communities experiencing the effects of poverty. Now, in *Towards an Active Nation*, Sport England is again proposing to concentrate resources in 10 pilot areas.

The *White Paper* continues: 'Our national heritage organisations will advise communities on how they can make best use of their historic buildings, including taking ownership of them' (part of the project to divest the local state of its resources). Meanwhile, Sport England intends to set up a Community Asset Fund to build on the success of the Inspired Facilities and Protecting Playing Fields initiatives, to take on responsibility for local authority infrastructure (Sport England 2016, 13). There is no mention of arts–sport collaboration here, although this would be in the spirit of the White Paper and could strengthen the social inclusion and public engagement impacts.

The White Paper also proposes a 'Cultural Citizens' programme to increase the number of disadvantaged children and young people having high quality cultural experiences. This initiative might be compared with *Sportivate* (receiving additional funding in 2017) and *Sporting Champions*, though those are not specifically for the disadvantaged. Again we see the different emphases on consumption in the case of the arts, and on active participation in the case of sport. There is then a commitment in the White Paper to encourage councils and owners to make empty business premises available to cultural organizations on a temporary basis, something from which sports bodies could benefit too. There is a later proposal (11) to establish a new virtual Commercial Academy for Culture. Anyone who has followed the attempts of governing bodies to impose financial discipline in response to off-field sagas at any number of professional football, rugby and cricket clubs in recent years might spot the potential for similar benefits in sport. Indeed, the sport documents also talk of the need for strong, visionary, more diverse leadership.

Missed opportunities?

One of the things shared by the sport and by the arts policy documents is a separation of the worlds of the arts and sport, revealed by very weak mutual recognition and appreciation despite similar remits: to promote excellence, widen engagement and deliver social benefits. Perhaps the closest they come together is in an observation that 'the Cultural Olympiad was a special opportunity to showcase our diverse talents & museum collections on the world stage and to make global connections' (ACE 2013, 26).

In addition, our assessment of government strategies is that they are better at exhortation than delivery. They are anxious to claim the benefits accruing from sport and the arts, but the details of delivery have yet to be decided. Although the White Paper does at least draw on research evidence to try to substantiate the claims of benefit (e.g. through the CASE programme), there is no consideration of what it is about the arts (or sports) that will deliver such benefits. For example, while diversity is addressed, there is little consideration of what might meet the needs of minoritized groups, never mind what might promote community cohesion. The view seems to be that getting more people involved will automatically deliver social returns, without a critique of what is capable of achieving success. This may be partly because there are other agencies closer to the delivery of services and partly because these documents are supposedly national expressions of UK strategy while the arts and sport are devolved responsibilities to Scotland, Wales and Northern Ireland. Matters are complicated by dealing with fuzzy concepts in a categorical way. While the arts are commonly referred to in the plural, sport is more commonly in the singular. We have heterogeneous concepts with porous boundaries ('arts' and 'sport', never mind 'recreation', 'leisure', 'physical activity' or 'creative industries') being defended by passionate advocates as though they are homogeneous, singular entities.

As already mentioned, the Strategy for Sport and the Culture White Paper both feature quotes from ministers in other departments in an effort to demonstrate potential linkages. However, despite various protestations of the virtue of partnerships there is no connection to the work of other departments. For example, there is no link to the Education White Paper or to the work of the Department for Business, Innovation and Skills (BIS) or of the Department for Communities and Local Government (DCLG). These serious shortcomings reveal a mismatch between the rhetoric of joined up government and the reality. This kind of disjuncture appears elsewhere too. Like the government's *Sporting Future*, ACE acknowledges the role of local authorities in addressing need: 'We must take account of the differing needs of different places. We will do this in partnership with local government, the largest investor in arts and culture in England' (ACE 2013, 29). However worthy, this seems oblivious to the constraints imposed by major 'austerity' cuts in government funding to local authorities experienced particularly since 2010.

As typified in the field of education there is a plethora of initiatives and good local examples, but no system-wide coverage. Even the 'national' network of Cultural Education Partnerships does not provide nationwide coverage. Meanwhile those in schools responsible for teaching the arts feel under threat.

Discussion

The occasions when the arts and sports have been brought closer together in policy terms, have been exceptional rather than the norm. Only one person has ever been on both the Arts Council and the Sports Council, Bernard Atha in the 1970s, and at that time there was one joint meeting of both Councils to discuss mutual interests.[6] Even then Atha's assessment was pessimistic:

> There was no desire that I could discern from anyone to become more closely involved with the Arts Council and its activities because, they would never say this, but it was rather effete and un-masculine. It was the arts and so it wasn't like sport and good for the mind and spirit. The Arts Council was much less receptive to any ideas than the Sports Council … The problem with partnership is that if you're in one of those two funding bodies you're very protective of what you've got … When it comes to sport or art there's closure almost immediately. (Research interview)

During that earlier period of economic adversity in the wake of the oil crisis, consideration was given to joint provision and it was the time of the Quality of Life Experiments. An examination of the proceedings of conferences organized by the Leisure Studies Association shows that the debate was lively in academia too. Still flush with enthusiasm stemming from the 1974 reorganization of government that gave impetus to the establishment of combined leisure services departments there was recurrent discussion of integrated organization, policy and provision. Talk was of common challenges and converging policies to overcome political and administrative barriers (Walker 1978). While Geraint John (1978, 5.1) protested that he did 'not personally believe in the "culture" gap between Sports and Arts', Fred Inglis (1978, 2.1) observed that

> we busy ourselves with worrying about the divisions between sport and art and are worried also about the implications below these divisions which set art above sport and do so in such a way as to give rise to charges of elitism.

Even in our supposedly classless society four decades later it seems likely that such presumptions regarding sociocultural positioning lie behind the twin-track policies discussed earlier. Despite calls by the New Labour governments for 'joined-up thinking' in public policy and practice (Pollitt 2003; Long and Bramham 2006) we find ourselves rehearsing strikingly similar arguments today.

Thomson, Stokman, and Torenvlied (2003) suggest a four stage model for the coordination of agendas: information sharing, proposing solutions, bargaining over the proposition and terminating bargaining. Our research suggests that national bodies have so far only taken tentative steps into the first stage (e.g. the Taking Part survey and the CASE studies), and that the rest of the sequence remains uncharted. Our reading of the policy literature highlights four interrelated reasons that accord with our own assessment of why those responsible for national policies for sports and arts tend to be so resolute in keeping the two fields apart.

First, Bouckaert, Peters, and Verhoest (2010) note the continuing *specialization* in the public sector that frustrates coordination. This encourages a presumption that 'others' lack the expertise to contribute to decisions and practices. Verhoest et al. (2010) suggest that those in the respective departments and agencies come to believe that they are *meant to be* separate and independent. Peters (2013, 572) argues that information sharing might be more likely with 'organisations that are perceived as more different from themselves, given that they will not be perceived as competitors within the same policy space'. This suggests a second reason: professional communities engage in *turf wars* to protect territory, power and autonomy (e.g. Thompson 2000; Adler and Wilkerson 2008; Pawlak 2009). It is not just a question of jobs, but also of status and perceived ability to make decisions. Atha, using military language, explains that the Arts Council and the Sports Council, and the professionals within them, 'defend entrenched positions in protection of their own'. Third, the various interest groups already represented in the decision-making are wary of new interests appearing 'at the table' for fear of having to spread what are seen as meagre *resources* ever thinner.

More fundamentally, Peters (2013) suggests that there are different *epistemic communities*. In our case, the arts and sports policy-makers just see things fundamentally differently, so leading to an inability to comprehend the other.

> The professional training and the expertise of individual organisations provide them with lenses through which they interpret the policy world. Even if confronted with a common problem, different organisations with different epistemic foundations may perceive the problems differently…and therefore have a limited foundation for cooperation with other organisations. (Peters 2013, 573)

Certainly, this was Atha's interpretation of his tenure at the Sports Council and Arts Council. Campbell (2002) suggests that what may appear to be obstructive behaviour may be rationalized as protecting the very concepts that underlie policy in a particular area. The problem is compounded when, as appears to be the case here, there is little overlap between the networks of the professionals involved.

The arts–sport nexus: potential contributions

By holding the worlds of sport and the arts separate the policy statements discussed earlier are 'missing a trick'. What would be the potential benefits of a more integrated strategy?

Crucially, sport and the arts both have magical powers to create a space of relatedness, a space of mystery and marvel. Just as the idea of competition is attracting increasing interest in the arts, so too is creativity in sports. Artists bring something different to sport and sport can present artists with inspirational ideas of physicality and movement. Members of the Fields of Vision network have identified new arts–sport hybrids that are 'interactive' and 'transformative' (Froggett in this issue). They can inspire and create a sense of magic through cultural experimentation and innovation, appealing to new audiences in the process. Such new images and experiences disrupt stereotypes of what constitutes art and sport. These stereotypes see (some) sports as being the preserve of working class men and (some) arts as appealing mainly to middle class women. Some will be encouraged by the greater opportunity for play and fun (the ludic dimension), as it is easier to play when not tied by what people think sports or arts should be. Play is central to the origins and essence of both arts and sports; it is a concept shared by theatre and cricket, music and rugby. Play is linked with risk, adventure, imagination and dreams. The arts are rediscovering their ludic origins, as shown for instance by the recent popularity of 'immersive theatre', practised in the UK by companies including Punchdrunk and dreamthinkspeak. Despite the theoretical recognition of the importance of learning through play, the underinvestment in this field is reflected in cuts in funding for playgrounds and the downgrading of playworkers' jobs. However, a ludic approach still offers chances for both artS and sportS to attract new participants or audiences. In this increasingly commercial age the associated potential to attract new sponsors is very appealing, as are the possibilities for efficiency gains, like sharing facilities and marketing, especially at a time when cuts in public spending reduce established income streams.

As the bulk of provision is still separate, research evidence tends to consider the benefits derived from separated sport and arts provision (e.g. PAT 10 1999; Long et al. 2002; Fujiwara, Kudrna, and Dolan 2014a, 2014b). The most clearly demonstrated benefits of any increase in engagement are found in improved mental and physical health (see, for example Taylor's presentation at one of the Fields of Vision seminars https://artsinsport. wordpress.com/resources/). However, the practical experience introduced at the seminars showed how sports and arts together can help to achieve social inclusion, with gains in education, employment, social cohesion and community safety as well as wellbeing. Although evolving, class remains an important factor influencing patterns of cultural consumption and participation in the UK (Savage 2015). One of the key advantages of mixed arts–sport programming could be the broadening and mixing of audiences, by introducing unfamiliar art forms to a sport audience and vice versa.

The appropriateness of the individual measures notwithstanding, we welcome the commitment in recent strategies to trying to assess impact. Just as any arts or sport project, the kind of integrated initiatives we advocate below need to be able to demonstrate the outputs claimed for them.

Possible policies

While there is a growing acceptance of 'Sci-Art', Sport-Art currently has little currency and, as demonstrated here, is not part of public policy. We struggle to comprehend implicit definitions of 'culture' in government and NDPB thinking and suggest that cultural policies at all levels should clearly recognize sport's contribution to our national culture.

The government, DCMS, ACE and Sport England all urge others to join in partnerships. This would command greater credibility if ACE and Sport England were to demonstrate greater evidence of their preparedness to work collaboratively. Where 'partnerships' are established to address community need there should be an expectation that both sport and the arts will be represented and that funding will follow. Similarly, as the White Paper talked of directing Lottery funding to initiatives led by a strong coalition of local bodies, we might speculate on why this good practice is not deemed to be appropriate at national level in promoting collaboration between the arts and sports. The development of Sport-Art would benefit from taking this a step further by funding organizations beyond the established worlds of sport and the arts (e.g. youth work, community development, social work and public health) to run initiatives, as it is they who often have a better understanding of the advantages of an integrated approach.

As suggested earlier, the search for new audiences and participants featured in the strategy documents would be assisted by new forms/practices. At local level, there are many arts organizations demonstrating their readiness to innovate in this way. From the world of sport comparable initiatives may sometimes take the form of 'extreme' or 'lifestyle' sports. Hitherto lifestyle sports have been little valued by policy-makers, but they are slowly winning acceptance as demonstrated by Sport England's recent 'recognition' of parkour (also called free running or art deplacement). Its founders refer to it as the 'art of moving fluidly from one part of the environment to another' (McLean, Houshian, and Pike 2006, 795). Dance, gymnastics and sports like parkour and urban exploration blur the boundaries between sport and the arts (Gilchrist and Wheaton 2011). For urban explorers, for instance, documenting the explorations through cutting edge videos and photography is as important as overcoming the physical challenges, and Gilchrist and Wheaton (2011, 117) identify projects in Brighton and Croydon where parkour receives arts funding as a form of physical theatre.

It is possible that trends like the increasing importance of women in sport (as both participants and audiences) will make the task of arts–sports collaboration easier. There is also potential in the use of 'movement' and 'the moving body' as integrating concepts. These concepts (successfully adopted by arts–sports collaboration projects like the Cultural Olympiad's imove) link sport and the arts with the increasingly important strategic objective of promoting physical and mental health and wellbeing by combating sedentary lifestyles at all ages and encouraging active ageing to counteract dementia and other conditions.

Proposals for co-location might encourage dialogue if extended to bring together sport and arts organizations, in a return to the joint provision that was briefly on the agenda in the 1970s. Equally the community asset transfers being precipitated by the squeeze on local government finances may also trigger combined Sport-Art initiatives as community trusts recognize the need to broaden their newly acquired facilities' appeal to make them financially sustainable. For example, to keep afloat, Bramley Baths, a community enterprise in Leeds, runs aqua-ballet sessions, hosts film shows and has had a string quartet playing in the swimming pool.

Such a shift in emphasis will take time to evolve, suggesting yet again the importance of planning for the longer term, not just short ('demonstration') initiatives. Experiments are all well and good, but it takes a lot to turn round oil tankers, especially if they are fully laden with the cultural baggage of established practice.

Conclusions

We examined national policy statements in the hope that they pointed the way to future integrated practices, only to find that they lagged behind what is happening on the ground. If the sport sector is showing more attention to arts policy than the arts sector is showing to sport policy, it is only marginal.

It is not just the four strategy documents discussed here that demonstrate a lack of integration of sport and the arts. A wider reading of the policy literature and party manifestos for the 2017 UK General Election suggests the same. However, at other levels, integration can be evidenced in more than just integration of cultural forms. For example, there may be integration of provision, as when community projects do not offer only sports or only arts, but can provide either as appropriate in the interest of securing community development. Equally, sport and the arts may be combined in an expression of cultural identity, whether by a socio-political elite (Henley, Glyndebourne, Covent Garden, Ascot...) or by a marginalized social group. In the case of the Leeds African Caribbean community this might be through Carnival, the Caribbean Cricket Club, Fforde Grene football, reggae and ska, even dominoes at the West Indian Centre. Equivalents might also be identified for LGBT communities and other groups keen to establish a sense of shared identity. Such processes do not constitute policy, but the seeds of new policies may lie outside established forums. This is why policies concerned with lifestyle, youth and public health may be more accommodating to combined arts/sport initiatives than the entrenched interests of traditional arts or sports policy communities.

Despite sharing the same building Sport England and Arts Council England seem determined to protect their separateness while at local level there are some keen to bridge across established boundaries, even though integrated local authority leisure departments are no longer the norm.

To date, we have found little evidence of looking to international experience to learn what might be most productive in creative and social terms. We can see a role for the Fields of Vision network here and suggest there may be potential in the developing concept of *culture urbaine* in France. This encompasses art forms like graffiti, rap, slam poetry, hip hop, beatbox, urban dance (including breakdancing), photography and video, as well as sports represented by the French League of Urban Sports, founded in 2009: parkour, skateboarding, BMX cycling, street basketball, street football, street golf, street surfing, urbanball, quick soccer and street fishing. We are aware that similar projects may be found on the ground in the UK, but since the late 1990s different French governments have recognized the potential of arts–sport collaboration within the framework of the concept of 'urban cultures', especially as a response to the problem of youth unemployment and marginalization, and to the risk of radicalization of young Muslims in the suburbs of French cities including Paris, Lille, Lyon and Marseilles. France now has a National Urban Cultures Observatory, several festivals cutting across the arts–sport divide, and institutions like the Centre Eurorégional des Culture Urbaines in Lille, inspired by an idea of Lille-born rapper Axiom and supported by Lille City Council.

The way in which differences between 'sport' and 'the arts' are reinforced by the strategies we have examined does not bode well for efforts to integrate the two. One of the problems we have noted is the paucity of 'intercultural mediators' (Bernard Atha being a rare example), who can encourage dialogue, encounter and exchange between the two policy communities. Like other forms of intercultural exchange and crossover (for example, in music, gastronomy, fashion and design) arts–sport collaboration could encourage aesthetic, conceptual, organizational and product innovation. It could form part of a bold rethinking of cultural policy, comprising mixed arts–sport public spaces and institutions. An uphill battle awaits in bridging the organizational chasm between sports and arts, yet that also offers scope for making an impact in an underdeveloped area of work. If sport and the arts are understood at policy level as alien concepts the challenge for those like us who want to bring them together is to reframe the issues involved. This can happen through further research on the benefits of collaboration and integration and through pilot projects – e.g. twinning schemes between museums and sports clubs, or experimental sport–arts centres.

The French experience and individual local initiatives in the UK suggest that perhaps the best chance of achieving greater integration lies somewhere beyond the rigidities of established arts and sports policy communities: in health, youth work, community development or other social policy arenas.

Notes

1. https://artsinsport.wordpress.com/
2. This echoes the Chief Medical Officer (DH 2011, 17): 'from a public health perspective, helping people to move from inactivity to low or moderate activity will produce the greatest benefit'.
3. https://www.gov.uk/government/news/new-ministerial-team-at-dcms-confirmed (last accessed 20 April 2017).
4. The National Council for Voluntary Organisations leads a consortium using funding from ACE to help improve the interaction between cultural organisations and public sector commissioners to develop greater awareness of the potential for cultural organisations to deliver social benefits.
5. According to the web site of the Chartered Institute for the Management of Sport and Physical Activity, it provides leadership, support and empowerment for professionals working in sport and physical activity, and a single voice for the sector: https://www.cimspa.co.uk/
6. We have been unable to identify record of a more recent equivalent.

Disclosure statement

No potential conflict of interest was reported by the authors.

Funding

The research was self-funded. The Fields of Vision network was supported by the Arts and Humanities Research Council in 2016/17.

ORCID

Jonathan Long ⓘ http://orcid.org/0000-0001-5220-1152

References

Adler, E. S., and J. D. Wilkerson. 2008. "Intended Consequences: Jurisdictional Reform and Issue Control in the US House of Representatives." *Legislative Studies Quarterly* 33 (1): 85–112. doi:10.3162/036298008783743318.

ACE (Arts Council England). 2013. *Great Art and Culture for Everyone, 2010–2020: 10-Year Strategic Framework*. 2nd ed. London: ACE.

Bouckaert, G., B. G. Peters, and K. Verhoest. 2010. *Coordination of Public Sector Organizations: Shifting Patterns of Public Management*. Basingstoke: Palgrave.

Campbell, J. 2002. "Ideas, Politics, and Public Policy." *Annual Review of Sociology* 28 (1): 21–38. doi:10.1146/annurev.soc.28.110601.141111

DCMS (Department for Culture, Media and Sport). 2001. *Building on PAT 10. Progress Report on Social Inclusion*. London: DCMS.

DH (Department of Health). 2011. *Start Active, Stay Active: A Report on Physical Activity for Health from the Four Home Countries' Chief Medical Officers*. London: Department of Health.

DoE (Department of the Environment). 1977a. *Leisure and the Quality of Life: A Report on Four Local Experiments*. vol. 1. London: HMSO.

DoE (Department of the Environment). 1977b. *Leisure and the Quality of Life: A Report on Four Local Experiments*. vol. 2, Research Papers. London: HMSO.

Froggett, L., J. Manley, A. Roy, and S. Hacking. 2013. *An Evaluation of Imove: Final Report*. Preston: UCLAN.

Fujiwara, D., L. Kudrna, and P. Dolan. 2014a. *Quantifying the Social Impacts of Culture and Sport*. London: DCMS. https://www.gov.uk/government/uploads/system/uploads/attachment_data/file/304896/Quantifying_the_Social_Impacts_of_Culture_and_Sport.pdf

Fujiwara, D., L. Kudrna, and P. Dolan. 2014b. *Quantifying and Valuing the Wellbeing Impacts of Culture and Sport*. London: DCMS. https://www.gov.uk/government/uploads/system/uploads/attachment_data/file/304899/Quantifying_and_valuing_the_wellbeing_impacts_of_sport_and_culture.pdf

Gilchrist, P., and B. Wheaton. 2011. "Lifestyle Sport, Public Policy and Youth Engagement: Examining the Emergence of Parkour." *International Journal of Sport Policy and Politics* 3 (1): 109–131. doi:10.1080/19406940.2010.547866.

HM Government. 2015. *Sporting Future: A New Strategy for an Active Nation*. London: Cabinet Office.

Inglis, F. 1978. "The Imagery of Power: Sporting Institutions and Sporting Individuals." In *Community Leisure and Culture: Arts and Sports Provision*, edited by B. Rees and S. Parker, 2.1–2.4. Eastbourne: Leisure Studies Association.

James, C. L. R. 2005. *Beyond a Boundary*. London: Yellow Jersey Press.

John, G. 1978. "Sports/Arts Building Design." In *Community Leisure and Culture: Arts and Sports Provision*, edited by B. Rees and S. Parker, 5.1–5.6. Eastbourne: Leisure Studies Association.

Long, J., and P. Bramham. 2006. "Joining up Policy Discourses and Fragmented Practices: The Precarious Contribution of Cultural Projects to Social Inclusion?" *Policy and Politics* 34 (1): 133–151. doi:10.1332/030557306775212160.

Long, J., and I. Strange. 2009. "Mission or Pragmatism? Cultural Policy in Leeds since 2000." In *Sport, Leisure and Culture in the Postmodern City*, edited by P. Bramham and S. Wagg, 63–82. Aldershot: Ashgate.

Long, J., M. Welch, P. Bramham, K. Hylton, J. Butterfield, and E. Lloyd. 2002. *Count Me in: The Dimensions of Social Inclusion through Culture and Sport*. Report to the Department for Culture Media and Sport. http://eprints.leedsbeckett.ac.uk/638/

Long, J., J. Parry, D. Sandle, and K. Spracklen. 2013. "Introduction." In *Fields of Vision: The Arts in Sport*, edited by D. Sandle, J. Long, J. Parry and K. Spracklen, v–ix. Eastbourne: Leisure Studies Association.

McLean, C. R., S. Houshian, and J. Pike. 2006. "Paediatric Fractures Sustained in Parkour (Free Running)." *Injury* 37 (8): 795–797. doi:10.1016/j.injury.2006.04.119.

Mennell, S. 1976. *Cultural Policy in Towns*. Strasbourg: Council of Europe.

Parnell, D., K. Spracklen, and P. Millward. 2017. "Sport Management Issues in an Era of Austerity." *European Sport Management Quarterly* 17 (1): 67–74. doi:10.1080/16184742.2016.1257552.

Pawlak, P. 2009. "The External Dimension of the Area of Freedom, Security and Justice: Hijacker or Hostage of Cross-Pillarization?" *Journal of European Integration*. 31 (1): 25–44. doi:10.1080/07036330802503825.

Peters, B. G. 2013. "Toward Policy Coordination: Alternatives to Hierarchy." *Policy and Politics* 41 (4): 569–584. doi:10.1332/030557312X655792.

Phillpots, L. 2013. "An Analysis of the Policy Process for Physical Education and School Sport: The Rise and Demise of School Sport Partnerships." *International Journal of Sport Policy* 5 (2): 193–211. doi:10.1080/19406940.2012.666558.

Pollitt, C. 2003. "Joined-up Government: a Survey." *Political Studies Review* 1 (1): 34–49. doi:10.1111/1478-9299.00004.

PAT 10 (Policy Action Team 10). 1999. *Arts and Sport: A Report to the Social Exclusion Unit*. London: Department for Culture Media and Sport.

Savage, M. 2015. *Social Class in the 21st Century*. London: Pelican.

Snow, C. P. 1959. *The Two Cultures*. London: Cambridge University Press.

Sports Council. 1982. *Sport in the Community: The Next Ten Years*. London: The Sports Council.

Sport England. 2016. *Towards an Active Nation. Strategy 2016–2021*. London: Sport England.

Taylor, P., L. Davies, P. Wells, J. Gilbertson, and W. Tayleur. 2015. *A Review of the Social Impacts of Culture and Sport*. London: DCMS. https://www.gov.uk/government/uploads/system/uploads/attachment_data/file/416279/A_review_of_the_Social_Impacts_of_Culture_and_Sport.pdf

The Culture White Paper. 2016 (Cm. 9218) London: DCMS.

Thompson, J. D. 2000. *Organisations in Action: Social Sciences Basis of Administrative Theory*. New Brunswick, NJ: Transaction Press.

Thomson, R., F. Stokman, and R. Torenvlied. 2003. "Models of Collective Decision-Making: Introduction." *Rationality and Society* 15 (1): 5–14. doi:10.1177/1043463103015001037.

Verhoest, K., P. Roness, B. Verschuere, K. Rubecksen, and M. MacCarthaigh. 2010. *Autonomy and Control of State Agencies*. Basingstoke: Macmillan.

Wagg, S., ed. 2002. *British Football and Social Exclusion*. London: Frank Cass.

Walker, G. 1978. "European Problems of Cultural and Sports Provision". In *Community Leisure and Culture: Arts and Sports Provision*, edited by B. Rees and S. Parker, 3.1–3.11. Eastbourne: Leisure Studies Association.

Participant experience in art-sport: Additive? Interactive? Transformative?

Lynn Froggett

ABSTRACT

imove, which became Yorkshire and Humberside's regional programme for the 2012 Cultural Olympiad, was inspired by 'the art of movement', and underpinned by the idea of transcending dualities of mind/body and art/sport. Art and sport were combined in various ways within the programme, and with different degrees and types of audience engagement and participation. This article draws on the evaluation data collected during the course of the programme to develop a typology of art-sport relationships: additive, interactive, and transformative. It defines and illustrates each instance with examples of particular projects and highlights the role of the participants/audience in determining the nature of the physical learning and new knowledge of the moving body that arises in each case. Finally, it considers the conditions under which hybrid forms of art-sport can innovate and flourish with reference to the concept of 'third space'.

Introduction

Do the changing conditions under which contemporary art and sport are practised favour a closer relationship between the two? Welsch (2006) identifies an aspect of contemporary culture which does in fact appear to facilitate a convergence: specifically the aestheticization of everyday social practices which has arguably contributed to the blurring of the boundaries between 'high' and 'low' art. Welsch's claim is that both art and sport can be transformative for spectators or participants in comparable ways. There has been an episodic discussion, especially in the fields of philosophy of sport and aesthetics, on whether sport can legitimately be regarded as art (for example Best 1974, 1980; Wertz 1986). The questions that concern us here are what hybrid forms can the interaction between art and sport take? How do they implicate audiences and participants in their development, and with what impacts on individuals and communities? Under what conditions can 'art-sport' flourish?

This question is addressed here by developing a typology of art-sport interaction. For purposes of illustration it takes examples from a single programme, imove – which combined art and sport in a number of different ways, and which became part of the Cultural Olympiad programme for Yorkshire and Humberside. The Psychosocial Research Unit at the University of Central Lancashire conducted a two-year evaluation of this programme (Froggett et al. 2013). The purpose of the present article is not to reprise the evidence for imove's achievements or shortcomings[1] but to think beyond the documented outcomes of the evaluation in order to produce a conceptual model of art-sport interaction. After the Cultural Olympiad, imove continued to support key projects that had demonstrated sustainability and was reconstituted as imove arts.[2] These projects are of interest by virtue of the fact that they continued to attract audiences, participants, funding and community profile long after the conclusion of the original imove programme, and therefore at the very least they afford localized examples of viable art-sport projects. Two of them: Runs on the Board and Sea Swim inform the model developed here.

Over a two-year period imove commissioned a range of projects inspired by 'the art of human movement'. The aims for the programme were ambitious and a strong accent on participation was central to their realization. From the outset people of the region were to be introduced to new cultural experiences in which physical learning and awareness of the moving body would follow from combinations of sport and arts based activities. It was intended that community and identity would be built through enhanced health and well-being and through the positive regional self-perception and regard that an enriched cultural offer could support. It was hoped that wider national and international links would follow, but more importantly, that culture would be repositioned as central and relevant to people's lives by drawing on and enhancing existing regional resources (especially in terms of sporting activities) and strengths (Figure 1).

The programme commissions were very diverse in terms scale, target audience, how they built on sporting and cultural traditions, and the use they made of urban spaces, landscapes and the coastline of the region. Most projects were arts led but involved sport in varying degrees. Examples were: *Runs on the Board*, the over 50's Grey Fox Trophy cricket series, with artists and writers working alongside the game and producing work inspired by it; Phoenix Theatre's *Score* and *Dancing with Rhinos* where the dance moves were inspired by football and rugby; *Games in the Park* which was aimed at children and young people in Bradford; *Stanza* Stones which combined walking with poetry in a contemplative

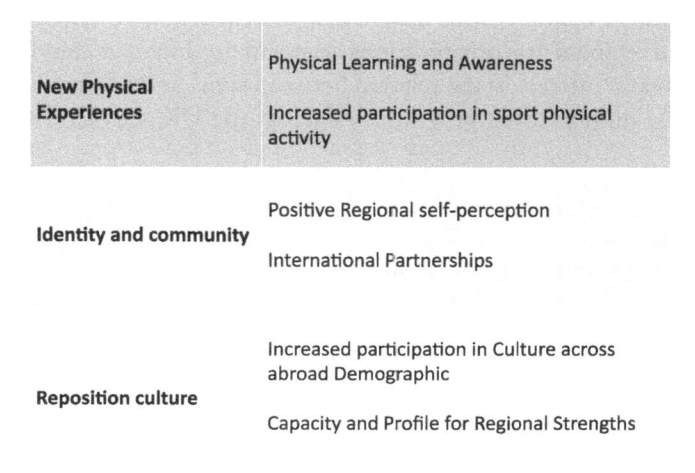

Figure 1. imove's key aims.

exploration of nature, led by poet, Simon Armitage; *Synchronised* which fused synchronized swimming and classical Indian dance in both performance and participatory Aqua Kathak workshops; *Cycle Song* a participatory operatic spectacle in Scunthorpe, based on a local cycling hero; *Sea Swim* in Scarborough where open water swimming continues to inspire a range of associated cultural activities.

The Psychosocial Research Unit at University of Central Lancashire became the research partner for the imove programme in its delivery phase, with a brief to evaluate psychosocial outcomes for individuals, groups, communities and the cultural sector. The complexity and diversity of the imove programme meant that a variety of research strategies were needed to capture process and outcomes at personal, project and programme level and these had to adapt to different forms of activity and event as the programme unfolded. Methods were ethnographic, narrative, observational, interview and survey-based, and they were used in combination in in-depth case-studies, extensive rapid capture surveys, and for programme overview. Much of the final report considers what imove achieved for participants, host communities and partner organizations (Froggett et al. 2013). However, at the heart of the programme lay a complex issue that can now be reconsidered with hindsight: the relationship between physical movement, especially in its sporting forms, and art.

The Programme Director, Tessa Gordzeijko, came from a predominantly arts background with a strong interest in dance, but was also prepared to take seriously and re-articulate for a contemporary regional context elements of Pierre de Coubertain's vision of Olympism (2014). In the idiom of his time (1863–1937) de Coubertain promoted the idea of combining in a balanced whole, exalted qualities of body and mind, through involvement in the Games. The Cultural Oympiad in its original conception was to provide an artistic avenue for the expression of the Olympic spirit (Muller 2000). It is fair to say that it has had a chequered history, variously attributed to the overtones of a now dated Nietzschean vitalism; de Coubertain's admiration for British public school education (1988); distaste among artists for ferocious public competition; and the fact that sport per se has proved to be a somewhat restrictive subject for art. The 2012 UK Cultural Olympiad was less concerned with Olympian competitive ideals than with offering an ambitious and diverse cultural programme in parallel with the Games (Garcia 2013). Among other opportunities, this afforded regional arts organizations access to funding that could be used to raise public awareness and interest in the relation between sport and culture. The Legacy Trust UK allocated £24 million to 12 programmes across the UK regions with the following explicit aims:

- to unite culture, sport, knowledge and learning, in line with the values and vision of the Olympics
- to make a lasting difference to all those involved
- to be grassroots projects, often small in scale, and uniting communities of interest at local and regional level.[3]

Gordzeijko's intention was to bring a clear philosophical perspective to the task of putting together a regionally relevant programme that would achieve these goals. In particular, she saw the opportunity to use human movement in its many forms to challenge Cartesian dualism – which she associated with the mind–body split endemic in Western culture. Cartesian dualism can be linked to low rates of participation in art and sporting activities alike, insofar as it supports a reductionist view of sport as a 'merely' physical activity and an elitist view of art as a 'cerebral' form of expression, accessible to the highly educated. The particularly low participation rates for physical activity in the Yorkshire and Humber region could be linked to deficits in health and well-being at a population level. By combining art and sport in new ways around the possibilities of the moving body, imove intended to ride the wave of interest in sport generated by the Olympics. It aimed to commission movement-based art, not only for known venues and audiences, but for communities in areas where cultural investment had been historically low. The notion of human movement was intentionally expansive so that the programme could draw on the diversity of cities of inward migration, such as Bradford, showing how it has been enriched by population flows, as well as settled, traditional white communities, and the skills of organizations that made up the cultural sector itself. imove was, among other things, an identity project, with a strong commitment to the healthy body in movement at its core and an implicit conviction that this was a goal around which people could unite.

Despite the strong intellectual underpinnings and coherent sense of purpose with which the programme set out, the imove vision proved hard to distil into simple messaging that the public could readily comprehend. The concept of mind/body integration has been promoted by popular 'wellness' psychology, and esoteric practices such as yoga, but the experience of the programme suggests it still has little local and regional purchase, at least in Yorkshire. Confusion as to what it might mean in the context of imove seemed to accumulate as activities gathered pace. Attempts were made to clarify the idea for the purposes of marketing but the problem appeared to be that in drawing on a philosophical framework which offered a challenge to habitual ways of thinking, and commissioning hybrid art-sport projects that were themselves unfamiliar, imove was unintentionally surrounding the problem of mind/body and art/sport with an aura of 'strangeness'. This compounded the split that it sought to overcome. Members of the public who were interviewed declared that they didn't have a clue what it was about, while the marketing consultants urged a simpler and more straightforward message. Gordzeijko referred to the problem of being dogged by the purity of the concept. As a result, messaging was simplified without, however, abandoning the core idea which continued to inform the more complex projects. Art-sport and mind-body relations, if they were to be worked through in the context of imove, would have to find practical expression in the activities themselves where they could then more easily be recognized. However, the problem of conceptualizing the different ways in which art and sport can in principle combine, remains. Art-sport projects within the imove programme suggest a typology that could be heuristically useful in identifying the underpinning modes of public engagement and participation.

With hindsight, and through examining its different expressions, a tripartite model has emerged that characterizes the forms taken by art-sport within the programme: additive, interactive, transformative (Figure 2). This model is here illustrated through projects that are instances of the combinations it describes. The discussion that follows the presentation of empirical examples will help to clarify the conditions of third space under which art and sport interact to produce transformative effects.

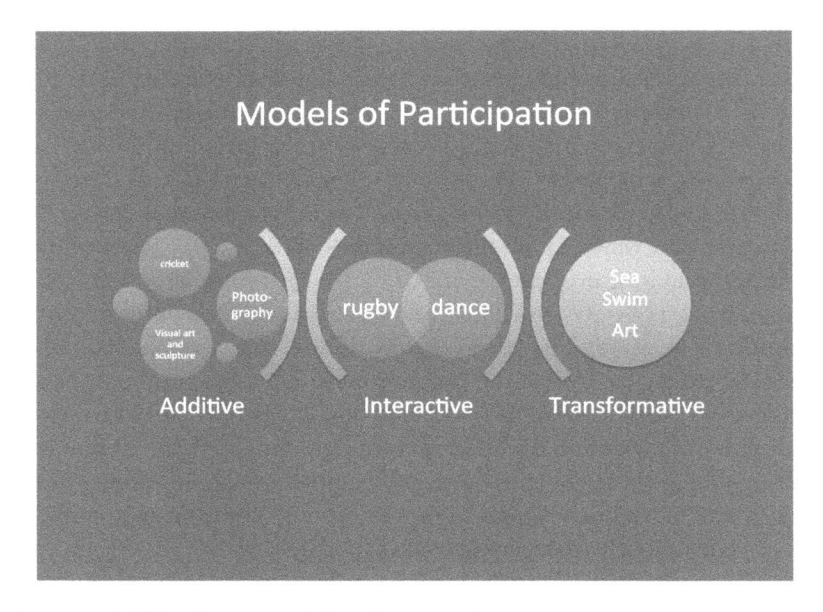

Figure 2. Art-sport: Additive? Interactive? Transformative?

Theoretical framework

The theoretical framework that informs this typology draws on a psychosocial conceptualization of third space as an 'in-between' arena of experience (Winnicott [1971] 2005) that arises at the boundaries of what is subjectively known but has yet to find a symbolic form that allows it to be shared with and communicated to others. This is the ground on which the unknown, which can be perceived as either full of potential, or threatening and alien, can be encountered without preconceptions, and therefore with curiosity and openness to discovery. It is essentially a ludic space favourable to emergence insofar as it allows for the suspension of habitual and taken-for-granted assumptions about the nature of play, games and other forms of creative activity, and the rules by which they are bound. From a developmental perspective Winnicott ([1971] 2005) who designates it 'potential space' saw it as the locus of creative exploration of the world, where subjective experience finds expression in shared cultural form. Third space or potential space is 'in-between' in the sense that it is a third area of experiencing, neither wholly subjectively conceived, nor wholly objectively perceived, and the originary location of culture. The capacity to make use of the space of cultural experience is elaborated throughout life in the reception and production of art, literature, sport and other cultural forms.

Psychoanalyst Christopher Bollas (1992) argues that self-expression within cultural domains, as well as in everyday life, allows for the refinement of personal idiom. Hence selection, participation and performance in art and sport can be regarded as expressions of personal idiom in a cultural form. Philosopher of art and music Suzanne Langer ([1942] 1990) argues that the symbolic activity at issue here is 'presentational' rather than 'discursive' and represents the articulation of knowledge as sensuous bodily practices, for the most part unavailable to verbal language. German cultural analyst Alfred Lorenzer (1986) regards this as the basis of sensuous symbolic 'scenic' experience that accounts for the vitality of cultural expression. His work, from a very different, depth hermeneutic, intellectual tradition, converges with that of Winnicott on identifying the in-between nature of cultural experience, and Lorenzer comments on the compatibility of Winnicott's concepts with his own theory of 'symbolic interaction forms' (Lorenzer and Orban 1978). Elsewhere in the context of sci-art I have argued that the concept of third space is useful in understanding what happens when knowledge is produced in the encounter between disciplines, where there is as yet no settled discourse (Muller et al. 2015, forthcoming).

Together with colleagues in the Psychosocial Research Unit at Uclan and in the arts sector, I have developed a new group-based methodology, the Visual Matrix, based on the principle that in order to understand a third space in any given context, we have to create one under carefully curated conditions (Froggett, Manley, and Roy 2015). This development occurred subsequent to the imove programme evaluation which, however, clearly revealed the methodological gap that it responds to. I shall refer to this again in the discussion and conclusions, though a full exposition of the methodology is beyond the scope of this article. I have also attempted to demonstrate that third space facilitates expressions where the aesthetic dimension of experience comes strongly to the fore as an 'aesthetic third' (Froggett and Trustram 2014) and that this accounts in part for the distinctively new knowledge that arises within it, and its transformative potentials. In the typology presented here the transformative model both requires and reproduces third space more consistently than the other two, although it is likely to arise provisionally and often with productive instabilities in all three instances. I shall attempt to show by means of examples, how art-sport in third space is likely to be characterized by a distinctive aesthetic that defines it as a new, hybrid, transdisciplinary practice.

Additive art-sport

Runs on the Board was a classic example of an 'additive' case where Art and Sport illustrate or interpret one another, but where each retains distinctiveness as a cultural form. The project featured a cricket series for teams with a combined age of over 550 and culminated in the award of the 'coveted' Grey Fox Trophy, a glass sculpture of a Victoria sandwich cake, at the Headingley Carnegie cricket ground in Leeds. The trophy was designed by *The Curious Guide* artists Rob Young and Tim Sutton and set the tone of the accompanying mobile installation (Figure 3). Over-fifty's cricket was rescued from nostalgia by a note of affectionate irony and self-deprecation in the art that graced the display cases, featuring, for example, the iconic 'Man of the Match' prize, The Combover Ball (Figure 4).

On a classical note, there was a limited edition hard copy book edited by Graham Roberts (2011) with poet Andrew McMillan and photographer Anton Want who attended dozens of local matches around Yorkshire, capturing the spirit, personality and aesthetic of game and its amateur older players. Portraits were accompanied by photographs celebrating scenes of pitch, figures and sky against cricket green and conversations recorded through a poet's ear (Figure 5).

Amateur cricket is woven into the warp and weft of Yorkshire life and local matches are social affairs. Audiences for the matches were diverse, as the sport attracts an enthusiastic South Asian following, whose experience of cricket may be less steeped in the aesthetic of Englishness that inspired much of the work on show. However, the additive model meant that the art and the cricket could in principle be enjoyed for their mutual enhancement, or separately from one another. The centrepiece and inspiration for the whole project undoubtedly remained the cricket itself, with the artwork as something of an embellishment;

Figure 3. The Series Trophy, Runs on the Board: The Book, Photograph by Anton Want.

Figure 4. Man of the Match Trophy, Runs on the Board: The Book, Photograph by Anton Want.

delightful and amusing to those for whom it was meaningful, but not indispensable to the *Runs on the Board* experience. This is not to gainsay the pleasure that the art afforded to those who engaged with it. In several short interviews conducted at the ground it consistently attracted curiosity and favourable comment. It could well be argued that the 'parallel' existence afforded by the additive model gives maximum freedom to both the art and the

Figure 5. Image from imove touring installation, Runs on the Board: The Book, Photograph by Anton Want.

sport since neither is constrained or qualified by the other. Members of the audience are at liberty to bestow their attention selectively according to taste and disposition. However, beyond individual preferences, the art aimed to expand the symbolic registers available for the game capturing the distinctive and elusive quality of events aimed at older players and their communities along with their good humour, sociability, localism and timeless devotion to the sport, where at a local level competitive success is regarded as secondary to love of the game for its own sake. Although not its primary purpose, the art aimed to find a form for these qualities that also enhanced marketing of the series. A measure of success, and the affection bestowed on the project, is the ongoing sponsorship that has allowed it to continue each summer, ensuring a lasting legacy.

Interactive art-sport

imove also commissioned a series of projects in which there was a more interactive relationship between art and sport in the sense that they combined to produce something genuinely novel which would not have existed except through this engagement. The mutual influence of art and sport in such instances occurs in settings where one is transposed into the other; usually, sport becomes the subject matter of participatory arts (rather than vice versa). Reflecting the Legacy Trust's commitment to 'Artists Taking the Lead' the interaction in the imove projects was arts-led. This is unsurprising in the sense that artists are professionally concerned with transgressing boundaries, exploring the as yet unrealized potentials of their materials, and confounding expectations. In this model the audience may either enjoy the outcome of the art-sport interaction, or become more actively involved in its processes.

In the blink of an eye

As an example of the former relation, imove supported the commissioning of two artworks for the exhibition at the National Science and Media Museum *In the Blink of an Eye*. *Forms* by Quayola and Memo Akten was based on digital analysis of the body in motion, in successive phases, as athletes push themselves to extremes of performance. The resulting forms are kinetic abstracts – volumetric sculptures of the relation between pure movement and

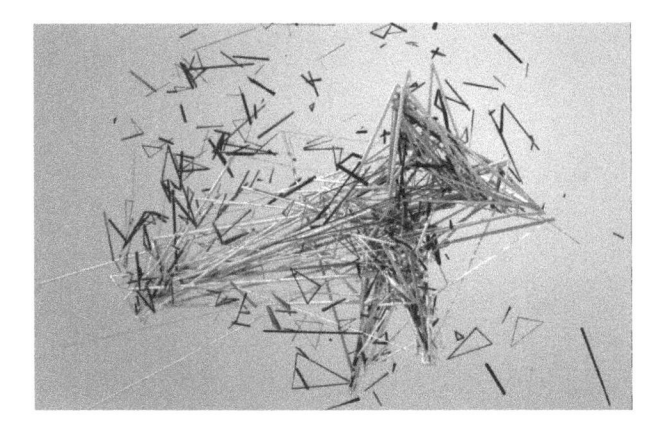

Figure 6. Still image from forms. Artists: Quayola and Memo Atken, Science and Media Museum https://www.scienceandmediamuseum.org.uk/what-was-on/blink-eye

surrounding element.[4] In this case the art-sport relationship is essential to the outcome, each being dependent on the other, and the audience is presented with a finished product, which by virtue of its scale and presence in a gallery setting is able to offer a vicarious experience to the spectator who, however, is incidental to the finished work (Figure 6).

Dancing on together

Dancing on Together effected a more participatory combination. Sharon Watson, Creative Director of Phoenix Dance Theatre, choreographed *Score* and *Dancing with Rhinos*, modelled on football and rugby moves respectively, and performed to enthusiastic young audiences at Leeds United FC and Headingley Carnegie Stadium (Figure 7). In the course of the programme, opportunities arose for young people from local schools and clubs, many of whom had no previous dance experience, but who would have been familiar with rugby and football, at least as spectator sports. Charis Charles, education coordinator for Phoenix was surprised by the impact on young people of performing in front of large crowds of sports fans

Figure 7. Dancing with Rhinos. Photogtaph courtesy of imove arts.

> … we didn't know how the audience was going to react and I prepped them, you know, one of them was as young as 13 … how do you prep a 13 year-old that you might, by over 10,000 people, potentially be booed off? … They were on the big screens, it was such an occasion and the audience response couldn't have been better … that is just sports audience seeing, you know, live art … (Charis Charles 13.07.12)

Community sport development officers from Leeds United supported the event with balls, flags, whistles and markers, so that at a community level barriers between the worlds of dance and sport began to be dismantled. The same was true of the gender divisions between dance and these overwhelmingly male dominated sports.

At an individual level the dance was enjoyed by young people who would normally have been excluded by fiercely competitive team sports, raising self-esteem. For example, in the case of one boy

> … he had Dispraxia and his mum came and spoke to me and she said I can't believe I've just watched him perform a dance piece in time, catching a ball and actually lead the steps, you know, I've never heard of that being achieved and I've got my son to prove it and actually he was told he would never do this… (Sharon Watson 13.07.12)

This interactive model realizes its full impact through participation. Given the status of football and rugby in these Northern English communities sport-themed dance would most likely have been of interest, even if performed solely by professionals, however the opportunity for young people to practise it raised enthusiasm for contemporary dance to a new level, while at the same time deepening public understanding of grace and choreography within the sports themselves. In this sense, the project was educational without being didactic, developing authentically new forms of self-expression and public appreciation of movement.

Transformative art-sport

The interactive mode is unstable in the positive sense that it opens the door to fuller more diverse and self-sustaining public engagement and therefore something enduringly transformative. Transformative art-sport is likely to depend both on a professional input that transmits key skills, ambition and confidence, while developing completely new cultural forms that depend for their realization on the full contribution of participants. The impacts are likely to be complex with the potential to bring about profound shifts in sensibility for individuals and communities, while the art and the sport are each expressed through the medium of the other and the environment in which they occur, to the extent that it is no longer possible to 'weigh' or 'disentangle' their respective contributions.

Sea swim

> Sea Swim is about process: documentation and display; sub-cultures; the movement from sensation to narrative; suspension to weight; the embodied imagination – the sea is the ultimate liminal space and Sea Swim moves back and forth between the sea and art. (Sea Swim website 22-08-17)[5]

The Sea Swim project in Scarborough ran from May 2011 to September 2012 and was codirected by artist, curator and swimmer, Lara Goodband, with poet and swimmer, John Wedgwood (Figure 8). It proved so popular that it gained ongoing support from imove, Legacy Trust UK and Arts Council England, and continues as an open (very cold) water

Figure 8. Sea swimmers and supporters: *photograph courtesy of imove arts.*

swimming club with an intrinsically cultural dimension. The project took inspiration from the fortitude of generations of cold water swimmers whose legacy is remembered in Scarborough through the organized forms it has taken, and through ancestral figures whose stories have passed into local family folklore.

The physical focus of the activities was where land and sea meet in the wet sands and chilly waters of England's North Sea shoreline. Equally indispensable, as a site of preparation, recuperation and sociability, were the two adjacent Edwardian bathing huts where poetry was read and written and where blue shivering flesh turned vibrant pink over hot tea, home-made cake and conversation. According to eight of the swimmers interviewed directly after a swim heightened sensation led naturally to creative self-expression, and this was visibly reflected in the comments, sketches and fragments of poetry pinned to the walls of the hut.

By infusing sea swimming with imove's commitment to the idea of body/mind integration, or embodied mind, and linking it to historical traditions, a sense of place, home and culture became integral to the experience. The basis, however, was the existential awareness that arises in startling liquid sensation and the exploration of separation, connection and borderline between terrestrial and aquatic perception

> There's something about...the way in which the water finds out every single part of your body ... You know where you are, you're not in some virtual world anymore, you're back right in your body... I'm kind of interested in those moments of transition from being on dry land to being buoyant and out in the sea...and the stories that have grown up out of that very simple experiential change of weight from the land to the sea ... a whole host of Mediterranean literature based on sea journeys, and I thought wouldn't it be great if we start with the actual experience of going in the sea and then build out of that towards stories that exist around that very basic experience, body experience, being in water. (John Wedgwood Clarke, Sea Swim Artistic Co-Director, 07.07.12)

> Openness, that infinity, that looking in one direction and seeing nothing and in the other direction and seeing the land and being anchored. To me it's all about... all the experience is about that sense of separation from the land. (Sea Swimmer, quoted in Damian Murphy's Sea Swim podcast[6])

The altered perspective, achieved through bodily experience in the present, found expression through the conversational exchanges of the group and was the most important outcome for individuals. It was directed simultaneously 'inwards' in self-reflection and 'outwards' towards a shared sensibility expressed in poetry and art, This was confirmed in our interviews and in public statements as swimmers gained heightened consciousness of self, environment and other people

> When you get out into the sea you have a completely different take on the place that you spend most of your time... (Sea Swimmer in Damian Murphy's Sea Swim podcast)

> When the sun's out, it's just absolutely amazing, just watching, watching the reflections on the surface of the water and I definitely am more appreciative of living here now. (Sea Swimmer in Damian Murphy's Sea Swim podcast)

> I have found that the beach and the sea form a greater part of my idea of home than I'd realized. (Sea Swimmer in Sea Swim self-evaluation, 25.10.12)

> As my head slips under the glass-like surface I think of friends, of family, of those who are far from me – yet we are all connected by the tide of water and time. (Sea Swimmer in Sea Swim self-evaluation, 25.10.12)

Finding shared artistic expression allowed the group to make full use of the swimming as a sensory and reflective experience. Swims – always in a group – would often begin by sharing a reading from Homer's Odyssey. Swimmers took these words with them into the water where they remained present in their minds and bodies, were 'salted' with the sea and emerged to be woven into new thoughts, stories, prose and poetry. These were recorded on post-cards, diary notes and sketches pinned to the beach-hut walls and some found their way into exhibits in the Scarborough Art Gallery in a show that included visual art, film and creative writing. The exhibition extended the presence of the project within the town and expanded its reach to visitor audiences. Variants of it travelled regionally to York and Middlesborough Institute of Modern Arts (MIMA). Wedgwood Clarke compiled and performed *A Swimmers' Manifesto*. Swimmers' reflections attested to sensory transformations, sociability and dramatically improved sense of well-being, recorded in podcast by sound artist Damian Murphy[7], in creative writing by swimmers themselves, and in an anthology by Wedgwood-Clarke (2014).

> We emerged from the sea as Odysseus did – but laughing at the nebulas of swirling mist that danced with us...No eagles, but distant gulls, as we stroked along, mammals in our element.' (Sea Swimmer's postcard, Sea Swim exhibition at MIMA)

However, the perceptual acuity that followed from each swim could take poetic cues from observed banalities of situation, as well as high art.

> Spilt sugar as action art; tea bags dropped on the concrete a gesture testing the immanent weight of saturated tea leaves – soft land art. (John Wedgwood Clarke, extracts from 'Splash. Towards a Swimmer's Manifesto')

Seventy-four seconds (by John Wedgwood Clarke and Lara Goodband, with a sound track in response to the film by Damian Murphy) was a digital installation taking up a large self-contained room. The film, shot at nose level of a swimmer while treading water, was projected along an entire wall, accompanied by sounds of the sea. The enveloping sensation allowed viewers an intimate sensation of swimmers floating in water and of the sea's movement, blueness and hypnotic musicality. This translation and mediation of movement through water aimed to help the audience, even if they were not sea swimmers themselves, to grasp the distinctive aesthetic of the experience.

Sea Swim's impact in the town depended on a significant set of local partnerships with the Local Authority, schools and community outreach and educational programmes. Surprisingly, it became clear the beach was for many people an underused and undiscovered resource, even for children who lived in the Scarborough coastal area. The project was also able to draw in the Stephen Joseph Theatre which transported dance out of the studio and onto the shoreline for a performance of Ballet Boys on the Beach.[8]

In summary, Sea Swim helped to realize a number of imove's key aims of transcending divisions between sport and culture. 'The artists have been brought to the water and the swimmers to art', (Lara Goodband 18.08.12). There is abundant testimony from the swimmers themselves that the experience was personally transformative in building physical and artistic confidence and encouraging people to do things they never expected of themselves. Among the changes wrought was an ability to see Scarborough itself in a new light, to appreciate how a particular relation between land and sea was intrinsic to the sight, sound, feel and temperature of the place. Sea Swim achieved this by articulating a distinctive relationship between body, mind and place produced by its activities.

Discussion

Instrumental and intrinsic art-sport values

There is a risk in describing art-sport interaction and transformation of focusing primarily on instrumental outcomes since these are most likely to support self-advocacy where funding is at stake. An important aspect of imove's pitch rested on the health and well-being that increased involvement in sport and other forms of movement could bring to individuals. Another strong suit, played to gain the support of financially beleaguered local authorities, was the potential of imove projects to bring together communities, offering activities to a range of demographics and abilities, and building a sense of connection and ownership of local environments and their resources, as well as strengthening the visitor economy.

> It had to be sold on the wider benefits, i.e. using arts and swimming as the tool for economic/ social benefits and potential for raising awareness as a visitor destination... the potential of the project having national status through imove rather than the artistic concept. (Rowena Marsden, Culture Events and Film Officer, Scarborough Borough Council 28.11.12)

There has been animated debate within the cultural sector on the distinction between instrumental and intrinsic values (Holden 2004, 2006). The arts sector has been, and remains, deeply mistrustful of the instrumentalism originally ushered in with New Labour's cultural policy and which has remained a key driver of DCMS[9] investment (O'Brien 2013). The AHRC's cultural value programme report (Crossick and Kaszynska 2016) attempted to move the debate beyond what it saw as a simplistic dichotomy, and many would now accept that intrinsic value is in any case vital for the realization of instrumental outcomes. Gordzeijko (2013) has made the same case with respect to imove. The examples in the tri-partite model outlined above suggest that the argument holds in art-sport of whatever kind. *Runs on the Board* has only been sustainable to the extent that it provided excellent and *meaningful* entertainment to the communities from which the players came, and who were the audience and support base for the project. The series gave expression to an embedded amateur sporting tradition and an enduring local passion. *In the blink of an eye* provided visual analysis that enhanced understanding of the athletic body at extremes of performance, but it depended for its impact on the visual/kinaesthetic abstractions that formed arresting artworks in themselves. The *Dancing on Together* projects enhanced appreciation of rugby and football moves, and expanded the range of opportunities available to local youth, not simply through an act of translation (sport to dance) but through an imaginative elaboration of an embodied intelligence that the art and sport held common, and that could be represented choreographically. In the transformative model we see an even closer alignment between the intrinsic quality of the experience of cold open water swimming as a participatory art-sport form and its health and community benefits. However, it was only in and through the cultural forms that swimmers found to express their experience that the mind-body integration took full effect and became available to thought and representation. The well-being induced was then felt in the body, registered in the mind, and expanded in the imagination into something that was both intimately personal, and yet at the same time cultural – which is to say it could be the object of a shared and communicable experience. This is likely to have been the basis for its health effects, which were both mental and physical, and also for its potential to enable new forms of community inclusion and solidarity.

Innovative participatory practices and new methods

It should be clear then that the audience/public are far from being incidental bystanders to art-sport. They are in the position of being not only recipients but active interpreters of these new and inherently 'unstable', or evolving, hybrid forms. The instability is inevitable to the extent that these are emergent practices that cannot be located in a particular cultural discipline, or governed by an established set of rules. There is a danger that in developing a heuristic model which attempts to define possible combinations of art and sport; practices that are still developing become artificially categorized and thereby fixed. Instability is desirable to the extent that it allows an open field of innovation but experimental practices still have to attract resources to develop. As the *Fields of Vision Manifesto*[10] observes there has been little cultural investment in art-sport, as compared to Sci-Art, for example. The latter has gained significant funding, and has prestigious peer reviewed publication platforms. Sci-art has succeeded in becoming a distinct field of both practice and transdisciplinary scholarship. Art-sport carries no such recognition, although a discussion of 'sport as art' has surfaced in various literary and philosophical debates (Wertz 1986). Wertz is one among several critics of David Best's argument that sport cannot be considered an art form because, although sport as a practice certainly has an aesthetic dimension, it does not accommodate expression of meaningful life issues (Best 1974, 1980). Although this discussion might still hold some interest, it is of limited use in building a field based on the aesthetics or art of movement that will attract public support. The study of art-sport needs, at the very least, to map or conceptualize the possible relationships at stake in order to produce strategies of engagement and a convincing account of where the public benefit might lie, and this might also shed light on the 'life issues' that gain expression through these forms of physical and cultural activity.

This article attempts to take a step in that direction, and in so doing argues that the public should be brought into the equation and that this implies a consideration of the conditions under which art-sport is produced, and very possibly a new set of methods with which to capture what is effectively a tri-partite rather than a dualistic relationship, in which audience or participant experience is key. The virtue of considering the transformative model in some detail is not that is in some way superior to the interactive or additive forms, but that it affords a higher degree of participation and the public becomes a direct partner in its development, as in the case of Sea Swim. By the same token, many of these formations will be unspectacular, embedded in the communities of which they are a part, and likely to attract relatively modest publicity. However, they may still have profound impacts, and provide a seed bed in which to nurture new genres – and because they create spaces of emergence – new sites of discovery (Figure 9).

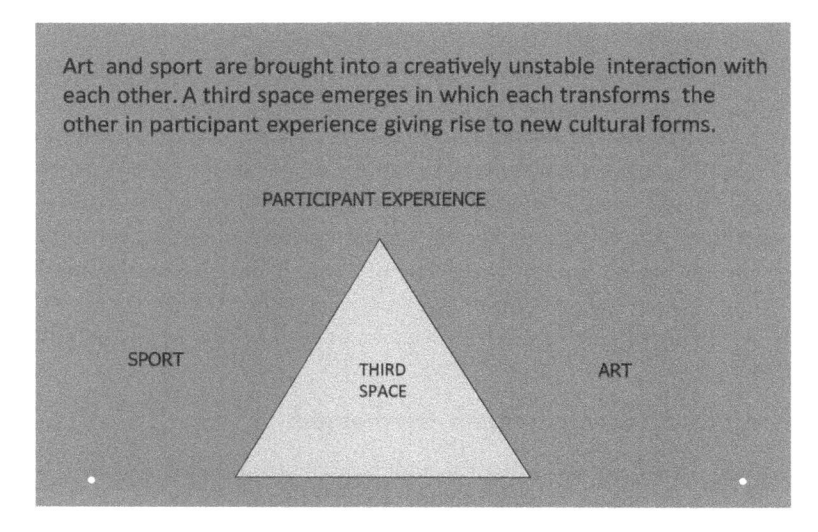

Figure 9. The Third Space of Art-Sport.

A further analogy with sci-art is that art-sport collaborations have the problem of evolving not only novel ways of working, but also representations of what they are producing out of their mutual influence. Elsewhere, with colleagues who work in the transdisciplinary arena of sci-art, I have argued for the necessity of 'third spaces'; essentially, curated epistemic spaces where new knowledge arises (Muller et al. 2015, forthcoming). In the case of art-sport this is experiential knowledge of the body in movement. The Visual Matrix method was developed by Froggett, Manley, and Roy (2015) specifically to respond to the gap in visual, sensory and kinaesthetic group based methodologies available to capture such experience, particularly in its aesthetic and affective dimensions. It has been successfully used in the field of Sci-Art to respond to emergent experience in third space where there is no existing discourse with which to articulate the new knowledge that emerges in the encounter between disciplines (Muller et al. 2015, forthcoming). There is considerable scope to apply it in art-sport contexts. As a method it aims to be 'experience near' (Geertz 1974) and depends on group-based associative thinking in response to a sensory or kinaesthetic stimulus (such as that provided in any of the examples described here) rather than analysis and opinion after the event. Critically, the visual matrix itself provides a third space in which experience is partially re-enacted and shared with others. The process is audio-recorded for later hermeneutic interpretation in a specially designed panel-based process (Froggett, Manley, and Roy 2015).

The conditions of art-sport: participation in third space

The particular inventive freedom that a third space confers arises from the fact that it is a space apart from existing disciplines and practices, a social, relational and intrinsically ludic space established so that new encounters and discoveries can take place (Figure 9). It is created physically in a setting, as well as psychologically in the mind. What happens within it is, initially at least, open, undefined, and unbounded by rules, although new conventions may evolve as a distinctive form of practice develops. Sea Swim depended in just such a space, intuitively facilitated by its co-directors in such a way as to keep open the ways and means to represent the swimming as an aesthetic practice – an affective, physical, lyrical and, for some, spiritual experience. The protective comfort of beach huts was essential to holding this space as was the sense of community forged in the group as a whole. Out of this it became possible to swim in the liminal space of the sea and find there a basis for a new form of bodily self-expression: the art of swimming and swimming as art.

What has been offered in this article is a specific case-based set of responses to the questions asked at the beginning. There are numerous ways in which art and sport can intertwine and the additive, interactive, transformative typology is a relatively crude instrument to impose on a field that is perhaps best characterized as one of 'creative chaos'. Nothing would be gained by shoehorning these hybrid forms into a schema that imposes more organization than reality will bear. However, its virtue as a heuristic device has been to throw into relief the essential role of audience engagement and participation in developing the possibilities and impacts of art-sport collaborations. If participants in the most radical, transformative model are to be taken seriously as co-producers of art-sport, then it needs to be understood in its complexity, not through schema that deconstruct experience into aesthetic, affective and physical dimensions but as a bio-psycho-cultural practice, with methods that are adequate for this purpose. Attention needs to be paid to the third space in which the intricate relationships that compose it can develop optimally. Creating these conditions demands a mind-set and skill that is learnt on the ground and that will only develop as collaborations mature, but there is a great deal to be gained from a strong philosophical standpoint that licences the transgression of boundaries between art and sport, and understands how these are underwritten by mind-body dualism. The Legacy Trust UK's assessment of the regional programmes it funded recognized the difficulty of working with these perspectives and concluded that other programmes had formulated simpler objectives and deliverables and therefore got off to a smoother start, but then struggled to identify what it all amounted to afterwards. Based on the fact that two of the examples discussed here have proved to be sustainable projects attracting continued participation, support and funding, it appears that at least in these instances imove's approach engendered a sense of direction for the longer term.

Notes

1. The original report can be found at http://clok.uclan.ac.uk/19648/1/imoveFINAL_WORD_300713_071013.pdf
2. imove Arts website https://www.imovearts.co.uk
3. https://culturalolympiad.wordpress.com/2012/05/17/the-legacy-trust-their-regional-programmes/ (accessed 22–08-17).
4. Some of these can be viewed on vimeo at https://www.scienceandmediamuseum.org.uk/what-was-on/blink-eye#&gid=1&pid=1 (accessed 20-08-17).
5. http://SeaSwim.co.uk/exhibitions/.
6. Damian Murphy podcast: Sea Swim Podcast, Sound Cloud (accessed 22–08-17) http://www-users.york.ac.uk/~dtm3/practice.html
7. http://www-users.york.ac.uk/~dtm3/practice.html
8. Ballet Boys at Sea Swim You Tube. Published 10–07-2012 https://www.youtube.com/watch?v=X_bZI7imPmM (accessed 22–08-17).
9. Department of Digital, Culture, Media and Sport.
10. Fields of Vision: a Manifesto for the Arts and Sport Together https://artsinsport.wordpress.com/a-manifesto-for-the-arts-and-sport-together/ (accessed 23–08-17).

Acknowledgements

The art-sport typology presented in this article has drawn on the data collected for the evaluation report of the imove programme completed by the Psychosocial Research Unit at the University of Central Lancashire. Thanks are due to Alastair Roy, Julian Manley and Suzanne Hacking for their role in that work, and to Lizzie Muller and Jill Bennett at the University of New South Wales for discussions on audience engagement and third space in trans-disciplinary fields.

Disclosure statement

No potential conflict of interest was reported by the author.

References

Best, D. 1974. "The Aesthetic in Sport." *British Journal of Aesthetics* 14: 197–213. doi:10.1093/bjaesthetics/14.3.197.

Best, D. 1980. *Art and Sport: Understanding the Value of Arts and Culture*. Swindon: Arts and Humanities Research Council.

Bollas, C. 1992. *Being a Character: Psychoanalysis and Self Experience*. London: Routledge.

Crossick, G., and M. Kaszynska. 2016. *Understanding the Value of Arts and Culture*. Swindon: The Arts and Humanities Research Council.

De Coubertain, P. 1988. *L'Education en Angleterre*. Paris: Hachette.

Froggett, L., and M. Trustram. 2014. "Object Relations in the Museum: A Psychosocial Perspective." *Museum Management and Curatorship* 29 (5): 482–497. doi:10.1080/09647775.2014.957481.

Froggett, L., J. Manley, A. Roy, and S. Hacking. 2013. *Evaluation of the imove Programme: Yorkshire and Humber Cultural Olympiad Programme*. Final Report, CLOK. University of Central Lancashire Research Repository. http://clok.uclan.ac.uk/19648/1/imoveFINAL_WORD_300713_071013.pdf.

Froggett, L., J. Manley, and A. Roy. 2015. "The Visual Matrix Method: Imagery and Affect in a Group-based Research Setting." *Forum Qualitative Sozialforschung / Forum: Qualitative Social Research* 16 (3): Art 6. http://www.qualitativeresearch.net/index.php/fqs/article/view/2308

Garcia, B. 2013. *London 2012, Cultural Olympiad Evaluation*. Liverpool: Institute of Cultural Capital. http://iccliverpool.ac.uk/wp-content/uploads/2014/04/Garcia2013London2012COEvaluation-Summary.pdf.

Geertz, C. 1974. "From the Native's Point of View: On the Nature of Anthropological Understanding." *Bulletin of the American Academy of Arts and Sciences* 28 (1): 26–45. doi:10.2307/3822971.

Gordzeijko, T. 2013. "Create the Physical: imove and the Art of Human Movement." In *Fields of Vision: the Arts in Sport*, edited by D. Sandle, J. Long, J. Parry, and K. Spracklen, Leisure Studies Association, 126, 163–174. Eastbourne: University of Brighton.

Gordzeijko, T. 2014. "The London 2012 Olympic Legacy and the Wonder Factor: Implications for Culture and the Intrinsic Versus Instrumental Debate." *Journal of Policy Research in Tourism, Leisure and Events* 6 (1): 80–84. doi:10.1080/19407963.2013.800375.

Holden, J. 2004. *Capturing Cultural Value: How Culture has Become a Tool of Government Policy*. London: Demos.

Holden, J. 2006. *Cultural Value and the Crisis of Legitimacy*. London: Demos.

Langer, S. (1942) 1990. *Philosophy in a New Key: A Study in the Symbolism of Reason, Rite, and Art*. Cambridge, MA: Harvard University Press.

Lorenzer, A. 1986. "Tiefenhermeneutische Kulturanalyse." In *Kultur-Analysen: Psychoanalytische Studien zur Kultur*, edited by A. Lorenzer, 11–98. Frankfurt/M.: Fischer.

Lorenzer, A., and P. Orban. 1978. "Transitional Objects and Phenomena: Socialization and Symbolisation." In *Between reality and fantasy*, edited by S. Grolnick, L. Barkin and W. Muensterberger, 471–482. New York, NY: Jason Aronson.

Muller, N., ed. 2000. *Pierre de Coubertain: Selected Writings*. Lausanne: IOC.

Muller, L., J. Bennett, L. Froggett, and V. Bartlett. 2015. "Understanding Third Space: Evaluating Art-science collaboration." In *Proceedings of 21st International Symposium of Electronic Art*, August 14–18 2015, Vancouver, Canada. (Archived CLOK: University of Central Lancashire Research Repository). http://clok.uclan.ac.uk/12024/1/12024_froggett_ISEA2015_submission_332.pdf.

Muller, L., L. Froggett, and J. Bennett. Forthcoming. "Emergent Knowledge in the Third Space of Artscience." *Leonardo*.

O'Brien, D.. 2013. *Cultural Policy: Management, Value and Modernity in the Creative Industries*. London: Routledge.

Roberts, G., ed. 2011. *Runs on the Board: An Artists' Celebration of Over 50's Cricket in Yorkshire*. Wakefield: RKL consultants.

Wedgwood-Clarke, J. 2014. *Sea Swim*. Scarborough: Valley Press.

Welsch, W. 2006. *Sport Viewed Aesthetically – And Even as Art*. Filosovski Vestnik online/Open: Humanities Press. Accessed August 21, 2017. https://ojs.zrc-sazu.si/filozofski-vestnik/article/viewFile/4076/3783

Wertz, S. 1986. "Representation and Expression in Sport and Art." *Journal of the Philosophy of Sport* 12 (1): 8–24. doi:10.1080/00948705.1985.9714425.

Winnicott, D. (1971) 2005. *Playing and Reality*. London: Routledge.

Subjectivity and temporality in literary narratives about sports

Stephen Carl Arch

ABSTRACT
This article explores the concept of embodied subjectivity in literary narratives about sport. While embodied subjectivity has been central to the methodology of sociologists of sport in recent years, it is also manifested in complex and fascinating ways in a special kind of literary sports narrative. Using narrative strategies developed by novelists in the early twentieth century, the authors discussed here aim to do more than simply describe sporting experience. They recount the deep physical, emotional, and psychic transformation of the self through athletic training and competition. They represent the sporting self as a construct layered over time through inclination, repetition, and habit. They characterize competition as a felt, embodied, and even sometimes disembodied experience. The lived experience of sport cannot be captured in simple narratives. The literariness of these narratives enables their authors to portray convincingly that lived experience.

Introduction

In the last 30 years, many sociologists and anthropologists of sport have rejected the Cartesian dualism of a mind-body split in studying sport as an embodied practice. This 'carnal sociology' (Crossley 1995, 43; see also, e.g. Kerry and Armour 2000) derives variously from a number of theoretical perspectives: the late work of Michel Foucault with his suggestion that the critical self can resist some structures of power; the work of Pierre Bourdieu, especially his conception of habitus as a set of mental and bodily schemata that define behaviour; and the work of Maurice Merleau-Ponty with his emphasis on the body as an incarnated subjectivity. Scholars such as Jacquelyn Allen-Collinson, Loïc Wacquant, John Hockey, Jesús Ilundáin-Agurruza, Pirkko Markula and many others have taught us to understand better the phenomenology of the sporting experience.[1]

I assert in the essay that follows that literary narratives represent some of our best accounts of the embodied practice of sports. There is a carnal sociology in some of the finest accounts of sporting activity. By 'literary', I mean a kind of writing that is valued because of the quality of its structure and style. In this essay, I analyse and discuss in detail two narratives that use complex literary techniques to convey in remarkable ways the felt, embodied experience of sports. It is through such literary techniques that authors can help us understand better the embodied experience of the athlete.

I recognize that my use of 'literary' is problematic. There is no objective measurement for what makes a novel or an autobiography or a play 'literary'. In the scholarship on language and literature, the term emerged in the nineteenth century as a way to distinguish 'high' culture from 'low' culture (see, e.g. Levine 1988). Lowbrow, or popular, literature took shape in the mid-nineteenth-century in a variety of new genres and sub-genres such as crime fiction, melodrama, the gothic and sports writing. In it, the sensational content took precedence over the manner in which the story was told. Authors of popular literature were relatively uninterested in *form*. They strove to reach a wide audience by emphasizing content, often in graphic or sensational ways, and simplifying form. In literary writing, on the other hand, authors experimented with structure, style, narrative technique, and other aspects of storytelling. *Uncle Tom's Cabin* was a popular novel, *Moby-Dick* was a literary novel. Edward Bulwer-Lytton was a popular novelist, Henry James a literary novelist.

The two terms have in most ways lost their usefulness in recent decades. Genres that were once dismissed by literary critics – graphic novels, mysteries, romances, etc. – are now the subject of intense study. Writers like Stephen King, who would have been dismissed by literary scholars in the mid-twentieth century, are now the focus of graduate seminars. Literary critics no longer see an easy or clear distinction between 'literary' and 'popular'. However, in the context of my discussion in this essay, I think the term 'literary' can still be useful. I argue that it is only through a certain kind of complex literary art that non-participants can glimpse from the inside the felt experience of high-level sporting activity.

Literary styles

When I teach university-level courses on sports literature, I offer students a wide variety of written perspectives on sport. In a single semester, I might include novels focused on particular sports, lyric poems with sports as a focus, autobiographies by athletes or coaches, historical narratives about a sport or a season or a single sporting event, scholarly studies by historians or sociologists or anthropologists and documentary sports films. Sports can engage us from multiple perspectives and through many disciplinary lenses, and there are complex, compelling accounts from every perspective on the sporting experience. In constructing my courses, however, I learned early on that a good deal of the writing about sports was completely ineffectual in explaining what athletes actually did and experienced.

Narratives of athletic endeavour are often told from an outsider's perspective. Insiders, after all, tend not to be writers; they are athletes first and foremost, or they are professionally committed to sports as coaches, managers, etc. Athletes like Dave Meggyesy (*Out Of Their League* [1970]) and Andre Agassi (*Open* [2009]) have written compelling and complex accounts that I often ask students to read. But the vast majority of 'classic' sports literature has been written by outsiders who are often compelled to subordinate sport to other concerns such as morality, politics, or social change. In Bernard Malamud's *The Natural* (1952), for example, the action builds dramatically through a series of moral choices that Roy Hobbs makes, and culminates in his failure to get a hit in his final at-bat (after agreeing one day earlier to throw the game). Malamud has essentially no interest in the game of baseball itself and how one prepares to play it well or how it feels to play it well. He is uninterested in the preparation, training and maintenance of athletic prowess. Baseball merely serves as a lens for a story of morality, hubris and American tragedy. Baseball as allegory displaces any sense of the lived athletic experience. *The Natural* is a terrific novel, but it is a lousy sports novel.

In *Friday Night Lights* (1990), to take another example, H. G. Bissinger immersed himself in the social and cultural world of Odessa, Texas, hoping to discover the meaning of the city's desperate commitment to American high school football. Covering one season from training camp to season-ending game, Bissinger claims to have been 'caught up' with the townspeople in the Friday night lights (xvi), yet at the same time to have seen the events with 'the clear eyes of a journalist' (356). His narrative offers a dual perspective as he shifts uneasily between the poles of insider and outsider. But his insider position is not the position of the *athlete*. Bissinger to some extent merges with the local community as a fan and observer, though even here as a northerner in the American South he is unable to overcome the townspeople's uneasy sense that he is a 'visitor' (130). But certainly as a white, northern, professional, 'thirtysomething' (xiii), he is very far removed from the athletes themselves. Tellingly, Bissinger begins his study with an epigraph from James Wright's poem, 'Autumn Begins in Martin's Ferry, Ohio,' in which the narrator is himself situated well outside the action taking place on a high school football field. That distancing effect is repeated throughout Bissinger's text, as when in his closing acknowledgements he reluctantly gestures toward the distance that separates him from the athletes: 'I remember how I thought of [the athletes] at the end, as kids that I adored' (359).

Objects of adoration are always distant from us. Hans Ulrich Gumbrecht notes in *In Praise of Athletic Beauty* that 'All that it takes to become addicted to sports is a distance between the athlete and the beholder – a distance large enough for the beholder to believe that his heroes inhabit a different world' (Gumbrecht 2006, 8). From just such a distance, Bissinger understands the athlete both as an adored object and as a pawn, being sacrificed on Friday nights to prop up the dreams of a decaying 'America that existed beyond the borders of the Steinberg cartoon … an America of factory towns and farm towns and steel towns and single-economy towns all trying to survive' (xv).[2] The game of high school football in Bissinger's account is a fantasy created by adults in post-industrial America. Having themselves fallen into adulthood, community members fetishize the violence and grace of those who have yet to fall. Bissinger ignores the felt, athletic experience of the sport of football to make a larger argument about post-industrial America.

The sentimentality of many sports narratives is predicated upon this distancing effect from the felt, embodied experience of the sport. Narratives about sport often depend on a broader, larger framework that gives meaning to the athletic endeavour, but that very framework often displaces the felt experience of the sport. *Chariots of Fire* (1981), for example, embeds the story of two British sprinters in the 1920s within a framework in which post-First World War (WWI) British society opens itself to class permeability and religious tolerance. The athletes' training process and practices receive very little screen time. Viewers may well remember the iconic opening sequence set to Vangelis' score, but the slow-motion, dream-like quality of that sequence is precisely designed to separate it from the felt experience and to move it into the realm of the ideal. Running never feels quite like *that*.

Writers and directors do this for a variety of reasons. After all, the repetition essential to all high-level athletic training is rarely dramatic, the purpose of drills or exercises often requires substantial explanation for outsiders, and the long, slow, even haphazard process of physical improvement and skill development works against the time constraints and narrative conventions of plot-driven narrative. To reach a broad audience, writers are often compelled to provide a non-sports 'hook' or framework of some kind. To reach a non-expert audience, writers 'package' the sport in ways that give it a higher, readily identifiable purpose. They cannot spend too much time on training or on incremental improvement or on the felt experience, except perhaps to demonstrate by synecdoche or montage the long, felt arc of lived athletic experience, as when famously in *Rocky* (1976) we see the protagonist's dramatic improvement over five weeks of training in a three-minute montage that culminates in his racing up the steps of the Philadelphia Museum of Art. (Indeed, all of the subsequent *Rocky* films contain a similar training montage.)

In this essay, I analyse two narratives of athletic endeavour that attempt to represent the complex embodied experience of sport. I want in particular to describe and explain particular moments in both narratives when the intensity of experience demolishes the linear, logical storytelling we associate with realistic description – when the irrational, even dangerous play of sports cannot be contained by the constraints of narrative exposition. At such moments, the athlete/narrator is challenged to explain, in words and images, just how it *felt* to be or to excel at a superior level as an athlete. I focus on narratives by athletes who offer a dual perspective on their experience, but a dual perspective that is quite different from Bissinger's in *Friday Night Lights*. As insider practitioners of a sport, these authors have access to the felt experience of intense athletic endeavour; at the same time, with training as a scientist or journalist, they are able to understand and explain themselves and their experience from a more objective viewpoint. I discuss two texts that focus on athletic achievement in (largely) individual sports: Bernd Heinrich's *Why We Run: A Natural History* (long-distance running) and Tim Krabbé's *The Rider* (long-distance cycling). Both of these works were written by adult athletes determined to describe the felt experience of sports. Both authors frame their accounts within or alongside other kinds of disciplinary knowledge: Heinrich as a biologist and Krabbé as a journalist and championship chess player. One book is a non-fictional narrative, the other is a novel, but the line between fact and fiction is irrelevant to me. What matters is how each author attempts to frame and convincingly describe intense athletic experience.

Their dual perspectives enable Krabbé and Heinrich to write narratives that describe a high-level athletic endeavour and, at the same time, enact for the reader the felt experience at the heart of their sport. At key moments, each narrator attempts to reach beyond realistic representation in order to demonstrate where, at its furthest reaches, sport can take its participants. To do this, they draw from the techniques of high modernist art (Virginia Woolf, James Joyce, William Faulkner, Norman Mailer and others) to enable the willing reader to experience vicariously the embodied pain, beauty and wonder at the heart of sport.

Representing embodied experiences: Krabbé

Tim Krabbé's short novel, *The Rider* (2002), recounts a competitive cyclist's thoughts and experiences in an invented 137 kilometre race in the Cévennes, the 'Tour de Mont Aigoual'. Krabbé is working in the style of New Journalism made famous in the 1970s by Tom Wolfe, Norman Mailer, Joan Didion and others, in which the line between fiction and fact is blurred. In long-form New Journalism, the narrative point of view is subjective, the narrator has immersed himself or herself in the action, and the tools of the novelist are brought into play to create tension or suspense. In *The Rider*, the race has been invented, but the narrator is a cyclist named Krabbé (14) who, like the author, plays competitive chess. He tells his story as a 'reporter' who happens also to be one of the race leaders. One unusual aspect of this novel is that it takes place in real time. Assuming that Krabbé's narrator is cycling at around 40 kilometres per hour, he recounts the three-to-four hour race in approximately the same amount of time that a reader reads the narrative. We are familiar with this use of 'real time' narration from films like *Rope*, *Run Lola Run* and *Timecode*, but of course the concept itself goes back to Aristotle's conception of the unity of time in drama. In prose narratives, it is the modernists who experiment with written texts that occur for reader and character alike in 'real' or perceived time, as when Virginia Woolf in *Mrs. Dalloway* (1925) details a day in the life of her protagonist or when James Joyce devotes an entire chapter ('Penelope') of *Ulysses* (1922) to the real-time interior monologue of Molly Bloom. Like Joyce in that chapter, Krabbé embeds the sensations, thought processes, emotions and logic of his narrator within a story that refuses to stray from what the main character can know in the moment, or might be thinking in the moment. For the duration, the 'rider' and the reader are clipped into the pedals, and everything we see, hear, smell, taste and touch is filtered through the narrator's consciousness.

A second unusual feature of Krabbé's novel is that the narrator juxtaposes the forward, linear trajectory of narrated events within the race itself against an interspersed, fragmented set of memories that move backwards in time through his life. The rider experiences the race as it happens, but his mind also traces in backward glimpses (that keep receding farther and farther back in time over the course of the novel) the path that led him to such a moment of exquisite suffering. In this dual movement of the narrative, Krabbé weaves two separate strands into one story: the perceptual immediacy of the experience of racing forward in real time and the simultaneous backward excavation of memories that delve the origins of this cyclist's desire to compete.

This double movement is *artful*, of course. Endurance athletes report that all kinds of things go through their heads during competition (see, e.g. Samson et al. 2015). But Krabbé's narrator is persistent in his meta-critical thinking: he is always thinking about the race and, at the same time, about himself as an athlete, about the sport of cycling, and about the purpose of his sport. He has an especially heightened consciousness about himself as an athlete. 'What I can do, no animal can: be the other and admire myself' (26). The very title of the novel gestures toward this self-consciousness: 'People are made up of two parts: a mind and a body. Of the two, the mind, of course, is the rider' (5). Invoking Descartes, Krabbé here sees the body as the machine or tool, and the mind as the planner and strategizer. For younger athletes, in particular, this split is embodied in the coach/athlete relationship. The coach not only plans and strategizes, but at a deeper level tries to embed a particular psychology and set of embodied actions/behaviours in the athlete, who then 'performs' at her or his behest. While the athlete must of course think on her 'own' during the event itself, even this is controlled to some extent through various kinds of training: inculcating work habits, repeating drills to embody certain responses, visualizing tactics, etc. Ideally, in some training scenarios, the athlete's body *is* a kind of machine or automaton and the mind is along for the ride.[3]

But note that, at the same time, this figure of 'the rider' challenges Descartes' neat dichotomy. To ride, in English, is to suggest varying degrees of physical and intellectual engagement. When I ride a London bus, I am largely passive; I am carried along by someone else's will after having made the decision to board the bus. At times, Krabbé's narrator expresses a similar kind of detachment, as if his mind is merely along for the ride after his body has logged tens of thousands of miles of training. But more often his narrator uses 'ride' in ways that suggest a complicated, embodied sense of self. Think of three kinds of 'riding' from the world of sports: riding a horse, riding a bike, and riding a wave. A horse is responsive to an experienced rider, and vice versa; person and animal communicate constantly. A bike is also responsive, but in a different way; it 'communicates' information to the rider but not as a knowing object. An ocean wave is completely unresponsive, but still there is a way in which the surfer 'communicates' with the wave. The surfer's body receives information from it and from the board, and the mind/body then modifies actions in response to it.

Krabbé's narrative actually posits three different aspects of the rider: a body that moves the bicycle and suffers pain; a mind that senses and perceives in the moment, and thinks and reasons about the race and the world around it; and a meta-critical, 'rational' mind that in the moment constantly thinks about the way that the mind/body is perceiving, feeling, and thinking. This third aspect of the self is conditioned by the fact that the narrator took up competitive cycling at the age of thirty – too late in life, he says, to be a 'natural' or to execute certain technical demands with a lack of self-consciousness, including (for example) descending without fear on steep downhills. That late start gave the narrator an intellectual perspective that not all insiders have; but through a commitment to high-level training and racing he has also gained an experiential perspective that few outsiders to the sport have. Krabbé's narrator has a peculiar and distinctive relationship to the sport, understanding it experientially but also seeing it from the 'outside' in a more objective way. The narrator trains and races with an ironic, distanced self-awareness that all younger, and even many older, athletes lack.

This self-awareness is disciplined by his training as a journalist and advanced chess player, facts which he reveals in the narrative. For example, the narrator remembers a conversation he once had as a journalist with Gerrie Kneteman, the 1978 world road race champion. Simply an outsider to cycling at the time, the narrator tells Kneteman that 'You guys need to suffer more, get dirtier; you should arrive at the top [of a mountain] in a casket, that's what we [the spectators] pay you for'. Knetemen's response is that the sport already has plenty of drama on the roads, but that the journalists 'need to describe it more compellingly' (29). There is a gap here between what the riders experience (but cannot or do not wish to articulate) and what any reporter and newspaper reader could potentially understand about the sport. At that time, Krabbé had no personal experience of racing; he simply wanted drama from the sport, fodder for the morning headlines. That is certainly how many fans experience sport. But as an insider, Kneteman knew that there was already plenty of 'drama' on the roads; journalists just needed to find a way to access and tell those stories.

Krabbé's meta-critical perspective as a reporter is what enables him to 'report' with an ironic, distanced eye, as well as to critique what he sees. Remembering how in a Dutch amateur classic race a huge gap once opened up early in the race, he describes how most competitors at that moment lost any chance of winning the race. He then comments that 'Racing customs develop the way dialects do; it seems only Dutch amateur classics start like that' (8). At such moments, the narrator understands his sport as a particular cultural construct, with its own customs and regional variations. He recognizes the distance between what competitors experience and what outsiders are told, and he analyses events for deeper meanings that escape his fellow competitors.

Similarly, the narrator mentions his former competitive (a)vocation as a chess player. 'A few years ago I was still sitting safely at the chessboard; no matter how many pawns and pieces I gave away, I was safe. Why am I [racing]?' (48). He is able to describe how a chess player's mind wanders during a match: 'Six new things every minute, to say nothing of the conversations with other players during the game that sometimes actually have subjects' (35). He contrasts that wandering distraction to his experience as a racer, when perception eventually narrows as fatigue sets in and consciousness shrinks only to what is immediately present: pain, suffering, the drive to win. His experiences as a chess player make him hyper-conscious about cycling race strategy. Like all competitive racers, he strategizes; but he also strategizes about his strategy, as it were. He is intensely conscious of how other racers race, of how different nationalities express different racing temperaments, and of the strengths and limitations of his own strategy. He does not simply race 'in the moment,' though he *is* doing that. Even as it is happening, he self-consciously analyses a race as a series of moves that, understood critically, have a logic, as do classic chess matches. He is racing in the moment, and at the same time also thinking about how one races, trains, and thinks about racing and training.

It is his lived experience as a high-performing athlete combined with the analytical skills brought from the outside that enable Krabbé to convey a sense of the physical demands of the sport. Having come to cycling late, he describes his initial training rides as a simple matter of time and distance. Without gps or even accurate and detailed maps, he remembers struggling to measure distances accurately. Even an odometer (in the early 1970s) was inconsistent. Once he figures out how to calculate distances accurately, he keeps detailed records of his progress. The narrative is filled with record-keeping statistics: number of races, length of training rides, number of pedal strokes per mile in a certain gear, even (jokingly) a reference to how many molecules there are in a gulp of water (22). This meticulous record-keeping is familiar to all self-trained athletes in cycling, distance running, cross country skiing, and other endurance sports. It is the first stage of his transformation from non-racer to racer. His body responds by 'achieving things I'd no longer thought possible. I was touched by its loyalty' (41). The limits he encounters in this transformation are both physical and psychological. Physically, he incrementally works his way up through the 'hierarchy of being dropped, of sticking with the bunch, of taking part in a break, taking part in *the* break, of placing, of winning' (42). Psychologically, he remembers a moment two years into his training programme when in the midst of a race he had to cross the line that separates one kind of racer from another: 'I would never make [the move across the gap between him and the lead pack] by any normal means. I had the extremely simple choice of either giving up (but then never racing again) or going straight through everything that was me' (64). Time narrows at that moment of decision:

> I fought my way into the wind … I bent to the bars in a cramp of exertion … And every time I looked up, I was closer. I could already smell the cosy, soothing odour of balsam on their legs … I coughed and slobbered … A few hysterical kicks on the thirteen, the clenched power of a mortal struggle. I was there. (65)

Unkindly, as soon as he makes the leap, the lead pack surges again and he is quickly dropped.

That moment is like many moments in *The Rider*: physical exertion, smells, the coughing and the slobbering, the thin line between control and fury ('hysterical' kicks, 'clenched power'). 'Body and spirit shook hands and moved to their corners', the narrator remarks; they are in the same ring, the same war, but one of them must win the battle at that moment. Krabbé asks us to connect that moment, when the narrator makes a leap of faith across a psychological barrier into a different 'me', to another moment in the narrative. In 1972, reading a newspaper in a small town in France, he impetuously decides to enter a bike race: 'Suddenly I sense that it was now or never' (20). This memory initiates the backward impulse of the narrative: while he cycles forward in his life from that moment and, more specifically, cycles forward in the race itself, he thinks back on the behaviours and conditions that made him a cyclist. What this reverse narration reveals is a deeply embedded competitive spirit. His earliest memory is of himself at the age of five, typing numbers on a manual typewriter: 'Each number was higher than the one before. My life was all about breaking records' (148). These are the final words of the novel, and in them Krabbé ties together a number of ideas and images: the psychological impulse to transcend a previous mark, the physical pleasure of tapping out the numbers, the meticulous act of record-keeping. It suggests that there is no rational explanation for the narrator's desire to compete as a cyclist: I compete, he says, 'purely and simply because it's road racing' (60). Referring to the cliché about why an alpinist climbs a mountain ('because it's there'), he remarks that the 'alpinist's will isn't prompted *by* the mountain, it's there even without a mountain' (89). For him, the desire to compete is enacted in the race, but it exists separately and inexplicably and always already in his identity, even at the age of five.

The complex temporal structure of this novel suggests how, at any moment in time, an athlete's performance represents multiple and different temporalities: a deeply embedded competitive instinct, decisions to pick up and commit to a particular sport, years of training sessions and competitions, the careful crafting over time of the body to do a certain kind of work, the experiential time of a training cycle and of a particular contest. And Krabbé offers yet one more temporality when, as he nears the summit of the steepest climb of the day, his narrator slips out of narrative time into a moment of transcendence, not of 'runner's high' but of an exodus from temporality when the mind retreats from the suffering and withdraws into itself. Modernist writers had first demonstrated ways of narrating such moments, as with Joyce's use of epiphanies in *The Portrait of the Artist as a Young Man* (1916) and Marcel Proust's conjuring of past memories through sensory experiences in *À la recherche du temps perdu* (1913–1927).[4]

In *The Rider*, this moment occurs between kilometres 113 and 114, very near the summit of the most difficult climb of the day. The narration shifts from the dual movement of the forward-looking experience of the race and the backward-looking memories into what purports to be a 'Little ABC of Road Racing', or handbook or primer of road racing. This six-page episode is surreal and illogical. Under the entry for 'Coppi, Fausto,' for example, the narrator 'remembers' climbing the iconic Mont Ventoux with Coppi: 'I had a book with me, and I held it against his back. It fit perfectly. That way I could profit most from Coppi's slipstream. So this was what was meant by "sitting on a wheel"' (106). In the entry for Eddy Merckx, the narrator watches the road in front of him in a race turning into 'a layer of fried mashed potatoes, which my mother had gone to the trouble to prepare' (109). The narrator here is cut loose from perception and from solid memories, and hence he is cut loose from time; his mind roams freely, unmoored from both experiential time and remembered time. Seemingly disconnected images and ideas pop up and disappear. Experiencing oxygen debt and the limits of physical pain, the narrator's mind retreats into fantasies unrelated to the race. 'On a bike your consciousness is small', the narrator remarks early in the narrative. 'The harder you work, the smaller it gets' (33). These fantasies in the 'Little ABC of Road Racing' are absurd, representing consciousness reduced to a space so small that it no longer narrates within the framework of time. Krabbé uses the fantasies to represent consciousness as it has shrunk completely within itself, to a place where external stimuli are absent and the mind sees no temporal distinctions between memories, images and thoughts. Though the experience itself is presented as surreal and irrational, Krabbé suggests that it is in fact a realistic effect that occurs to some endurance athletes at some moments of competition. Cresting the mountain at kilometre 114, the narrator begins his recovery and re-enters normal competitive and narrative time. Over the final 23 kilometres, he returns to the dual forward/backward narration that structures the novel.

Representing embodied experiences: Heinrich

In *The Rider*, Krabbé employs a number of strategies to create a narrative representation of felt, embodied athletic experience: the narrator's *perception* is limited to the immediate experience of the contest; he is constantly aware of his *body* and the signals it is sending to his brain; his *consciousness* is sometimes engaged with immediate facts but at other times it wanders in and out of memories and random ideas; and at a moment of supreme effort his consciousness narrows to a space so small as to be absent. In that surreal moment at the top of the final climb, Krabbé the rider essentially disappears into a non-representational space of memories and images and fantasies, a space that is in a sense absent of the conscious self. This narrowing of consciousness at a moment of supreme effort is represented in language through techniques developed by modernist fiction writers; it is experienced as non-realistic, fantastic, non-linear and poetic. I want now to look at a similar kind of moment within a long non-fictional narrative by Bernd Heinrich.

In *Why We Run: A Natural History*, Heinrich combines and interlaces his physical and psychological development as a competitive runner, his intellectual development as a field biologist, and his and others' research in evolutionary biology to create a complex layered explanation of 'why we run'. *Humans* run, he argues, because of 'our ancient heritage and residual capacities as endurance predators' (Heinrich 2002, x). Heinrich theorizes that our ancestors were 'endurance predators' (x, 174, and elsewhere), capable of chasing down prey that cannot sustain planned, continuous, steady running. He analyses and discusses physiological research about oxygen consumption, sweat glands, muscle fibres, blood temperature and oxygen-carrying capacity and anatomy to make that argument; he even conducted and published some of that research himself, as he recounts in the narrative. But in order to answer the question from a different perspective – why, now, when there is no need to run, do many people choose to run? – he also adduces his own training and fitness as he prepared to race an ultramarathon. Thanks to evolution, all able-bodied human beings have an inherent ability to run, but like Krabbé's narrator Heinrich also wants to explain why *he* runs, why he chooses to expend a supreme amount of effort in an event that carries no monetary reward or cultural prestige (much less the reward of food that our ancestors pursued). The ability to run does not explain why any particular human being now chooses to do so.

Heinrich's book ends with a chapter devoted to his victory at the U.S. 100 kilometre national championship in 1981. In this final, 15 page self-contained narrative (245–259), he uses those six hours of athletic effort to pull together the interlaced threads of his study, dramatizing his arguments about the body, aerobic training, physiology, his own intellectual development, his mental preparation, and our species' evolution. He begins in a reportorial style, focusing on external stimuli, as when he notes that 'I heard the five mile split' (246) and 'Jack came alongside me at the first aid station' (246). But soon, he is inside his head, talking to himself: 'Keep those thumbs up, I told myself' (247). Then, quickly in narrative time, he has fallen into a metronomic running rhythm and his 'mind goes blank' (248) for long stretches. Using the passive voice, he reports that 'The body's metronome has been fine-tuned by … tens of thousands miles', miles that 'have long been deleted from consciousness' even though 'the feeling of [them] remains' (248). The race becomes more difficult as the miles pass though Heinrich cannot always tell whether he is slowing down or speeding up.

At about the midpoint of his narrative of the championship race, Heinrich steps out of the moment to meditate on why, as humans, we exert supreme athletic efforts even though in modern, developed nations we do not need to do so anymore. His answer is that in order to go beyond the normal limits of pain and endurance, we have to self-delude ourselves: 'Logic is less an instrument for finding truth than a tool that we use to help us justify what our lower emotional centres direct or demand' (250). But even this kind of logical rationalization of our deepest impulses only explains so much. After 20 or 30 or 40 miles of racing, one reaches a point at which there is simply no logical explanation for what you are doing as an ultramarathoner. It simply makes no sense. Heinrich turns to something he calls 'faith – a combination of ignorance, deliberate blindness, hope, and optimism' – suggesting that it might be just the sort of non-logic that defines us as human, that makes us different from a 'computational machine' (250). It might, he theorizes, have been the logic that our ancestors used to chase antelope until they tired and could be killed. It should not work, but it did.

As he recounts the second half of the race, the narrator shifts back and forth from such meta-critical thinking to the felt realities of ultramarathoning: the thirst, the random thoughts popping into the head, the stink of sweat, the glazed eyes, the remembered knowledge of how mercifully wonderful it would feel to just *stop*. Like Krabbé at the top of the mountain, Heinrich tries to paint a realistic picture of what is, at certain moments of competition, a sensible but not logical experience. The narrator's mind descends into specific memories to rationalize the pain: a dying friend who *had* to have been suffering more than he is (257), a Vietnam veteran he once glimpsed from afar who *had* to have been (he imagines) painfully disfigured by napalm (255). Time shrinks: 'My entire life is compressed into this little life of several hours … I'm dipping into pain, gradually, inexorably' (254). Space is altered: 'The very landscape has changed. The distance between trees has expanded, the ground has hardened, the scenery is fading … The universe is contracting, constricting' (258). The narrator searches desperately for a 'medicine' in memories or songs or ideas that can numb the pain and repetition.

Heinrich's study is sub-titled 'A Natural History', and I do not want to downplay the then-groundbreaking research that undergirds many of the chapters of his book. But what I find most compelling is his complex interweaving of temporalities. On one extreme, he writes about our long evolutionary history as a species; on the other extreme, he writes about his own embodied joy and pain at a specific moment in a specific race in 1981. Other temporalities are layered in between: his buried childhood memories of post-Second World War (WWII) Germany, his story of taking up running and biological research, his long bout of conditioning for that one race, his accounts of the remarkably long migratory flights of birds and butterflies. As in *The Rider*, a complex narrative structure permits the author to represent the apparent clock time of a single sporting time as multiply layered from the participant's subjective point of view. Any single event like a bike race or an ultramarathon is comprised not just of clock time or scoreboard time, but of multiple subjectively experienced times: physical development, training schedules, perceptions of time, dreams of time, cultural time, even evolutionary time. 'Time and timing is everything', Heinrich says (234). The complex narrative structures of Heinrich's study and Krabbé's novel offer readers the opportunity to see how such different subjective temporalities overlay and interact with each other within a complex network or system that we refer to, too simply, as the 'experience' of sport.

Similarly, both Krabbé and Heinrich use the narrative structure to show how the body and the mind are sculpted over time. They paint the contours of an ascetic regimen of training that strips away fat and conditions the body's muscles, a process that is aided and abetted by the mind's own 'toughening' – its willingness to push through conceptual boundaries that, days or weeks earlier, seemed unbreachable. Both narratives track the inculcation of the habits necessary for success. 'Inculcate' comes from the Latin word for 'pressed in', the word stem 'calcare' deriving from the word for 'heel'. These sports narratives understand that the regimen of sport, when it is pursued assiduously, demands the 'pressing in' of habits, the ingraining of certain gestures (running, pedalling, swinging a golf club, etc.) as well as the ingraining of certain thoughts and thought processes. The word's etymology points to the embodied aspect of that process: the heel steps in to leave an imprint; the things themselves (body, mind) are altered by the pressing in of habits and repetition.

The academic research on embodied subjectivity has without question given us a better understanding of the sporting body/mind. In the third and final section of his now-classic sociological study of boxing, *Body and Soul: Notebooks of an Apprentice Boxer*, Loïc Wacquant narrates his own experience in the boxing ring. Titled '"Busy" Louie at the Golden Gloves', this short section of his study is presented as a 'sociological novella' (Wacquant 2004, 8).[5] In it, Wacquant attempts to 'erase the traces of the work of sociological construction [in the first and second sections of his study] … while preserving the insights and results of that work' (8). His first-person narration in '"Busy" Louie' is shot through with allusions to his arguments earlier in the book. His own felt experience of a competitive boxing match echoes and amplifies his overtly sociological observations. For example, when he remarks in '"Busy" Louie' that 'Becoming a boxer, training for a fight is a little like entering a religious order' (235), readers understand the simile in the context of his earlier observations about the 'collective ascesis' (108) of the gym: the functional and efficient training space (32); the 'monastic devotion' and self-denial of a boxer peaking for a bout, including the forsaking of sexual contact (67); the muzzling of 'certain feelings (of anger, restiveness, frustration)' in the ring (91); and the 'practical mastery of time' as the boxer patiently learns and embodies the craft (143).

Wacquant turns to the conventions of storytelling ('novella') as a particularly useful way to weave together the insights he gleaned from his research. What he offers in his concluding chapter is a version of what Krabbé and Heinrich offer in their books. Each author writes from a completely subjective point of view, layering the narrative with 'insights and results' that give readers a sense of the complex temporal depth and multiple convergences of influence on any single contest: the years of training, the gradual sculpting of the body, the inculcation over time of habits, the ascetic discipline demanded to excel in the duration of a bout or in the time of a race, even the evolutionary development of the dispositions of our species. In some manner, of course, most sports are contrived as temporal contests: races against the clock, runs scored across a number of innings, points scored in a set amount of time, first one to three (or five, or seven). Given that narrative is an account of a set of related events in which an initial situation undergoes change, sporting events are inherently narrativized.[6] Always, an initial situation undergoes change. But Krabbé and Heinrich use a complex literary structure to demonstrate that the narrative of clock time is only a small and often 'hidden' part of the subjective experience of a sporting event.

Conclusion

Earlier, I cited Gumbrecht's idea that the typical sports fan perceives 'a distance between the athlete and [himself] – a distance large enough for [him] to believe that his heroes inhabit a different world' (Gumbrech 2006, 8). For Gumbrecht, that distance creates an aesthetic appreciation of the beauty of sport, an appreciation that is not all that different from the point of view of sports narratives like *Friday Night Lights* or *The Natural* that are sentimental or allegorical or moral. After all, to make the athlete a 'hero' is to put him or her into a certain kind of narrative that separates the protagonist from the audience. In ancient Greece, heroes were demi-gods, like humans because one parent was human but unlike humans because one parent was a god. Readers could understand and sympathize with the hero, but could never *be* one in the everyday, human world. Bissinger's 'pawns' are no different in that sense from Gumbrecht's beautiful, isolated athletes: 'the rules of different sports confirm and consolidate the insularity that separates athletics from the everyday world' (77).

Gumbrecht's aesthetic appreciation is that of the viewer or fan, not the participant. It always puts the athlete on a pedestal. In contrast, Krabbé and Heinrich offer rich accounts of the complex, embodied practice of sports. They teach us to understand from the inside that sport is inescapably an embodied experience of multiple intersecting temporalities, and from the outside that we can best reconstruct the pleasures and pains of such subjective human endeavours through the complex tools of literary narrative.

Notes

1. For broad commentary on the use and promise of embodied subjectivity as a method of understanding sports, see, for example, Ravn and Høffding (2017), Allen-Collinson (2009) and Hockey and Collinson (2007).
2. Saul Steinberg's famous cartoon, 'View of the World from Ninth Avenue,' appeared on the cover of *The New Yorker* on 29 March 1976. It shows Manhattan as the centre of the world.
3. In his sociological study of boxing, Loïc Wacquant describes the 'mutual imbrication of corporeal dispositions and mental dispositions' achieved in training. 'In the accomplished boxer, the mental becomes part of the physical and vice versa; body and mind function in total symbiosis' (95, 96). He notes that experienced boxers can continue to fight after being knocked out, or knocked into semi-consciousness: 'the body continues to box on its own, as it were', until the boxer regains his senses (96).
4. To offer another very specific example, Ambrose Bierce in his 1890 short story, 'An Occurrence at Owl Creek Bridge', focuses on a main character who is being hanged by the Union army. In the split second between being dropped from the bridge with a noose around his neck and the moment when his neck is broken, the character imagines his escape and then his improbable return to his wife and family. Lived experiential time expands, through the imagination, into a rich, long narrative time.
5. The third part of *Body and Soul* was published in French in a French journal 10 years before the book-length study itself was published (Wacquant 1991). His use of narrative to analyse sporting experience is an early example of a sports research methodology developed by Andrew Sparkes and others. See, for examples, Sparkes 2001; and Smith and Sparkes 2009.

6. Miller (1995) argues that all narratives have three basic elements: characters with agency, an initial situation that changes, and repetition. Sporting events share those same three elements and thus are, by their very nature, narratives.

Disclosure statement

No potential conflict of interest was reported by the author.

References

Agassi, Andre. 2009. *Open: An Autobiography*. New York: Knopf.
Allen-Collinson, Jacquelyn. 2009. "Sporting Embodiment: Sports Studies and the (Continuing) Promise of Phenomenology." *Qualitative Research in Sport and Exercise* 1 (3): 279–296.doi: 10.1080/19398440903192340.
Bissinger, Harry Gerard. 1990. *Friday Night Lights: A Town, A Team, and a Dream*. Boston, MA: Da Capo Press.
Chariots of Fire. 1981. Directed by Hugh Hudson. Burbank, CA: Warner Brothers, 2011. DVD.
Crossley, Nick. 1995. "Merleau-Ponty, the Elusive Body and Carnal Sociology." *Body & Society* 1 (1): 43–63. doi: 10.1177/1357034X95001001004.
Gumbrecht, Hans Ulrich. 2006. *In Praise of Athletic Beauty*. Cambridge: Harvard University Press.
Heinrich, Berndt. 2002. *Why We Run: A Natural History*. New York: HarperCollins.
Hockey, John, and Jacquelyn Allen Collinson. 2007. "Grasping the Phenomenology of Sporting Bodies." *International Review for the Sociology of Sport* 42 (2): 115–131.
Kerry, Daniel S., and Kathleen M. Armour. 2000. "Sport Sciences and the Promise of Phenomenology: Philosophy, Method, and Insight." *Quest* 52 (1): 1–17.
Krabbe, Tim. 2002. *The Rider*. Trans. Sam Garrett. New York: Bloomsbury.
Levine, Lawrence. 1988. *Highbrow/Lowbrow: The Emergence of Cultural Hierarchy in America*. Cambridge: Harvard University Press.
Malamud, Bernard. 1952. *The Natural*. New York: Harcourt Brace.
Meggyesy, Dave. 1970. *Out of Their League*. New York: Harper Collins.
Miller J. Hillis. 1995. "Narrative." In edited by *Critical Terms for Literary Study*, 2nd ed. Frank Lentricchia and Thomas McLaughlin, 66–79. Chicago: University of Chicago Press.
Ravn, Susanne, and Simon Høffding. 2017. "The Promise of "Sporting Bodies" in Phenomenological Thinking – How Exceptional Cases of Practice Can Contribute to Develop Foundational Phenomenological Concepts." *Qualitative Research in Sport, Exercise and Health* 9 (1): 56–68.
Rocky. 1976. Directed by John G. Avildsen. Beverley Hills, CA: MGM Studios, 2014. DVD.
Samson, Ashley, Duncan Simpson, Cindra Kamphoff, and Adrienne Langlier. 2015. "Think Aloud: An Examination of Distance Runners' Thought Processes." *International Journal of Sport and Exercise Physiology* 15 (2): 176–189. doi: 10.1080/1612197X.2015.1069877.
Sparkes, Andrew C. 2001. *Telling Tales in Sport and Physical Activity*. Champaign, IL: Human Kinetics.
Smith, Brett, and Sparkes Andrew C. 2009. "Narrative analysis and sport and exercise psychology: Understanding lives in diverse ways." *Psychology of Sport and Exercise*. 10 (2): 279-288.
Wacquant, Loïc. 1991. "Busy" Louie aux Golden Gloves." *Gulliver* 6: 12–33, April–June.
Wacquant, Loïc. 2004. *Body & Soul: Notebooks of an Apprentice Boxer*. Oxford: Oxford University Press.

The art and artifice of early sports photography

Mike O'Mahony

ABSTRACT

The rise of modern sport in the mid-nineteenth century coincided with the emergence of photography as a new image-making medium. Thus, both practices developed in parallel. Notably, many early photographers turned to sport as a subject for their work, despite the early technological limitations of the medium. Histories of photography have, however, tended to overlook this. Similarly, sport historians have tended to regard these early photographs simply as illustrative material rather than important innovations in the formation of new visual conventions for the representation of sport. This paper seeks to redress this by exploring, in close detail, examples of sports photography produced in the mid- to late-nineteenth century. More importantly, it examines the visual vocabularies deployed by these early photographers within the context of contemporary art practices, demonstrating how artistry and artifice were deployed in the production of some of the earliest, and finest, examples of sports photography ever produced.

The 71st Royal Academy of Arts annual exhibition held in London in 1839 has become famous as the occasion on which JMW Turner exhibited one of his best known works, *The Fighting Temeraire, Lugged to her Last Berth to be Broken Up*, recently voted by BBC audiences 'The Greatest Painting in Britain'.[1] However, also on display at the exhibition that year was another work by a less well-known, though nonetheless influential artist, Thomas George Webster. Like Turner's contribution, though in contrast to many of the works exhibited alongside, Webster's *A Football Game* (Figure 1) eschewed classical and historical subjects in favour of a contemporary theme.[2] It represents a large group of over a dozen boys, all piling on top of each other in a melee on a stretch of scrubland with a handful of rural dwellings in the background. The summer setting, and indication of other festivities taking place in the background, suggests the kind of carnivalistic celebration typically enacted on holidays in English villages up and down the country in the early nineteenth century. Two boys emerge from the front of this chaotic crowd, one kicking a ball forward, the other raising his arm defensively in a gesture that modern rugby fans might describe as a hand-off. A diminutive lad stands as the only barrier before this crowd, though his apprehensive, hesitant posture suggests that he will be able to do little to prevent further forward motion. The game here being played seems far from organized or regulated and

Figure 1. Thomas Webster, A Football Game, 1839, oil on canvas, National Football Museum, Manchester.

the clutching of injured heads, elbows and shins certainly implies that aggressive combat is a core element in this competition. However, the overall mood is one of exuberant bucolic pleasure. This is manifested through the cleanliness of the players, the broad smile of the figure at the apex of the composition and the energetic enthusiasm of the small boy on the right of the scene, too young to participate yet barely able to contain his desire to do so.

As a representation of popular sporting activities practised amongst small rural communities, Webster's work is unusual in early nineteenth-century art and carries much significance for both art historians and sport historians. Certainly few other paintings, produced at this time, represented sport conducted beyond the Arcadian setting of Ancient Greece, or the playing fields of England's public schools. In this context, the work has acquired a reputation as the pre-eminent and iconic representation of pre-codification sport, a visual signifier of a moment immediately preceding the transition from the leisurely sporting pursuits of the early modern era to the increasingly regulated and commercialized practices that we now define as modern sport.

The date of the production and first display of this work is here of some significance. By 1839 the first shoots of what is now referred to as organized sport were beginning to appear, facilitated by the expansion of urban populations as part of the broader industrialization process. For example, that year saw the first staging of what would later be dubbed the 'Grand National' at Aintree racecourse in Liverpool (Pinfold 1998, 146).[3] Popular attendance at this early sporting spectacle was certainly boosted by the recent opening of railways connecting Liverpool not only to Manchester but also to the Midlands and London (Pinfold 1998, 148). Henley on Thames also played host to its inaugural regatta in 1839, the same year that Surrey, Britain's oldest county cricket club, was founded. It has recently been argued that Barnes Rugby Football Club also came into being that year, making it one of the earliest clubs established in any footballing code (Inverdale 2005).

Yet, much as modern sporting practices were beginning to acquire a significant status by the end of the fourth decade of the nineteenth century, departing from the folk origins of the more casual kind of sport represented in Webster's painting, so too would the very process for documenting such activities in visual form. 1839 was also the year that the French artist and physicist, Louis-Jacques-Mandé Daguerre, publicly announced a new image-making process, which he called the Daguerreotype. Contrary to popular conceptions, this event did not proclaim the invention of the new medium of photography – Daguerre's colleague Joseph Nicéphore Niépce, the French-Brazilian Antoine Hercules Romuald Florence and the Englishman William Henry Fox Talbot had all produced earlier examples of photographic imagery (Frizot 1998, 21–23). The arrival of the Daguerreotype, however, followed shortly by Fox Talbot's calotype process, acted as a major catalyst for the development and expansion of photography in the modern era. Within a few years, photographic processes were being widely deployed throughout Europe and beyond, thus making 1839 the generally accepted landmark year in photographic history.

What seems intriguing here is the extent to which the early development of photography largely coincided with the rise of sport as a significant form of social activity. This article seeks, therefore, to examine how early photography was deployed in the representation of sporting activities during the mid- to late-nineteenth century and how this contributed towards shaping conventions for sport photography as a genre. Given this alignment, it is hardly surprising that, from its very inception, photography was widely deployed to document sport and sport-related activities, though few popular histories of the medium acknowledge this fact.

Technical limitations, not least the necessity for long time exposures, inevitably limited the potential of photography to record sport in action, especially where speed and dynamic movement characterized practices. Yet, despite these limitations, sporting photographs were produced from very early on, initially in the form of staged genre scenes and portraiture of both famous and anonymous sportsmen and sportswomen. Later, as the technical capabilities of the medium developed, new vistas of visual possibilities opened up and photography was widely deployed to explore the high-speed movement of bodies in action. With the emergence of the halftone printing process during the 1880s and 1890s, photographs representing sport became more widely disseminated, not least as they began to appear regularly in a swath of new popular publications dedicated to sport.

Valuing the history of sports photography

The important role played by sport within the early history of photography has generally been ignored. For example, as recently as 2011, Lynda Nead claimed,

> Sports photography has been completely overlooked in the history of photography. It is unclear why this has been the case, but perhaps it is to do with its everyday nature and its association with the world of leisure; its place on the back pages rather than the front pages of news reporting. If sports photographs are the subjects of exhibitions, as, for example, in the exhibition of photographs of boxer Muhammad Ali in London in 2010, it is usually because of the identity of their subjects, in which the nature of the image changes from sports photograph to portrait. (Nead 2011, 309)

Nead's point regarding the potential re-classification of photographs of sport when displayed within an exhibition or museum context, is an important one, not least because it raises the question of what the term 'sports photography' might generally signify. Here, perhaps, the claim that this 'has been completely overlooked' might need some minor qualification as the last couple of decades have witnessed a number of exhibitions and publications that have explicitly claimed to offer a history of sports photography. In 1996, for example, during the Centenary Olympic Games in Atlanta, an exhibition and catalogue entitled *Visions of Victory: A Century of Sports Photography* set out to redress the fact that 'photographing sports has been underappreciated in comparison to photography's other genres' (Livingston 1996, 5). Similarly, *Sportscape: The Evolution of Sports Photography*, published in 2000, claimed on its inner sleeve to offer 'the most comprehensive look at the art of sports photography ever produced' (Wombell 2000). Both publications, it should be added, are characterized by a paucity of textual content and critical or analytical engagement, whilst a glance through their contents indicates that their definition of sports photography, though rarely explained or justified, is rather narrow. In essence, this is largely confined to images of famous sportsmen and women either in action, in training, or as celebrities away from sporting activity; or photographs taken during key sporting events that are assumed, to a significant extent, to derive their value and meaning from an awareness of the event rather than the intrinsic values of the image itself. Perhaps more troublingly, the tendency here has been to assume that sports photography essentially began in the late nineteenth or early twentieth century. A more recent exhibition at the Brooklyn Museum in New York, *Who Shot Sports: A Photographic History 1843 to the Present* (2016) (Buckland 2016) does, as the title suggests, include responses to sport by early photographers though the extent to which these works are taken seriously is perhaps reflected in the fact that they are confined to the appendix in the catalogue.

Here, I want to examine in detail photographic works representing sport produced during the very earliest days of the new medium, the period that has to date been most overlooked. In particular, I want to consider what visual conventions these early photographers of sport adopted for this new medium. As Gunning has recently argued, the emergence of new media typically results less in an overthrow, than in a 'convergence' with older media. As they argue, 'If emerging media are often experimental and self-reflexive, they are also inevitably and centrally imitative, rooted in the past, in the practices, formats and deep assumptions of their predecessors' (Gunning 2004, 7). Similarly, these pioneers, whose work constitutes the foundation for the subsequent emergence of sports photography in the twentieth and twenty-first centuries, embraced the possibilities and limitations of the new medium whilst simultaneously drawing extensively from the conventional art practices of their predecessors, engaging both artistry and artifice in their work to forge a new and dynamic genre. In this way they made a significant, though largely unacknowledged, contribution to the establishment of new visual forms and conventions in the development of sport photography's own visual aesthetic.

The first sport photographs

The first photographic representation of a sporting subject was, perhaps unsurprisingly, produced in the sport-loving United Kingdom. This, however, was not in the leafy surroundings of the English metropolitan centres, where some of the earliest sports clubs had been established, but rather in the east lowlands of Scotland. As is widely acknowledged, two Edinburgh-based photographers, David Octavius Hill and Robert Adamson, were among the most prolific and artistically significant early practitioners to adopt the new medium. Widely esteemed in their day and then largely forgotten for a century, Hill and Adamson are now much celebrated for their early use of the calotype (or Talbot-type), a process developed by the Englishman William Henry Fox-Talbot in the 1830s (Ford 1976, 10, 11). As this process had been patented in England, but not north of the border, Hill and Adamson freely exploited the new medium to produce, amongst other works, portraits of the elite in Edinburgh and St Andrews, topographical representations of the region and genre scenes of local fisherfolk at Newhaven harbour just north of the Scottish capital. Much less well known are their representations of figures explicitly identifiable as sportsmen, despite the fact that these images constitute the very earliest examples of photographic representations of sport.

In 1843, for example, shortly after establishing their partnership, Hill and Adamson produced a striking photograph of a serious looking young man, believed to be a Mr Laing or Laine, posed as a tennis player (Figure 2) (Stevenson 2002, 88). The sitter adopts a dramatic posture, holding a tennis racket at waist height. His right leg is thrust forwards to the very edge of the composition while his torso leans back, his eyes focusing beyond the picture frame as if looking towards a ball in play. The dark-and-light striped shirt, white trousers and soft canvas shoes signify participation in leisurely pursuits, though it is instantly clear that this is a carefully, even artfully, staged pose that has little to do with actual sporting action. The exposure time necessary at this stage to capture such an image required the sitter, as Fox Talbot himself would declare in the first volume of *The Pencil of Nature* published the following year, 'to maintain an absolute immobility for a few seconds of time' (Fox Talbot 1844-6). While this technical requirement is typically highlighted as a limitation in early photography, it might be argued here that the tension between stillness and movement achieved as a consequence of this, contributes significantly to the impact of Hill and Adamson's work. To facilitate maintaining the pose for the duration of the exposure, the sitter was perched on a stool or tripod. This prop, though disguised by retouching, nonetheless remains evident in the final image.

Equally important is the blurring of the racket-head, the only area of the photograph that is not in relatively sharp focus. As the retouching was executed later with full awareness of this blurring, it seems clear that Hill and Adamson did not perceive this as a failure, spoiling the overall effect. Indeed, while the blurring may well have been unintended, the overall effect is to add a sense of movement and dynamism to what would otherwise remain a rather stilted pose. Like the majority of Hill and Adamson's photographs, this image was captured out of doors. Unlike many of their portraits, however, this is here made a virtue, not least by the compositional emphasis on the sharply defined shadow on the background wall, echoing the profile of both player and racket and adding a further dynamism to the image. The length of shadow suggests a late afternoon or early evening, a time when tennis would typically be played, in contrast to the midday scenes more conventionally deployed to maximize light and disguise intrusive shadows.

The space occupied by the player is also worthy of analysis. The sitter is represented standing on paving slabs in front of a solid wall, probably a consequence of capturing the image in an area adjacent to Hill and Adamson's Edinburgh studio (Ford 1976, 26). This detail, however, also suggests an important historical context for the sporting subject matter. Produced fully three decades before Major Walter Clopton Wingfield first patented the game he called *Sphairistike*, the forerunner of modern Lawn Tennis, this work accordingly represents a participant in the traditional game subsequently referred to as Real Tennis (Gillmeister 1998, 174–177). Long associated with monarchy and aristocracy, this game was played within an enclosed, walled space derived from the medieval cloisters that are believed to be the original setting for the French game *jeu de paume* (Gillmeister 1998, 28). Here, it

Figure 2. David Octavius Hill and Robert Adamson, Mr Laing or Laine, 1843, photograph, National Galleries, Scotland.

might be noted that the oldest (Real) Tennis Court still in existence, the open-air, walled court at Falkland Palace in Fife, built for James V of Scotland in 1659, is situated midway between Hill and Adamson's studio in Edinburgh and the latter's native St Andrews, the two sites most strongly associated with the early photographers. While there is no evidence to document Hill and Adamson's awareness of this local site of major significance for the history of tennis in Scotland, nor to indicate whether or not they had a personal interest in the game itself, the broader links between sport and the aristocratic and intellectual communities of Edinburgh and St Andrews were much in evidence at this time.

Hill and Adamson's portrait of Mr Laing as a tennis player might thus be seen both as an early image of sport and as part of their wider artistic project to produce theatrical *tableaux vivants* of contemporary scenes with historical resonances, designed to capture the attention of a popular, image buying audience. Notably, the work also borrowed from more traditional artistic sources, such as Étienne Loys' 1753 *Portrait of Guillaume Barcellon*, professional tennis player to King Louis XV of France. As the earliest known example of a photograph representing a sporting subject, Hill and Adamson's tennis player forges a clear link between the representation of sportsmen in traditional and modern media, thus contributing to the early establishment of visual conventions for the photographic representation of sport. It is difficult, however, to determine who precisely were the audiences for these early images. The reproducibility of photographs certainly meant that Hill and Adamson could produce multiple copies that they sold to collectors, artists and consumers interested in the subject matter represented. Equally, in the absence of documentary evidence, it is impossible to determine what motivations consumers of these images had. It would be another half-century before the development of means to disseminate these images through publication in popular illustrated journals would generate a wider audience and consumer base for sport photography.

Imaging golf at St Andrews

Hill and Adamson's focus on tennis clearly signifies the social importance of sport in Scotland in the mid-nineteenth century. In this context, however, tennis is perhaps not the first sporting activity to come to mind when considering the reputation of St Andrews. Golf has been practised in Scotland, and at St Andrews in particular, since at least the mid-sixteenth century and probably as early as a century before that (Carradice 2001, 142). Indeed by the end of the seventeenth century, the town was already being referred to as a 'metropolis of golfing', though interest in the game would decline over the following century (Carradice 2001, 142). However, when Hill and Adamson first established their photographic business, golf was notably experiencing something of a revival, having gained the Royal Patronage of William IV as recently as 1834 (Malcolm and Crabtree 2010, 22). A further indication of the growing cultural significance of the game was the publication in Edinburgh between 1833 and 1843 of three editions of *Golfiana, or Niceties Connected with the Game of Golf,* George Fullerton Carnegie's volume of collected poems about the game (Carnegie 1843).

Given this context, it is perhaps unsurprising that Hill and Adamson's camera would focus on this most quintessential of Scottish sports. For example, between 1843 and 1847, Hill and Adamson produced a multi-figure composition showing a group of golfers and caddies gathered around a central figure about to make a putt (Figure 3). Once again, the outdoor setting implies an action shot, though the scene is clearly staged with all figures standing in a single horizontal line to form a balanced composition, focusing the viewer's attention on the dramatic moment of the putt itself. Here, the staging of the image makes it more reminiscent of a classical frieze than a subject of modern life. An original print of this work in the collection of National Galleries Scotland has notably been annotated, though perhaps some years later, to indicate that the players represented constitute an elite of St Andrews golf at this time. Most significant amongst these is the central figure with club in hand, identified as Major (later Sir) Hugh Lyon Playfair. Having spent the best part of his career as an Officer in the East India Company, Playfair returned to Scotland in 1834 and in 1842 took up the post as Provost of the University of St Andrews. He was also a prolific golfer, regularly winning competitions and medals in tournaments held at St Andrews, including the Gold Medal in 1840 and 1842 (Lewis and Howe 2004, 40). Later he would Captain the Royal and Ancient Golf Club and be the driving force behind the building of the new clubhouse, still an iconic visual signifier of golfing history at St Andrews. Playfair was also a highly influential member of the intellectual community in which Hill and Adamson circulated (Lewis and Howe 2004, 40). Along with physicist, Sir David Brewster, a close friend of Fox Talbot, and physician John Adamson, older brother of Robert, Playfair was instrumental in founding the first-ever photographic society, the Edinburgh Calotype Club (Ford 1976, 17). He thus straddled the two worlds of photography and golf.

Figure 3. David Octavius Hill and Robert Adamson, St Andrews Golfers, 1843–1847, photograph, University of St Andrews.

Amongst the other figures identified in Hill and Adamson's photograph are two of the most famous players in golfing history, Allan Robertson and Tom Morris senior (popularly known as 'Old' Tom Morris), second and third from the left. Robertson, widely held to be the first professional golfer, and the finest of his generation, made a significant living by winning bets against opponents (Carradice 2001, 145). His most famous apprentice was Tom Morris who frequently partnered Robertson in competitions and took over the mantle of professional and green-keeper at St Andrews after Robertson's death. Others identified in the photograph include Capt David Campbell (far left), and the professional golfers, Bob Andrews, (behind Playfair) Willie Dunn and Watty Alexander (second and first from the right, respectively). Yet, it is Playfair who occupies centre-stage in the composition, even amongst this exalted golfing company. Social standing is thus given precedence over golfing ability, and both Robertson and Morris, the most highly regarded professionals of their day, are relegated to the sidelines. That these players, as well as Alexander, are posed carrying clubs, serves visually to associate them more with the role of caddy than player, thus reinforcing a social hierarchy elevating the amateur gentleman above the professional player.

It is also important here to consider what might have been the original purpose of Hill and Adamson's golfing photograph. In 2002, the Scottish National Portrait Gallery acquired a major new work, a large-scale oil painting entitled *The Golfers: A Grand Match played over the Links of St Andrews on the day of the Annual Meeting of The Royal and Ancient Golf Club*. The work, described by then Director Sir Timothy Clifford as 'one of the greatest icons of the game of golf', is a modern-life, multi-figure composition produced in 1847 by the Scottish portraitist, Charles Lees (Lewis and Howe 2004, 9). This work preceded more famous grand narrative paintings produced in early Victorian Britain, such as Ford Madox Brown's *Work* (1852–1865) and William Powell Frith's *Ramsgate Sands* (1851–1854) and, more pertinently for its sporting subject, *Derby Day* (1856–1858). Here, however, it is its significance for Hill and Adamson's photograph that is of interest. Like the photograph, Lees' painting positions the top-hatted Playfair (centre-left, having just struck the ball) as the focal point of the composition. Campbell also appears as the most prominent figure amongst the background group on the far right while the golfer, Dunn, peaks around the shoulder of the elderly seated figure in the lower right foreground. More importantly, Robertson also occupies a prominent position standing immediately behind the foreground crouching figure to the left of Playfair. Robertson again carries clubs underneath his arm and stands in a posture virtually identical to his appearance in the Hill and Adamson photograph. The similarity between the representations of Playfair (though reversed) and Robertson has led Lewis and Howe to speculate that Lees used the photograph as an aide to his composition and may even have commissioned it explicitly for this purpose (Lewis and Howe 2004, 28). Indeed, one of the key roles photography served in its earliest days was to provide material from which artists could work, so this conclusion seems particularly convincing.

A key question here, is whether the decision to differentiate, in visual terms, gentlemen and players was initially made by Hill and Adamson, in the original photograph, or was a requirement of Lees. It is certainly the case that the two prominent figures also represented carrying clubs in the right foreground of Lees' painting were professional golfers (Sandy Pirie and Sandy Pirie Jr). Either way, it is clear that while golf and photography both played a significant role in bringing different classes into the same social frame, this visual shorthand nonetheless ensured that a distinction was both maintained and communicated visually to the spectator. This differentiation of class would shape much sport photography throughout the remainder of the nineteenth century and beyond.

The close relationship between sport and photography in early Victorian Scotland would continue well into the second half of the nineteenth century, a factor evidenced in the photographic archive at the University of St Andrews. In the 1850s and 1860s, for example, Hill and Adamson's staged, panoramic portrait format was widely replicated by photographers such as Thomas Rodger and George Middlemas Cowie. Rodger, additionally, would modify Hill and Adamson's strict class juxtapositions by bringing professional golfers into his St Andrews studio and representing them independently. As early as 1850, for example, Rodger photographed Robertson, at this point at the apex of his golfing career, striking a dignified, upright pose framed on the right by hanging drapery (Figure 4). Here, the sitter holds a club firmly in his right hand, partly as a means to secure support for the time of exposure, but also to replicate the appearance of a gentleman's walking cane. As Roy Strong has argued in relation to the work of Hill and Adamson, early Scottish portrait photographs

> belong to a definite stylistic tradition of portrait painting in Scotland. In many ways, much of what has been described as the their 'enigmatic charm' springs from the fact that these photographs represent the final flowering of a concept of recording human likeness first established as a style by Sir Henry Raeburn at the close of the century. (Ford 1976, 51)

To reinforce this point, Strong compares Hill and Adamson's photographic portrait of Thomas Duncan with Raeburn's portrait of John Crichton Stuart, Second Marquess of Bute (1821), a comparison that might equally be made with Rodger's portrait of Robertson. Certainly, the posture adopted by Robertson echoes the earlier portrait of a major landowner and member of the aristocracy, whilst the confident gaze beyond the picture frame

Figure 4. Thomas Rodger, Allan Robertson, 1850, photograph, University of St Andrews.

suggests an individual of much self-assurance. Yet, other details reinforce Robertson's less socially elevated status. The presence not only of an additional club, but also of two golf balls lying in a prominent position to the right, serve to signify Robertson's status specifically as a professional player. Moreover, the weight of Robertson's right hand pocket implies the likely presence of further balls. As Rodger, and indeed any contemporary viewer who recognized the golfer would be aware.

Robertson's reputation at this time lay not only in his playing ability. He was also an established tradesman, having taken over his father's business manufacturing and selling golfing equipment not just locally, but all over the world. Without doubt, his most significant product was the so-called 'featherie' golf ball, a hand-stitched, leather sphere stuffed with boiled-down chicken or goose feathers. Robertson, assisted by his apprentice Tom Morris, had effectively cornered not only the local, but also the global market for this expensive product. However, in 1850, Robertson's virtual monopoly was under threat following the development of a new ball known as a 'gutty'. Manufactured from gutta-percha, a rubber-like substance found in Malaysia, the 'gutty' was significantly cheaper to manufacture than the hand-stuffed 'featherie'. Further, many believed that its aerodynamic qualities were a significant improvement on the older model. Though aware of the threat to his commercial enterprise, Robertson belligerently resisted the new 'gutty' ball, even falling out with Morris after discovering that his apprentice had used one in a match (Malcolm and Crabtree 2010, 33, 34). Shortly after this, Morris left Robertson's employ to set himself up in England. In this context, the presence of the 'featheries' in Rodger's portrait of Robertson acquires an additional significance. They thus become attributes to signify not only Robertson's status as golfer, but also as a manufacturer of a major product, and one happy to use his own image to promote his commercial interests. Indeed this image might be seen as one of the earliest examples of the photographic image of a sportsman deployed, at least in part, to endorse a commercial product. Ultimately, however, Rodger may also be alluding to a weakness in Robertson's character, a steadfastness, perhaps even an inflexibility, in the face of technological and commercial change.

The Morris dynasty

In the mid 1870s, perhaps one of the most famous photographic portraits of early sportsmen, and golfers in particular, was produced (Figure 5).[4] This double portrait by an unknown photographer, possibly named Sawyer, represents the Morris dynasty, including in the

Figure 5. 'Sawyer', Old Tom Morris with Young Tom Morris, c.1870–1875.

background, Robertson's former apprentice, 'Old' Tom Morris, and beside him, wielding a club, his son, 'Young' Tom Morris. The image, once more, was clearly produced in a studio, the golfers posing against a painted backdrop. Both wear hats, the former a cap at a jaunty angle, the latter a glengarry, which he was known to wear during tournament play. The senior figure stands upright, like Robertson, his club simultaneously reminiscent of a walking cane. His posture, however, is far less rigid than in Rodger's earlier portrait. While this may be a consequence of a significantly shorter exposure time, it perhaps also suggests a greater informality of character. The younger Morris is represented addressing a golf ball with an open stance typical of the chip shot for which he was particularly renowned. Here, however, the three-quarter-body posture also facilitates a near-full face representation. Indeed, the adoption of this open stance, halfway between action shot and posed portrait, had previously been introduced in 1855 in an outdoor portrait of the aforementioned Captain Campbell taken by Rodger. Clad in tartan jacket and also wearing a glengarry, Campbell here poses in front of the doorway to a humble cottage door, a setting perhaps more intended to suggest a specifically Scottish rural setting than a bad lie. Campbell's focus is straight towards the camera, thus constructing the viewer as the target towards which the shot is aimed. The low crouch suggests the pent-up energy about to be released by the swing of the club. In contrast, the pose of 'Young' Tom Morris is more upright and relaxed, suggestive of a golfer with little to prove to the spectator. The presence of Morris senior, here literally backing up his son, confers upon the portrait an aura of easeful confidence, one that reflected the position of both players within their sport.

They had more than sufficient cause for such confidence. Following the foundation of the British Open Golf Championship in 1860, 'Old' Tom Morris had dominated the early years of the competition winning in 1861, 1862, 1864 and 1867. His failure to win in 1868 was as a consequence of defeat to his then 17-year-old son, who also won in 1869, 1870 and 1872 (no competition was held in 1871). Thus, by the early 1870s the Morrises, father and son, had occupied a position at the very pinnacle of their professional sport for over a decade. But this, as things transpired, was not to last. In September 1875, while partnering his father in a team match, 'Young' Tom Morris received a telegram requesting his urgent return as his pregnant wife had gone into labour. Before reaching home, however, he learned that both his wife and the child had died (Malcolm and Crabtree 2010, 137–141). In October of that year, Morris himself fell ill and died suddenly on Christmas Day 1875, less than four months after his initial loss. He was just 24 years old (Malcolm and Crabtree 2010, 147).

The tragedy endured by 'Young' Tom Morris has had a significant impact upon the status and legacy of this photograph, inevitably shaping the image of the champion golfer in the public domain. Shortly after his death, for example, a proposal was made to honour Morris by erecting a funerary monument at the site of his grave in St Andrews' Cathedral cemetery. The Edinburgh-based sculptor John Rhind was commissioned to produce the work, which was subsequently unveiled in 1878 (Figure 6). Intriguingly, Rhind abandoned the allegorical approach more conventionally deployed for funerary monuments and instead designed a relief sculpture representing Morris in the exact pose adopted in the photograph. Indeed the similarity between photograph and monument – the sole exception being that Morris' jacket, undone in the original, has here been buttoned – makes it clear that Rhind used this photograph as his primary source material. The other key difference, of course, is the excision of 'Old' Tom from this representation, thus isolating the deceased golfer and diminishing the original message of dynastic continuity. As Tom Gunning reminds us,

Figure 6. John Rhind, Monument to Young Tom Morris, 1878, author's photograph.

> The ties of frozen images to death have been widely remarked upon from the beginning, when photographs took on an important role in memorial imagery, to the recent eloquent characterization by Roland Barthes of photographers as the agents of the image of death. (Thorburn and Jenkins 2004, 49)

Here, the literal transition from photograph to material monument situated in a graveyard further reinforces this connection between the photograph and death as elaborated upon by Barthes (Barthes 1981, 13–15).

The last few decades have witnessed a global explosion in the production of civic monuments dedicated to sportsmen and sportswomen (Stride, Wilson, and Thomas 2013, 148–160). Significantly, many of these monuments have also been based directly on photographic sources. At the front of this long line, however, stands Rhind's 'Young' Tom Morris funerary monument, the earliest manifestation of photography's direct impact upon the production of a public monument to a sporting hero.

William Notman and early sport photography in North America

In the latter part of the nineteenth century, yet one more Scottish photographer, this time an émigré to Canada, would make another significant impact on the development of early sporting photography. In 1874, William Notman produced the earliest photographic representation of team sports in action (Figure 7). *Harvard* vs. *McGill Football Match* represents a groundbreaking moment in North American football history. In May that year, the Redmen team from McGill University in Canada travelled south to Cambridge, Massachusetts to play the Crimsons from Harvard in a series of three intercollegiate games, the first two played in Cambridge on 14 and 15 May, the third in Montreal on 23 October. As the rules of football had yet to be standardized, the teams initially agreed to play two matches, the first deploying the 'Boston rules' adopted by Harvard, the second, McGill's own regulations (Zukerman 2012). The former was a round ball, kicking game broadly following the Association (later dubbed 'soccer') rules that had been established in England in 1863. The latter, based more on English rugby, allowed handling and running with an oval ball. Harvard secured a 3–0 victory in the first match while the second ended without score (Zukerman 2012). Subsequently, Harvard abandoned the kicking game in preference to McGill's handling version and thus these contests have gone down in popular sporting folklore as the catalyst for the subsequent development of North American style football. Notman's photograph thus commemorates this iconic moment in American sporting development and is frequently reproduced in histories of the game. However, even at first glance, it is clear that this is a far cry from a straightforward image documenting a specific historical moment. By the mid-1870s, Notman had become one of the most prolific and pre-eminent photographers in Canada, having established professional studios in Montreal, Toronto, Ottawa and Halifax and further secured seasonal branches in the north-eastern United States photographing students and faculty at Vassar College, Princeton and Harvard (Parsons 2014, 7).

Figure 7. William Notman, Harvard vs Mc Gil, 1874, composite photograph, McCord Museum, Montreal.

Like most professional photographers of this era, Notman's stock-in-trade was portraiture. As a member of Montreal's artistic community, however, he was also committed to producing more creative works, many of which notably embraced sport, particularly local winter sports, as a popular theme (Poulter 2009, 166–174). Initially these works, like Hill and Adamson's early 'action' shots, were carefully staged affairs. His *Tobogganist* (c. 1875), for example, reveals how Notman constructed complex, purpose-built studio sets with specially painted backdrops for dramatic effect (Figure 8). *Group of Curlers* (1867) was similarly composed and shot in the studio with the figures posed on a plate of zinc, highly polished to resemble ice (Parsons 2014, 17). *Harvard* vs. *McGill Football Match*, however, reveals an alternative practice widely embraced by Notman at this time. The image is, in fact, a composite, constructed from multiple individual photographs staged and shot separately, usually in a studio, and then montaged to create a carefully preconceived final composition (Hall, Dodds, and Triggs 1993, 166, 167). The following year, Notman produced an even more elaborate composite photograph notionally representing the same event. It is noteworthy here that Notman's work, though constructed from photographs, bears more than a passing resemblance to the compositional conventions deployed by the graphic artists who regularly illustrated sporting events for the contemporary press. These, in turn, also

Figure 8. William Notman, R. Stevenson and Friends on a Tobaggan, 1870, studio photograph, McCord Museum, Montreal.

drew significantly on the compositional devices developed in painted scenes of sporting play, epitomized by Webster's *A Football Game*, with which this article opened. Notman's studio had acquired considerable expertise in the technique of composite photography, a practice originally developed in the 1850s in Britain (where it was more typically referred to as combination printing). The most famous exponents of this were Oscar G. Rejlander and Henry Peach Robinson, whose works, such as *The Two Ways of Life* (1857) and *Fading Away* (1858) have acquired renown within photographic histories. Unlike his predecessors, however, Notman was happy to paste his figures onto painted backdrops as evidenced here, thus aligning his images more closely with contemporary paintings and adding an artistic prestige to his work.[5] By the time of his death in 1891, Notman's studios were turning out both staged and composite photographs in the thousands, with sporting scenes featuring significantly. These were eagerly purchased by the burgeoning collectors of photographs, many of whom built up their own albums of images. A catalogue of sports represented in Notman's studios would include, in addition to the above-mentioned activities, athletics, boxing, cricket, fencing, ice hockey, lacrosse, polo, skating, tennis, wrestling, rowing and yachting.[6] After his death, Notman sporting composites even began to appear in the sporting press where they were presented as if they represented live action.[7]

Conclusion

The period from 1839 to the mid 1870s played a pivotal role in the establishment of visual conventions for the representation of sport in photographic form. Initially, this was confined to traditional forms of portraiture, or to posed shots that contrived to represent sporting action. Here, the relative stillness conventionally adopted by tennis players and golfers shortly before engaging in play provided a suitable opportunity for photographers to reference sporting practices. When more dramatic action was required, the composite technique could compensate for the technical limitations of the medium. In both cases, art and artifice were openly and creatively deployed not only to enhance the visual representation of these modern activities, but also to establish clear links to visual conventions within a broader history of art. In the years that followed this period, both technological and aesthetic advances would transform the possibilities for photography's relationship with sport. From the high-speed photography of Eadweard Muybridge and Étienne-Jules Marey to the mass publication of specialist photo-illustrated sports journals, facilitated by the development of the halftone printing process, photographic representations of sport would play an increasingly important role in the visual landscape of the fin-de-siècle world and beyond, shaping popular perceptions of sport as an integral aspect of modern culture.[8] In 1898, the Frenchman Pierre Lafitte launched what might be considered as one of the most innovative and visually striking of these early photo-illustrated journals, *La Vie au grand air*. In the true Anglo-French competitive spirit of the time Lafitte explicitly set out to counter the perception that 'les Anglais' were the dominant sporting nation by demonstrating how France had now become 'le Pays du Muscle par excellence' (Lafitte 1898, 1). His goal, however, was not only to foreground France's sporting excellence but also to link this to his nation's well-established reputation as a global centre for art, thus producing what he explicitly described as 'un album tout aussi artistique' (Lafitte 1898, 1). Yet, while competing with 'les Anglais', Lafitte had perhaps forgotten the achievements of 'les Écossais', the true artistic pioneers of early sports photography.

Notes

1. http://www.bbc.co.uk/pressoffice/pressreleases/stories/2005/09_september/05/painting.shtml.
2. Amongst the works most widely discussed by contemporary critics were: William Etty's *Diana and Endymion;* Daniel Maclise's *Robin Hood and his Merry Men Entertaining Richard the Lionheart in Sherwood Forest;* and Turner's *Ancient Rome, Agrippina Landing with the Ashes of Germanicus* and *Pluto Carrying off Proserpine.*
3. Earlier races, referred to as the Liverpool Grand Steeplechase, had been staged at Aintree between 1836 and 1838. See Pinfold (1998).
4. The loose attribution to 'Sawyer' is based on the inscription 'Sawyers Collection' on an early print dated 1875 in the collection of the photograph archive of the University of St Andrews.
5. For more on Notman's composite works see, Triggs (2005).
6. An extensive number of Notman's photographs can be accessed via the McCord Museum online archive at www.musee-mccord.qc.ca, accessed 15 March 2016.
7. For example, in 1900 the French sporting periodical *La Vie au grand air* published two of Notman's studio staged bobsleigh photographs alongside a composite representing an ice hockey match in Montreal to accompany an article reporting on winter sports. See Lange (1900).
8. For a fuller account of the history of early photo-illustrated sports journals see O'Mahony (Forthcoming).

Disclosure statement

No potential conflict of interest was reported by the author.

References

Barthes, Roland. 1981. *Camera Lucida: Reflections on Photography*. Translated by Richard Howard. New York: Hill and Wang.

Buckland, Gail. 2016. *Who Shot Sports?: A Photographic History, 1843 to the Present*. New York: Alfred A. Knopf.

Carnegie, George Fullerton. 1843. *Golfiana, or Niceties Connected with the Game of Golf*. London: William Blackwood and Sons.

Carradice, Ian. 2001. "'Swiping … and Daguerreotyping': Photographing Golf at St Andrews." *History of Photography* 25 (2): 142–154. doi:10.1080/03087298.2001.10443450.

Ford, Colin, ed. 1976. *An Early Victorian Album: The Photographic Masterpieces (1843–1847) of David Octavius Hill and Robert Adamson*. New York: Alfred A. Knopf.

Fox Talbot, William Henry. 1844-6. *The Pencil of Nature*. London: Longman, Brown, Green and Longmans.

Frizot, Michel, ed. 1998. *A New History of Photography*. Köln: Könemann.

Gillmeister, Heiner. 1998. *Tennis: A Cultural History*. London: Leicester University Press.

Gunning, Tom. 2004. "Re-newing Old Technologies: Astonishment, Second Nature, and the Uncanny in Technology from the Previous Turn-of-the-Century." In *Rethinking Media Change: The Aesthetics of Transition*, edited by David Thorburn and Henry Jenkins, 39–60. Cambridge, MA: MIT Press.

Hall, Roger, Gordon Dodds, and Stanley Triggs. 1993. *The World of William Notman: The Nineteenth Century through a Master Lens*. Boston, MA: D.R. Godine.

Inverdale, John. 2005. "My Assumptions about 'Oldest' Were Confounded by Barnes." *The Telegraph*, November 2. http://www.telegraph.co.uk/sport/rugbyunion/2367614/My-assumptions-about-oldest-were-confounded-by-Barnes.html.

Lafitte, Pierre. 1898. "La Vie au grand air." *La Vie au grand air* 1. April 1: 1.

Lange, Géo. 1900. "Sports d'Hiver." *La Vie au grand air* 70. January 14: 232.

Lewis, Peter N., and Angela D. Howe. 2004. *The Golfers: The Story behind the Painting*. Edinburgh: National Galleries of Scotland.

Livingston, Jane. 1996. *Visions of Victory: A Century of Sports Photography*. New York: Pindar Press.

Malcolm, David, and Peter E. Crabtree. 2010. *Tom Morris of St Andrews: The Colossus of Golf 1921– 1908*. Edinburgh: Birlinn Ltd.

Nead, Lynda. 2011. "Stilling the Punch: Boxing, Violence and the Photographic Image." *Journal of Visual Culture* 10 (3): 305–323. doi:10.1177/1470412911419755.

O'Mahony, Mike. Forthcoming. *Photography and Sport*. London: Reaktion Books Ltd.

Parsons, Sarah. 2014. *William Notman, Life and Work*. Toronto: At Canada Institute.

Pinfold, John. 1998. "Where the Champion Horses Run: The Origins of Aintree Racecourse and the Grand National." *International Journal of the History of Sport* 15 (2): 137–151. doi:10.1080/09523369808714032.

Poulter, Gillian. 2009. *Becoming Native in a Foreign Land: Sport, Visual Culture and Identity in Montreal, 1840–85*. Vancouver: UBC Press.

Stevenson, Sara. 2002. *Facing the Light: The Photography of Hill and Adamson*. Edinburgh: National Galleries of Scotland.

Stride, Christopher, John Wilson, and Ffion Thomas. 2013. "From Pitch to Plinth: Documenting the United Kingdom's Football Statuary." *Sculpture Journal* 22 (1): 148–160. doi:10.3828/sj.2013.9c.

Thorburn, David, and Henry Jenkins. 2004. *Rethinking Media Change: The Aesthetics of Transition*. Cambridge, MA: MIT Press.

Triggs, Stanley G. 2005. "The Composite Photographs." Accessed May 21, 2017.http://collections. musee-mccord.qc.ca/notman_doc/pdf/EN/COMPOSITE-EN.pdf

Wombell, Paul. 2000. *Sportscape: The Evolution of Sports Photography*. London: Phaidon Press.

Zukerman, Earl. 2012. "This Date in History: First Football Game Was May 14, 1874," May 14. https:// www.mcgill.ca/channels/news/date-history-first-football-game-was-may-14-1874-106694.

The art of face-saving and culture-changing: sculpting Chinese football's past, present and future

Christopher B. Stride ⓘ and Layne Vandenberg

ABSTRACT

In this paper, we consider the football statues of China, whose football team has dramatically underperformed relative to its population size and economic power. Although China lacks a participative grassroots football culture and has struggled to establish a credible domestic league, recent government intervention and investment has seen football's profile rise dramatically. China's many football statues are largely atypical in comparison to the rest of the world, including their depiction of anonymous figures rather than national or local heroes, the incorporation of tackling scenes in their designs, and their location at training camps. Through four specific examples and reference to a global database, we illustrate how these statues reflect the tensions and difficulties inherent in China's desire to integrate itself into global football, and achieve its stated goal of hosting and winning the FIFA World Cup, whilst simultaneously upholding national, cultural and political values such as the primacy of hard work and learning, and saving face in defeat.

In his 1950 compendium, 'The Appreciation of Football', Percy Young mused on the great English footballers of the era, asking 'Why do these men have no statues erected?' Young's call-to-arms was belatedly heeded. By August 2017 the world's football statuary numbered 563 full-body figurative statues or statue groups depicting players (467, 83%), managers (48, 9%) or, occasionally, chairmen, founders, referees or fans.[1] Eighty two per cent of these statues have been erected in the past 25 years. Seventy countries have so far embraced figurative football sculptures, though there has yet to be a statue featuring a professional female player, with just a handful of anonymous figures at United States colleges depicting women's football.[2]

Football statues represent the largest single-sport collection within the wider phenomenon of contemporary sports statues, which encompasses almost every athletic activity from speed skating to surfing.[3] In their deeply traditional figurative form, these modern monuments to athletic achievement represent artistic revival rather than innovation, harking back to ancient Greek sculptures of Olympian heroes (Miller 2004), and in smaller form, to the Mesoamerican ballgame of 1500BC (Mint Museum 2011). The modern accumulation of sports statues has invigorated an already developing scholarly interest in sporting art (Guttmann 2011). Academic studies on sports statues have focused on established, traditional and successful national sporting cultures, such as US baseball or UK football (Stride et al. 2012); or on the representation of exceptional athletes with wider social relevance, such as war heroes (Smith 2012), or barrier-breakers (Osmond, Phillips, and O'Neill 2006; Schultz 2011). This research has identified numerous motivations for these monuments, including nostalgia and authenticity-centred marketing by sports organizations and cities (Stride, Wilson, and Thomas 2013), the creation of local and national identities through heritage (Bale 1994), memorials to tragic early deaths (Stride, Thomas, and Chamorro 2017), and even reparations to formerly marginalized communities (Smith 2009). Despite these contributions, there has not been an examination of international heterogeneity in the production, style and meanings of figurative sports sculptures.

The world's football statuary is unusual in reaching beyond successful nations, and internationally renowned clubs or athletes. Countries regarded as minnows on the pitch, such as India, Indonesia and Venezuela, have erected multiple football statues (Stride, Thomas, and Wilson 2012). On a basic level, this ubiquity demonstrates football's worldwide reach and appeal, further suggesting that football sculpture is – at least in part – driven by a desire to reflect, celebrate and exploit the popularity of the sport regardless of success. Such a global distribution also offers the opportunity to investigate the designs, motivations for, and interpretations of football statues within developing soccer cultures, where past football success is at best relative, and where growing the sport is a work in progress.

This paper considers the football statuary of China, a nation that has underperformed in international competition despite its population size and investment in the sport. Generally, football statues are most often erected to evoke nostalgia, celebrate traditions, leverage a club's or town's heritage, or bask in past successes. Football's historic low status and fractured progress within China makes those motivations unlikely. However, notwithstanding an ongoing struggle to establish a competitive national team and reputable domestic league, China has over 30 football statues or statue groups.[4]

In this paper, we utilize a unique database of the world's football statues developed by the first author and colleagues (Stride, Thomas, and Wilson 2012), to illustrate how China's football statues are atypical in subject choice, design aesthetics, locations, motivations and messages. Using four specific statues as examples, we argue that these differences depict China's unique football culture, which combines ancient roots with interrupted development, rapid recent change, and the overarching control of a one-party state. We also consider how China's football statuary reflects current challenges in Chinese football, including integration with a global, largely alien sporting community; championing national strength despite sporting weakness; and embracing an international sporting culture whose philosophy and behaviours run counter to national traditions.

Chinese football past: pre-history, birth-pains and stagnation

Despite being a relatively late starter in international football, China was recently acknowledged by football's world governing body FIFA as the birthplace of the earliest form of football (Goldblatt 2007, 5; Connor 2015). Cuju, which literally means 'kick ball', was a ball game that largely eschewed ball handling in favour of kicking, and featured opposing teams and goals. Cuju was popularized in the Han dynasty from 200BC as a form of military training, and remained part of Chinese culture for the next 1800 years (Timm 2015).

Written records and sculptural artefacts indicate that cuju was played by men and women (Williams 2007), and supported by successive Han emperors (Timm 2015). Rules and equipment evolved, with the original feather-stuffed leather ball replaced by an inflated ball, changing configurations and positioning of goals, nets and pitch boundaries, and an imperative to keep the ball in the air. Ball juggling was considered an essential skill (Cui 2016). Cuju grew throughout the Tang dynasty (618–907), becoming a non-contact sport, with teams aiming to kick the ball through a small hole in a centrally located goal-net. Popularity peaked in the Southern Song dynasty (1127–1279), with the establishment of cuju leagues, professional players and a transfer market (Barr 2009).

Cuju's social status declined over the following centuries. The Qing dynasty, which began in 1644, preferred individual sports, fearing subversive elements within team sports. The resulting nation-wide ban on cuju, with resistance punishable by cutting off a player's feet, unsurprisingly heralded the sport's demise, some years before the arrival of modern football. Given this lack of a direct lineage, cuju is best classified as one of a number of unconnected football-like sports played by ancient civilizations from around the world, that form football's pre-history (Goldblatt 2007, 5, 6). FIFA's support for China's claims as the ultimate birthplace of football can be better analysed in the context of FIFA's internal politics – specifically generating support for Sepp Blatter's continued presidency and FIFA's attempts to build relationships with the Chinese government, and hence the burgeoning Chinese TV and media market (Connor 2015).

Modern football spread to mainland China in the late nineteenth century (Hong and Mangan 2006, 47), via foreign workers and Christian missionaries, of whom 3000 were in China by 1900. By 1907 English expatriates in Shanghai had created a league, and along the eastern coast similar enterprises sprang up amongst immigrants from other established football-playing nations. Native adoption led inexorably to a Chinese football association and national team, formed in 1924 and affiliated to FIFA in 1931, marking China as a slow but not irretrievably late starter (Jones 2004, 54; Simons 2008, 144, 145).

In fact, China achieved a measure of international success from the mid-1930s to the late 1940s, including Olympic qualification in 1936 and 1948. The nation's football development, however, was severely hampered by the Second Sino-Japanese War (1937–1946) and the resumption of the Chinese Civil War that resulted in the establishment of the People's Republic of China (PRC), a one party communist state, in 1949. FIFA formally recognized the PRC in 1958, when China debuted in the Asian qualifying competition of the FIFA World Cup, but the following year China withdrew from international competition in response to FIFA's further acknowledgement of the independence of Chinese Taipei. As a result, China's involvement in international football from 1959 to 1980 consisted mainly of friendlies with sympathetic political regimes. Beyond this 'two-China' issue, China's involvement in international competition was limited by the internal purges and breakdown in society that marked Mao Zedong's Great Leap Forward and the Cultural Revolution. It was not until 1982 that the nation once again took part in World Cup qualifiers (Jones 1999, 186; Goldblatt 2007, 540, 541).

The Cultural Revolution also dealt a heavy blow to China's internal sports development, as sports institutions were broken up and leading athletes and coaches were sent to the gulag (Goldblatt 2007, 541). As a result, domestic football suffered a similarly stunted and intermittent development to that of the national team. Although China's social upheaval and vast size had prevented the organic development of a national competition before the PRC was established, a state-orchestrated Chinese football league emerged in the 1950s. Membership was restricted to government organizations such as the railways, navy and trade unions (Goldblatt 2007, 540). The league was halted in 1966 by the Cultural Revolution, and only re-established in 1973 (Goldblatt, 541). Factory clubs were allowed to join from the early 1980s, bringing greater competition and funds, but fully professional national competition, the Jia-A League, did not begin until 1994. Chinese domestic football mirrored the national economy in transitioning rapidly from almost complete state-sponsorship and central planning to a more diverse market-oriented system, with commercially sponsored teams, transfer fees, and even a handful of overseas players (Jones 1999, 186, 193).

Though late by western standards, the development of a Chinese national professional league came less than a decade after similar developments in the Republic of Korea (South Korea) and Japan (Moffett 2002). Given China's booming economy and accompanying rise to global superpower status – and its population's growing enthusiasm for watching televised football, particularly the proliferating coverage of European leagues – there was hope, even anticipation that football would become a source of national pride. The exploits of China's national women's football team, the 'Iron Roses', who were FIFA Women's World Cup runners-up in 1999 and perennial Asian champions in the 1990s (Hong and Mangan 2006), further raised expectations.

Instead, China's men's team has struggled, and been comfortably outperformed by its similarly late-developing East Asian neighbours South Korea and Japan, for the past two decades.[5] China's only qualification for the men's FIFA World Cup finals tournament came in 2002, but it lost all three games. Since then it has lurched between brief flickers of promise and abject failure, including humiliating defeats to Thailand and United States Major League Soccer (MLS) club Real Salt Lake (Minter 2013), even dropping out of the top 100 of the FIFA World Rankings in 2013. As of August 2017 it languishes in 77th place, sandwiched between Sierra Leone and Qatar ('FIFA World Ranking' 2017).

Simons (2008) argues that China's failure in football results from the lack of grass-roots-level participation that sustains traditional football nations. Despite its vast population, very few Chinese citizens actually play football. The absence of informal football activity is partly due to lack of places to play. Even by 1998, Beijing had only 30 football pitches for its 12 million inhabitants, mostly owned by universities (Simons 2008, 202). Amateur football has also been suppressed by laws requiring state approval for gatherings of 10 or more people (Simons 2008, 17).

Rather than encouraging all its citizens to kick a ball about for fun, developing public football facilities, and generally stimulating wider interest and involvement in the game, the Chinese government has focused on achieving international success as quickly as possible. To do this it has applied the top-down sports development model implemented successfully for Olympic sports, devoting its resources to identifying and hothousing elite talent at a very young age. Coaching has often been outsourced to foreign coaches hired from whichever nations were successful in world football at that time, as opposed to the more sustainable model of China developing its own coaches (Simons 2008). Furthermore, after an encouraging start to the professional era, even China's domestic football has offered little to inspire would-be young footballers to take up the game (Simons 2008, 179, 223). Despite a 2004 rebranding and reformation of the Jia-A League to become the Chinese Super League, the competition was increasingly beset by corruption involving gambling and match-fixing (Goldblatt 2007, 849; 'Little Red Card' 2011).

By the late-2000s, China's national football team and league were considered a source of shame ('Little Red Card' 2011; Minter 2013). Failures in football were not only a symbol of wider, seemingly intractable societal problems with corruption, but something so blatant and shameful that it could be publicly mocked without fear of reprisal, in a society where criticism of state institutions is typically unspoken. This stagnation in Chinese football occurred despite government efforts to develop football and utilize it as a tool in building national pride and asserting global superpower status. Football's increasing commercialization and hegemonic status amongst world sports throughout the 1990s and 2000s had coincided with China's extraordinary economic development. The transition to free-market capitalism had proved more successful for the wider economy than for football; by 2003 China had become the world's second largest economy (and is forecast to overtake the United States by the late 2020s; Maddison 2007). The international recognition and respect gained from hosting the 2008 Beijing Olympics has set the tone for China's continuing plays in international soft power politics and sports-related diplomacy. Beyond the Olympics, only the football World Cup offers similar levels of global exposure and prestige.

Chinese football present and future: tensions, ambitions … and statues

No doubt stung by Chinese football's failure to progress, former president Hu Jintao (2002–2013) and most notably current incumbent Xi Jinping, a keen football fan, eventually brought new impetus to China's football project. In 2009, when serving as Vice-President, Xi initiated an anti-corruption campaign that spanned the Chinese government and its agencies. Though not solely nor explicitly targeted at football, the campaign began with football because, as sport sociologist Xu Guoqi puts it, it was a 'safe' target: '… everyone knows [sports] officials are corrupt … everyone hates them' (Guoqi 2008; Guoqi 2015). Football was an ideal arena for testing the public's, and the government's, reaction to an anti-corruption campaign. If the campaign had begun with the Party that would have signalled 'a problem with the Party' (Guoqi 2015). Though beginning with the arrests of 16 low-level football administrators, by 2012 five top officials of the Chinese Football Association had been jailed for between 10 and 12 years, and a number of players were handed lesser custodial sentences (Watts 2009; 'Little Red Card' 2011; Beam 2012).

Having cleaned up domestic football, in 2015 the Chinese government set out a blueprint for developing the sport, including the intent to bid for the World Cup ('China sets goal' 2015). This was followed 12 months later by a strategy to become a 'world football superpower' by 2050, with plans to get '50 million children and adults playing the game … [and] at least 20,000 football training centres and 70,000 pitches in place by 2020' ('China aims to become football superpower' 2016). As a result, football has been widely introduced as part of the school curriculum from an early age. Although the Chinese authorities had issued many previous blueprints for football success, the grassroots flavour of this most recent policy suggests a break from top-down and top-only strategies.

Since this overt presidential intervention, China's domestic football league has also received rapid and substantial investment, both from government and, especially private enterprises and entrepreneurs, who see such munificence as a way of garnering favour with the ruling party and its football-loving president. Newly aggrandized Chinese Super League clubs have even begun to compete for the world's best players alongside the richest western clubs, paying salaries reported to exceed £500,000 per week.[6] Domestic attendances have grown considerably: in 2016 the Chinese Super League average of over 24,000 per match made it the sixth best supported football league in the world. Despite this domestic growth the Chinese football authorities – no doubt prompted by the government – have primarily focussed on the national team's success, restricting the use of overseas players in an attempt to encourage home-grown talent ('Chinese Super League' 2017). As well as extravagantly funding domestic teams, billionaire businessmen have created football training academies and purchased stakes in overseas clubs, notably in England and Italy.[7]

However, in its rapid and seemingly wholehearted embrace of the global game China faces twin conundrums. First, China's greater engagement in world football needs to be matched with a measure of success, or at least respectability, for the national team – and by dint of association, the nation itself and its leaders – to avoid continued loss of 'face'. Although a universal concern, saving face is particularly salient in Chinese culture, referring to being able to present oneself in a positive light whatever the truth of the matter (Lin 1939; Bond 1991; Faure and Fang 2008). As Li and Wang (2010) note, 'The importance of shame in Chinese culture is associated with the dominant social and moral thought of Confucianism', including the importance of one's ties to family and society: 'when people fail, they do not simply lose their own face, but they shame all those around them'. Others' perception of an act is therefore more crucial than whether that act is good per se. Shame has primacy over guilt in this way: how one is viewed by others is more important than how one views oneself (Wilson 1981). Furthermore, face operates as a group concept as well as a personal one (Li and Wang 2010). Since seizing power in 1949, the ruling Chinese Communist Party (CCP) has often invoked the idea of a past era or 'century of humiliation' (China's perceived previous failures and subjugation by other nations prior to the revolution) to place itself as China's liberating leader (Kaufman 2010). Football represents an awkward last remnant of this national humiliation.

Even if China does get its footballing act together, football and face-saving are not long-term bedfellows. China is unlikely ever to be viewed as the definitive world football leader in the same way it has swept the Olympic medal table in many individual sports. Football's international hierarchies are built on traditions of sustained success as much as on contemporary performance. Moreover, football is a national obsession in many countries, making any World Cup extremely competitive. Football is also a relatively unpredictable game, with the weaker team often able to scrape a draw or victory due to the difficulty in scoring a goal compared to, say, a basket in basketball. If and when China becomes a football giant, a potentially shameful giant-killing still awaits someday, somewhere.

The second conundrum is that, whilst China has adopted much of the free-market capitalism that underpins world football's transfer system and general business ethos, football has several other globally ubiquitous cultural tenets and characteristics that run counter to China's political strictures and national philosophies. The size of crowds that professional football matches attract, in a relatively spontaneous way, might be considered a threat to state control. Over and above the large numbers, the passions aroused at a football match, and particularly the occasional outbreaks of hooliganism, are unsettling to a government that fears and penalizes citizens who openly challenge authority and conventional behaviour

(Jones 2004, 63). Nevertheless, for international credibility China needs a well-attended and enthusiastically supported domestic league.

Furthermore, the commonplace glamour, adoration and exaltation of footballing heroes around the world, and the material and celebrity cultures encircling them, runs contrary to traditional Chinese patterns of rational influence from educators and intellectuals (Tan 2004, 98). Engagement with world football potentially endangers values and behaviours previously protected by China's relative isolationism. Also, based upon the Confucian hierarchical ethics that heavily influence the order of Chinese society, lower-ranked members of a team or collective must wait for clear instructions from their seniors before acting (Goldblatt 2007, 589). Chinese athletes have found Olympic success in individual sports with strong hierarchies and authoritative coaching, where repetitive training and mastery of specific, repeatable techniques are emphasized. The open game of football, however, also requires instinctive, proactive and imaginative behaviours, which are rarely acquired via formalized coaching routines and hard work (Jones 2004, 63). These abilities develop from the daily informal street or park games of football played by youngsters around the world, but not in China. It is also arguable that they require, or are at least strongly correlated with the type of free thinking incompatible with both China's traditional ethics and present government system.

As China has increasingly embraced football, it has also appropriated the modern fashion for commemorating the game through sculpture. This is an easier fit with Chinese cultural norms than many other aspects of global football culture, given China's long history of, and modern proclivity for, erecting figurative public art. In 1999 art historian John T. Young estimated that over 10,000 such artworks had been installed since the Cultural Revolution, the vast majority after 1980 (Young 1999, x). Traditional figurative portraiture, usually depicting political leaders, heroes, artists and poets has typically prevailed over abstract designs (Young 1999, 6).

Before the 1980s the state organized and funded large groups of sculptors, enabling the quick and easy collaborative creation of giant statues and statue groups (Young 1999, 22–24). Sculpture for political propaganda purposes dominated, with many heroic war memorials and statues of Mao unveiled. Although the government still exerts a veto over content and message, the variety of subjects depicted and images created has increased dramatically as China has opened up. As in the west, funding for China's public artworks now comes not only from government but from public donations and construction budgets, with commissioning and siting administered by local government arts committees (Young 1999, 39). As much as contemporary sculptures promote political ideas, they are also ostensibly erected to enhance civic identity, celebrate the hosting of regional or national events, and provide a visual point of reference in China's rapidly expanding utilitarian urban landscapes.

The national popularity and ubiquity of public sculpture, and the availability of funding and organizational infrastructure to support it, is one reason why China has accumulated football sculptures. Yet, given China's lack of engrained participatory football culture at the grassroots level and its underachievement at the international level, it is puzzling that the sport has been a subject choice for public art to the extent that China now boasts more football statues or statue groups (37) than all but the United Kingdom and Brazil (Figure 1). Furthermore, other nations with similar numbers (e.g. Argentina, Germany, the Netherlands, Spain) are established giants of the world game, previous FIFA World Cup winners or runners-up with historically well-supported club teams and domestic competitions.

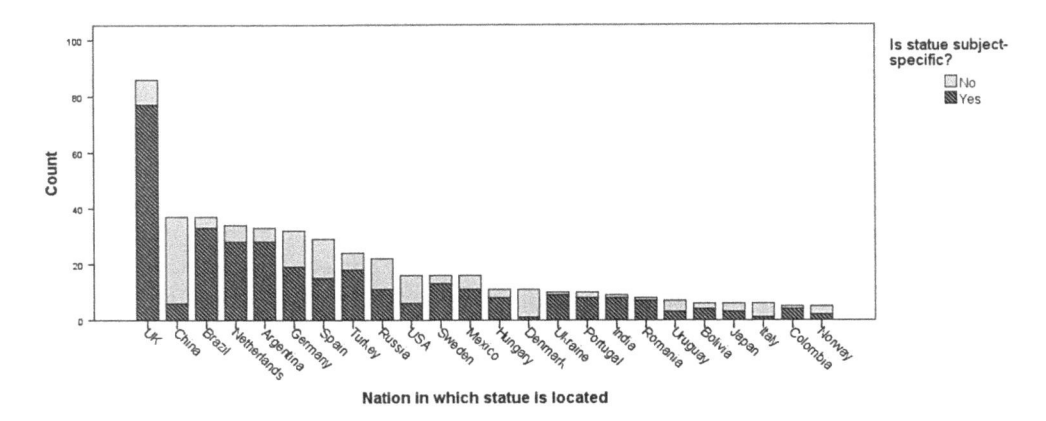

Figure 1. Numbers of footballer statues, *in situ* as of August 2017, by nation* and subject type.
Note: *Only nations with 6 or more statues or statue groups are displayed. 46 further nations have 5 or fewer statues.

Chinese football statues: anonymity and design

The most obvious explanation for the proliferation of Chinese football statues is hinted at by their relative recency (almost all have been installed since 2000), the anonymity of the subjects, and the accompanying abundance of anonymous statues depicting other sports. These statues are most likely part of wider government-promoted attempts to popularize sport, and the game of football in particular amongst Chinese citizens (Bo Qian 2017). This general promotion of sport through sculpture is likely to have been inspired by the run up to, and subsequently a desire to celebrate the success of the 2008 Beijing Olympic Games. Indeed, several of the football statues erected in this period are just one element of a multi-sport tableau.[8] With China's subsequent attempts to boost the state profile of football it has become a natural choice for single-sport athletic sculptures.

As Figure 1 indicates, China's football statuary has a disproportionate number of anonymous subjects. Globally, such non-subject-specific monuments comprise 33% of all football statues. This percentage rises to 84% in China. Furthermore, of China's six statues or statue groups that portray specific footballers, the three single-subject examples all honour the same player, Li Huitang (Lee Wai Tong) who starred for the national team in the 1930s. Though Li was an active player many decades before national television coverage of, or even the existence of a national league, he is probably the only world-class footballer produced by China and certainly the most revered (Guoqi 2009; Potts-Harmer 2015). Hence the anonymity of Chinese football statue 'subjects' other than Li may not just reflect state aims to popularize a sport as opposed to venerate an individual, but also suggest an absence of star players worth honouring by a single-subject statue, as is common in the west. This is partly due to the relatively brief history of China's professional clubs and the disrupted development of Chinese football as a whole. It may also express a wider national cultural norm of collectivism in which the individual is subservient to the team or even the game itself.

The use of anonymous figures instead of specific subjects also gives a statue an ambiguity of interpretation that enhances the relative importance of the design. Statues of anonymous players are depictions of the game, not of an individual. They are not only a promotion of football but also tell us how those who commissioned and funded the statue, which, in the vast majority of cases in China is national or local government authorities, themselves see, or want the public to see football. As such, the very distinctive design aesthetic of China's football statuary is as critical as its frequent subject anonymity. Across the global statuary, footballers are most often depicted in action (65%), followed by posed designs, e.g. standing with a ball under their arm (24%) and by celebratory portrayals (11%), often lifting a trophy. Though all but four of China's footballer statues and statue groups are action poses, of these, over half (56%) show players tackling or contesting the ball, a very rare composition elsewhere in the world (only 10% of action designs outside China portray tackling).

A typical Chinese statue of anonymous footballers tackling (Figure 2) was erected in Dalian in the early 2000s. The two monumental figures, cast at approximately two and half times life-size, dominate both their low, triangular plinth and the harbour-front plaza on which the statue is sited. One player strides forward purposefully with a ball at his feet: the other player is at full stretch, tackling from behind, with his leading leg finishing adjacent to both the ball and his opponent's shin, suggesting he has managed to toe-poke the ball away and will bring his rival down in the process. The sheer size of the figures radiates power, strength and aggression, enhanced by the physical interaction between the players, and especially by their muscular detail and contorted facial expressions. This is football portrayed as a battle.

Dalian was the home of China's most successful football club of the professional era. Dalian Wanda FC – later renamed as Dalian Shide due to a change in sponsor – triumphed in the inaugural 1994 season of the professional Chinese Jia-A league, and went on to win a further seven Jia-A and Super League titles. Dalian also has a deep involvement in Chinese football history: Wanda was a transmutation from Dalian Shipyards (1955–1982) and semi-professional Dalian FC (1982–1992), who played in the previous state-orchestrated national leagues. In 1988, Dalian FC had been the first Chinese team to announce themselves as a 'football club', that is, a private entity as opposed to a government-sanctioned and organized sports team (Simons 2008, 177). Hence, Dalian is a natural location

Figure 2. Anonymous Footballers, Lvshunkou, Dalian, China. Source: Photo by Eva Farrelly ©.

for a statue promoting football through public art, but there is no inscription to explain the statue's provenance, or celebrate Dalian's football history.

In fact, as with the anonymity of subjects, the portrayal of players tackling as opposed to individual figures demonstrating skills, is a national phenomenon. It may partly be attributed to nation-wide mimicking and contagion. However, China's geographical size and the number of different tackling designs, some of which feature more than two players competing for the ball, suggest that further explanation is required.[9].

One argument is that the absence of tackling statues elsewhere in the world is in part due to economic factors. Tackling designs might be considered desirable in that they enable a realistic match scene to be depicted, but they also require multiple figures, and hence cost more to sculpt and cast. They are affordable in China due to the surfeit of government-funded sculptors and access to relatively cheap raw materials. Moreover, subject-specific statues are more common outside China. The star players honoured are rarely lauded for their great tackling: fans typically want to be reminded of an iconic goal celebration, or skills such as shooting, dribbling or passing, so a single figure is all that is required.

Second, depicting tackling might be an attempt to promote football by association with sports and traditions that are already embedded in Chinese culture. Martial arts, such as Kung Fu, are an integral element of both traditional and twentieth century Chinese popular culture. The majority of Chinese football statues with a tackling scene composition show the challenging player making a straight-legged lunge, not entirely dissimilar to a kung fu kick. Linking football to martial arts by portraying football's combative dimension and similar movement elements is a potential way to engage viewers with little prior knowledge or interest, and boost football's recognition and acceptance as a sport for which China has natural affinity.

However, the most likely explanation for China's surfeit of tussles for the ball cast in bronze is the deliberate portrayal of football as a metaphor for, or reflection of political and cultural motifs. In an attempt to boost football's public appeal (and maintain their status as a state-favoured artist by adding a sympathetic political dimension to the image) Chinese artists have deliberately chosen to portray football as combat, a battle, a great struggle for victory, and its players as selfless warriors. It is unlikely to be coincidental that the other nation with multiple football statues portraying anonymous players contesting the ball is Russia – where we have identified five such monuments, most dating from the Soviet Union era of a one-party communist state.[10] These statues reflect the instrumental role of sport in pre- and post-Second World War Soviet society: after being frowned upon in the immediate post-revolution era, sports clubs and activities were soon encouraged, in an effort to enhance fitness for work and military strength (Zilberman 1982; Alexandrova 2014). This made participation in sport akin to a civic duty as much as a leisure activity. Thus, Soviet images of football often feature football's most combative, physical element, i.e. tackling in the process portraying strength and discipline in battle as core qualities of sport, and drawing a parallel between the struggle for communism against enemy forces.

We argue that modern Chinese sculptors, having been influenced by the same recurring themes of conflict and struggle in wider post-revolutionary Chinese politics, art and culture, have chosen to represent football in a similar way to their Soviet predecessors. Furthermore, the government still exerts influence over the subjects and themes of public art, albeit less so than its complete control prior to 1979 (Young 1999, 24). Therefore, it is unsurprising that much of China's public sculpture is in a propagandist vein promoting the longstanding and ongoing CCP narrative of the 'great struggle': through the 1949 revolution and subsequent hard work and courage, China has finally thrown off the yoke of foreign invaders, and ended the 'century of humiliation'. Such art often features noble characters, typically workers or military figures striving for their country, with clear political undertones about national service (Young 1999, 21, 24; Ma 2016). A recurring example is the depiction of a semi-mythical figure, Lei Feng, who was held up by the CCP as the ideal worker in Communist China, and is typically portrayed as a selfless citizen heroically exceeding his work quotas and generally going beyond the call of duty for the nation (Osnos 2013). For a footballer, tackling is a relatively selfless action, putting one's body on the line as a duty to the team, as opposed to displaying the individual skills that most often gain adulation from the crowd. This ambiguous yet heroic depiction of footballers and football is consistent with telling a story of collective struggle and eventual triumph, but also one in which self-sacrifice and the primacy of team victory supersede personal pleasure. This is football as work, not leisure.

China's football statues differ from those elsewhere in their designs but not in their absence of female subjects, whether considering specific players or anonymous figures.[11] Considering the chasm of achievement between its men's and women's teams, it might have been expected that China would celebrate its female football heritage, unlike other nations. Their absence may partly be a question of timing: the majority of China's football statues have appeared over the past two decades, during which the Iron Roses have fallen back in the world standings. Ironically it is China's push for success in the men's game that has negatively impacted its women's team. State encouragement for the men's national team and club game has prompted huge investment from commercial sources, whereas the women's game remains reliant on state support. This same state support gave it a relative advantage in the 1980s and 1990s, but while women's football has advanced elsewhere in the world due to both government funding and business sponsorship, in China this funding is now flowing entirely into the men's game (Hong and Mangen 2006).

Chinese football statues: triumph, failure and political expediency

These resources have, as yet, yielded just one FIFA World Cup finals appearance for China's men's team. Their decisive qualifying group victory, which confirmed their qualification for the 2002 finals, came against Oman in October 2001, in a match played at the Wulihe Stadium in Shenyang. Following this victory the Shenyang Green Island Hotel and Resort, which hosted the squad training camps during the qualifying campaign, commissioned a 44-strong statue group. The statues depicted the players in training, alongside the manager, coaches and officials that made up the national team entourage. This statue group (Figure 3 below), designed by Lin Xu and Zhang Feng but sculpted by 40 artists given the short time frame for production, was unveiled in May 2002 at the grounds of the Green Island Resort, prior to the team departing to the finals ('Chinese football players unveiled their bronze statues' 2002; 'Green Island Sculpture Group' 2011). Team statues are an admittedly rare subgenre, but this statue group is the largest such football monument in the world, featuring twice as many figures as its nearest challenger.[12]

Not content with this display of largesse, China's collective excitement at qualification resulted in the creation of a further monument. An immense 30 tonne statue, standing over 15 metres tall (Figure 4 below), comprised a giant steel 'victory V' placed on a bronze football, itself on a large black plinth inscribed with the results from the qualifying campaign. The V featured a fibreglass relief of 11 players (designed to be portrayals of typical

Figure 3. Part of the China World Cup 2002 Squad statue group, Shenyang, China. Source: Photo by Ji Jiao ©.

Figure 4. China World Cup 2002 Giant-V statue, Shenyang, China. Source: Photo by Ji Jiao ©.

footballers as opposed to specific players) and the manager Bora Milutinović. The V was the brainchild of Shenyang football fans association leader Sun Changlong, funded by the Shenyang Municipal Government and Sun himself, and sculpted by Guo Zhaoyang. It was first unveiled outside Wulihe Stadium in May 2002 ('Wulihe V-type Monument' 2002 [2013]; Chen 2007; Yao 2012).

China's first World Cup finals appearance, however, was a substantial blow to national pride. China lost all three games without scoring a single goal. The loss of face was exacerbated by regional rivals and joint tournament hosts Japan and South Korea winning through to the last-16 and the semi-final respectively, and naturally provoked a negative reaction in China. The reputations of several 2002 World Cup squad players and officials suffered further when they were implicated in football corruption investigations (2009–2012). These included Nan Yong, an administrator who had progressed to become director of the Chinese Football Association, who was jailed for ten-and-a-half years. Goalkeeper Jiang Jin and midfielder Qi Hong were each given five-and-a-half year sentences ('China football ex-chiefs' 2012; 'Former soccer head' 2012).

As the team fell from national grace, their statues were largely forgotten and neglected. When Wulihe Stadium was slated for demolition in 2007, there was little consideration given to the giant V (Chen 2007). Sun Changlong negotiated its rapid dismantling and removal to storage in a local factory warehouse just days before the stadium was razed to the ground, to be later replaced by a shopping mall. Rumours abounded that the sculpture had been destroyed in the demolition and even that Sun had perished in trying to save his beloved sculpture and the stadium ('Wulihe V-type Monument' 2002 [2013]; Yao 2012).

The team group statues remained at Green Island, but the Chinese national team no longer used the facility. Later Shenyang University purchased the site. The statues were retained by the university, albeit with their context removed, and without any promotion of their existence. They were partially rehabilitated in 2011 as part of a 10th anniversary commemoration of World Cup qualification, primarily organized by Chinese Super League clubs and the media. The figures were cleaned up, and were visited by Bora Milutinović and members of the 2001–2002 squad. Despite Milutinović's pleas for its restoration as a representation of a glorious success, the giant V remained in storage ('Green Island Sculpture Group' 2011; 'National football to commemorate' 2011; 'The fate of athlete sculpture' 2012).

However, in June 2012, the Liaoning region was awarded the right to host the following year's Chinese National Games, with Shenyang to stage many of the events. With the Shenyang Municipal Authority eager to celebrate their role in China's sporting history, the giant V was restored, pieced back together and erected at the front of the park facing Shenyang City Library ('Ten strong commemorative sculpture' 2012; Yao 2012; 'Wulihe V-type Monument' 2002 [2013]). The team group statues were moved from the university and installed in front of the giant V, with the original designers brought in to rearrange the training camp scene into one where the manager was more prominent. Surprisingly only 32 of the 44 statues were re-erected: the players, the manager, and the coaches. Statues of the team officials, many of whom were involved in the match-fixing scandal, were not installed ('Top 10 V-shaped sculpture back' 2012; Yao 2012). A further set of anonymous figures were placed on the hillside behind the V and a plaque was installed adjacent to the training scene, giving a brief, prosaic outline of the statue group's history in both Mandarin Chinese and English, unsurprisingly sidestepping the team's performance in the finals tournament.

The story of the 2002 World Cup statue group and the giant V reflects the changing place of football within Chinese culture over the past 15 years. Whilst the sculpting of a team group rather than a single player supports collectivism, the effort of erecting a statue of any sort just for qualification alone marks this as a key point in Chinese football history *and* betrays the lack of previous success. Likewise, while the very size and scale of these monuments matches Chinese tastes in public art, and indicates the availability and affordability of the materials, it also suggests a certain naivety about the global game. This is manifest both in the grandiose celebration of an achievement that football superpowers would consider a minimum expectation, and in raising expectations that the Chinese players would be able to continue their all-conquering form at the finals tournament.

The statues' subsequent abandonment is a metaphor for Chinese football's lost decade, as the raised expectations of 2002 turned into an overwhelming disappointment. Compared to China's booming economy and successful hosting of the 2008 Olympic Games, football's failures were a national embarrassment and best kept hidden to avoid loss of face. From the failure to qualify for the 2006 and 2010 World Cup finals to widespread corruption within domestic football, the sport was unable to display the successful image required by an emerging global superpower. Even on the 10th anniversary of qualification, it was primarily the media and the ex-manager cheerleading past achievements, while football and state authorities remained silent.

Likewise the statue group's (and the giant V's) rehabilitation in 2012, albeit by city rather than national authorities, coincided with the state-sanctioned push to improve Chinese football. While the aim of this process is future success, it is harder to hide Chinese football's past considering the game's increasing profile and establishment in the national psyche. Despite China's attempts to bury its football failures, this push for success inadvertently emphasizes it; if it was already as successful as it wished to be, such state-sponsored largesse would not be so necessary.

The re-emergence of these statues, which can be read as totems of at least relative success (as China's first and only World Cup qualification) as well as failure (the humbling at the final's themselves), might be seen as China tiptoeing towards reconciling the need for saving face with the twin realities of its low standing in world football, and the capricious balance between footballing triumph and disaster. For some fans, the confidence of future progress may allow the 2002 qualification to be celebrated as a national high point – and for Shenyang a source of local pride just five years after the stadium where qualification was achieved was swept away without a backwards glance. These statues might, therefore, illustrate the balance between local and national face saving: at present, while the 2002 World Cup is a memory China wishes to forget, it is a source of pride in Shenyang.

A further interpretation considers how the positive media coverage around the 10th anniversary of qualification event may have led to the resurrection of the monuments. Through demonstrating to the local authorities how, after a decade had passed, the joy of qualification overshadowed failure (at the World Cup itself), Shenyang might begin to embrace a collective nostalgia for the 2002 squad. However, nostalgia, a longing for a better past, is partly stimulated by present failure – making it a moot point whether any positive feeling towards these figures from 2002, at least nationally, would survive a contemporary Chinese football success.

The removal of certain figures from this statue group after its relocation is an indication of how China has begun to absorb some elements of global football culture – specifically the erosion of collectivism in favour of populist hierarchies. The original casting and erection of team officials and backroom staff alongside players suggested equality and teamwork, as well as a state that cherishes administrators as party comrades. The decision to remove non-players who were guilty of corruption but retain similarly indicted footballers further exalts the relative status of players. This reflects acquiescence to the hegemonic dynamics of global football culture, where individual players and the occasional team manager are deified far above other roles within domestic or national football.

However, the design and arrangement of the statue group to depict a training scene, a unique composition across the world's football statues, illustrates China's distinctive belief that progression in sport can be achieved *purely* through organized, formal practice, coaching, and national strengths of dedicated learning and hard work, as opposed to frequent casual, informal play and instinctive skills. The contrast with the only other national team group statue not sculpted in a team photo style (the Netherlands, at the Netherlands Football Association headquarters, Zeist) provides a stark illustration of how China's football culture differs from that which pervades much of the rest of the world. The Netherlands players are sculpted performing the individual attributes for which they are famed, such as a dramatic save, an overhead kick, or in the case of Johann Cruyff, directing the pattern of play with an imperious arm gesture.[13] Coaches and commentators have suggested that the absence of players with imaginative flair and an instinctive appreciation of tactics is a major reason for China's failure to progress to the higher echelons of world football, and is partly attributable to the lack of any 'street football' culture within the nation's youth (Sevastopulo 2014; Stayton 2016).

Chinese football statues: training minds and bodies for future glory

As well as its impact on design, China's focus on training explains why the location of its football statues differs from the wider world's football statuary. The comparative absence of statues from club stadia in China (just 8% of footballer statues) compared to the rest of the world (44%) is perhaps unsurprising given the combination of the typical drivers of stadia-sited sports statues, namely nostalgia- and authenticity-based exploitation of heritage. Chinese professional clubs lack a lengthy heritage of great players and triumphant moments to recreate in bronze. The municipal ownership of many stadia also limits clubs in stamping their mark upon the concourses and surroundings. China compensates for this shortfall with a disproportionate presence of football statues at both sports schools and state and private training facilities (17%, compared to just 3% across the rest of the world).

Examples of such statues can be found at the Evergrande Football School in Qingyuan, 75 miles north of the city of Guangzhou, whose Chinese Super League team is also sponsored by the Evergrande Real Estate Group. Run in partnership with Real Madrid, who supply the coaching staff, the school is probably the world's largest such venture. The campus contains 50 pitches, and at present hosts approximately 2500 mostly-fee-paying pupils, providing them with both an academic and footballing education (Sudworth 2014; Stallard 2016; 'President Xi's great Chinese soccer dream' 2017).

On the school's opening in 2012, several statues were installed in the palatial grounds. Their presence amongst fountains and manicured lawns only adds to the hyper-reality of a complex designed to resemble an English public school or country house (Simons 2017). Three of these statues depict anonymous players, including the ubiquitous tackling design, though with players seemingly of European rather than Chinese descent. However, two further statues are of particular interest. Both were produced by Saishang Design Group of Hubei, who specialize in film-sets and model-making as well as sculpture ('Humanities Sculpture Series' 2012). One portrays two legends of the global game with strong links to the World Cup (Figure 5): England captain Bobby Moore lifted the trophy in 1966; Brazil's

Pelé, widely regarded as one of the greatest players of all time, won the World Cup in 1958 and 1970, and was part of the winning 1962 squad (but didn't appear in the final). Pelé is depicted hoisting the trophy aloft. Moore is posed, with foot on ball. Both figures are attempted copies of existing statues: specifically the Bobby Moore monument, sculpted by Philip Jackson and sited at Wembley Stadium, and the Pelé statue by Lucy Viana, in Pelé's home town of Três Corações.[14] A fourth Evergrande Football School statue, also produced by Saishang, was prominently sited outside the school gates, and depicted the FIFA World Cup trophy, surmounted by figures of three anonymous players (Figure 6). This statue was removed in 2016, apparently on FIFA's request, probably due to copyright issues (Sabrié 2016).

The number of statues at training facilities and sports schools can be explained prosaically by the popularity of public art in China, but also by the nation's continued adherence to elitist sports development. This approach is modelled on that of the former Soviet Union and its communist satellite states (and latterly China itself) in achieving Olympic glory. While soccer schools and academies exist in many countries, they typically represent the top of a pyramid of youthful footballing endeavour. In China, with minimal informal or formal junior club football, and a wider push for football to be included in regular school curriculums only just beginning, ventures such as the Evergrande School are currently the principal tool in producing young footballers.

The designs of the Evergrande statues reveal the primary motive behind the school's existence. As privately funded art on private land, the Evergrande statues must be considered in a different light from public installations, such as those in Dalian and Shenyang. Superficially, these statues might be viewed as an attempt to inspire the children attending the school. However, perhaps more than this, they will reflect the image that Evergrande wants to project of their school (and by extension themselves as a business). Erecting a huge sculpted World Cup trophy and a statue of winning captains is an overt message that the school will produce winners, and indeed that Evergrande is a winner. This is despite the school having no track record of producing world class footballers to date. President Xi's

Figure 5. Pele and Bobby Moore statue, Evergrande Football School, Qingyuan, China. Source: Photo by Gilles Sabrié ©.

Figure 6. FIFA World Cup Trophy statue, Evergrande Football School, Qingyuan, China. Source: Photo by Gilles Sabrié ©.

stated aim to both host and win the World Cup has galvanized Chinese businesses to very publically and visibly invest in football, garnering government favour and smoothing their interactions with China's internal bureaucracy. By featuring the FIFA World Cup trophy in two statues, Evergrande is also explicitly supporting the president's aims.

These statues also betray the elite-focused approach that has historically blighted China's football development. National ambition to reach the ultimate prize has overshadowed and dwarfed the enjoyment of playing the game, and is presented as the reason both for the school's existence, and to play football at all. Yet not everyone can win, and if winning is the primary reason to participate, inevitably defeat will demoralize and discourage young footballers. Building football schools as big as Evergrande is an extremely expensive way of barely scratching the surface of China's potential junior football participation; the expansion of informal, public facilities and coaching systems aimed at access and involvement for the many, would be more likely to breed potential star players (Simons 2017).

Finally, while the presence of Moore and Pelé statues speaks of Evergrande's ambition, it also echoes a lack of self-confidence derived from the absence of a Chinese footballer within living memory to portray as an inspiration to the school's pupils; and reflects China's impatience to solve this problem. This impatience is manifest in the reflexive yet superficial copying of contemporary success from abroad, an instinct prevalent at Evergrande, across Chinese football and society more generally. Just as the Chinese FA has variously, over the years, employed Brazilian, Hungarian and German coaches to train their young players, Evergrande School employs a coaching team from Real Madrid, currently the world's most successful club football team. The school is built to resemble a palace from another conti-nent. So it is befitting that, rather than offering a home-grown inspiration or perspective, its statues are copies of other statues, featuring other countries' players. Chinese industry has long been renowned for its ability to replicate and reverse-engineer products developed in the west, and produce them more cheaply. This process has fuelled China's rapid eco-nomic gains but has hampered its ability to develop the next version, or at least diminished any motivation to do so (Stevenson-Yang and DeWoskin 2005; Guy 2016). Applying this approach to football, however, will be unlikely to result in China developing their own natural style of play that will match national attributes. The successful football nations have each evolved traditions regarding styles and tactics that have been influenced by cultural characteristics and playing conditions. It could be argued that, for China to achieve sustained football success, it needs its own unique football culture, not a facsimile from abroad.

Chinese football statues: kickabout diplomacy and saving face

In August 2016, city officals from Rio and Beijing unveiled a statue on the fringes of the Olympic Park in Rio de Janiero ('Chinese Sculpture' 2016). Sculpted by Huang Jian, entitled CMB Football Friendship, and presented as a gift from Beijing to their twin city of Rio, the statue (Figure 7) depicts Han dynasty emperor Wudi (漢武帝), dressed in full imperial robes, kicking a ball. The ball (Figure 8) is notably different from a modern football, its rough nature rather closer to the imperfect, sewn seams that were used to construct the hull of a *cuju* ball. Alongside Han Wudi is Pelé, who is aiming a kick at the ball but, to his evident amusement given his wide sculpted grin, has been beaten to a touch by the emperor. The statue departs slightly from the traditional, realist figurative portrayal adhered to by almost all sculptors of football statues. Instead it includes a motion blur effect, popularized by American sports sculpture firm Studio Amrany in their depictions of basketball and baseball stars, to enhance the sense of movement and action.[15] The Chinese press reported the unveiling as

> expressing the Chinese people's good wishes for the Olympic Games in Rio, commemorating the 30th anniversary of the twinning of the cities of Beijing and Rio, carrying forward the spirit of the Olympic Games, the inheritance of sports, enhancing Sino-Brazilian friendship and promoting world peace. ('Chinese Sculpture' 2016)

The two figures, which are sculpted at approximately one-and-a-half times life-size, are set on a low metal plinth that has been allowed to accumulate a rust finish. A wide plaque is affixed to the front of the plinth. The plaque inscription reads as follows:

Figure 7. China–Brazil Friendship Soccer Match statue, Rio De Janeiro, Brazil. Source: Photo by Leonardo Marques ©.

China-Brazil Friendship Soccer Match. By Huang Jian from China. 2016. The sculpture 'China-Brazil Friendship Soccer Match' is presented by Beijing Municipal Government to the city of Rio de Janeiro as an official gift to extend the sincerest blessings to the Rio Olympic Games and to commemorate the 30th anniversary of the sister city relationship between Beijing and Rio. The Sculpture, created by Ms. Huang Jian, a world renowned sculptress depicts two prominent figures from the two countries – China's 'Soccer Emperor' and 'Pioneer of the Silk Road' Emperor Hanwu and Brazil's 'King of Football' Pelé, who have travelled over 2.000 years through time and space to the Olympic Park in Rio and played a friendship soccer match. Hopefully this sculpture will help promote the long-lasting friendship between the two countries.

As the inscription and press reports suggest, this statue is as much a monument to the diplomatic value of sporting relations as it is to the combatants depicted. Post-revolution China has a long history of sporting diplomacy, though its early football-centred forays were more about strengthening ties with political bed-fellows in Eastern Europe than extending its global reach. In the early 1960s, despite having withdrawn from FIFA and hence, competitive international matches, the Chinese national team played hundreds of friendlies with the communist states of Eastern Europe and Soviet-sponsored or sympathetic regimes in Asia and Africa (Simons 2008, 212). However, as Chairman Mao's Cultural Revolution began to fade and China looked to reintegrate with the rest of the world, sport became an important conduit for re-establishing diplomatic ties and trade relationships with the previously demonized capitalist and democratic west. The most famous example in Mao's era was early 1970s 'ping-pong diplomacy' through table-tennis encounters between China and the USA (Griffin 2015), but similar relationship building was conducted through football. In 1977, the first western club invited to China was the star-studded New York Cosmos team featuring Pelé and Franz Beckenbauer. The Cosmos' two encounters with the Chinese national team ended with, as Simons (2008, 216) notes, a pair of 'perfectly diplomatic' results: a 1–1 draw followed by a 2–1 win for the hosts. Further match-ups with English club sides and a series of relationship-building tours in the USA and the UK occurred at the turn of the decade.

Figure 8. Detail from China–Brazil friendship soccer match statue, Rio De Janeiro, Brazil. Source: Photo by Leonardo Marques ©.

As China's economic stock rose inexorably, the balance of power in these diplomatic relations changed. Seeking contacts, influence and a 'foot in the door' is no longer such an imperative for China. As an established global superpower it has become more the master of its own economic destiny than the servant of western whims, and can make trade deals on its own terms. Instead China focuses on the importance of soft power, the public relations and sense of acceptance and recognition as a world leader that is important to its image of itself and in the wider world. In this sense football still presents opportunities, but is also an end in itself. The ultimate glory surely lies in hosting, and winning, a World Cup. It is no longer just the taking part in order to build relationships that matters, but the winning (or at least being spared the humiliation of frequent defeat). The current failure of the national team undermines China's status, making football an awkward, potentially shameful diplomatic pitch to play on.

The 'CMB Football Friendship' statue further highlights China's rewriting and subjugation of its traditional sporting heritage to position itself as a relevant nation in world football, suggesting it is only worthy of consideration as a forerunner to football rather than on its own merits. First, the statue inscription does not distinguish between cuju and modern football. It describes Han Wu, a keen player/sponsor of the game whose dynasty founded cuju, as the 'soccer emperor' without any mention of cuju. Likewise the Chinese media describes this statue as celebrating the 'inheritance' of football, by Brazil, from China.

Second, matching Pelé with an ancient figure who is largely unknown outside China, and with very little supporting context provided by the inscription, again highlights the lack of truly great Chinese footballers to stand alongside Pelé. The inclusion of references to 'the Silk Road' is a compensatory reference to China's historic business and trading prowess, rather than football capability. Ultimately, in creating a football themed statue, China, despite its economic might, chooses to meet Brazil at a cultural reference that is very much Brazil's, not China's. This indicates a lack of self-confidence in Chinese football, or at least in how it is perceived in the west – and a certain creativity in presenting a gift that promotes Chinese football and culture by depicting the impossible, China winning a footballing tussle with Brazil.

Conclusion

As Savage (1994) notes, monuments such as statues speak as much to the values, attitudes and beliefs of those who produce them, as they do of the subjects depicted. Societies rarely erect images of unknown or unpopular figures or practices. The existence of so many football statues within China, almost all dated post-2000, is in part due to a continuing fashion for figurative public art, but also a desire of local government arts committees to dovetail with the increased national promotion and public interest in football over this period.

China's use of football statues, and the statues themselves are as distinctive as China's undeveloped yet hyper-accelerated football culture. Much in the styling and placement suggests a strategic use of sculpture to promote Chinese football, but, rather like China's attempts at improving the nation's football performance, these statues also betray a number of inherent contradictions and tensions. Ultimately China's football statues seek to inspire progress, whether through portraying perceived national attributes of hard work and commitment to training, the strength and power needed to achieve an anticipated future triumph, or the trophy that the nation craves. However, the statues' subject anonymity or use of foreign stars, associated propaganda regarding China's past football influence, and the statues' own tangled back stories reveal a lack of tangible success or confidence, and the inherent problems in reconciling this lack of success with China's desire for preserving face. China's football statues and its football culture embody the tension between the need to avoid perceived sporting humiliation in the present with the longer-term reforms needed to build a sustainable football base; and between saving face locally whilst losing it nationally, as seen in Shenyang.

The consequences of a face-first approach are also borne out by the statue designs, which foreground hard work in the pursuit of victory to the complete exclusion of playing football for fun: whether in the determined expressions of the anonymous players, the victory V of the Shenyang World Cup sculpture, the images of the FIFA World Cup itself at Evergrande School, or the depiction of the 2002 World Cup squad in training. In one respect, this makes China's football statues more honest than those found elsewhere in the world. Fans may take pleasure from the moments of skill and improvisation, but ultimately they would prefer to see their team 'win ugly' than lose flamboyantly.

However, China's rigid focus on victory both stifles grassroots development and is an awkward perspective to maintain in a nation where football success has yet to be achieved. Collectively, these statues reflect the juxtaposition of this underachievement with the urgent need to be seen to succeed in world football, or at least be relevant in it. Whereas the global football statuary is typically one of self-confidence, with careful reading China's ultimately displays a lack of confidence. Statues are associated with permanence, but whether the football statues that have taken root in China over the past two decades mark a permanent change in China's relationship with football remains to be seen.

Notes

1. For the purposes of this paper, statues are defined as three-dimensional full-body figurative monuments, with the figures being both at least half-life-size and permanent installations (as opposed to waxworks and museum models). Statue groups feature multiple such figures arranged in close proximity, almost always constructed and unveiled together, presented as a single exhibit, e.g. with a single plaque or inscription, and with the figures typically but not always interacting.
2. Between January 2013 and March 2014, the first author and a colleague constructed a database of existing statues of football players, managers, and chairmen as part of a wider project into commemoration in sport, which they have continued to maintain and update. Data and images were obtained through a literature, archival and online search, and via interviews with sculptors and project organizers. Variables collected included the precise location, date of unveiling, design type (broadly classified as 'action', 'posed' or 'triumph'), the full plaque or plinth inscription, and the identity of the statue project promoters and funders, as well as further demographic and performance information on the subjects depicted. Since April 2014 the primary elements of the database (the statue location, sculptor, unveiling date, inscription and photos of the statue showing the design) have been publically available through the project website at http://www.sportingstatues.com (Stride, Thomas, and Wilson 2012).
3. For some examples, see the project website http://www.sportingstatues.com, which gives details of many less popular UK sports that have had statues erected in their participants' honour, including lawn bowls, water polo and wheelchair basketball.
4. For a full listing see the sporting statues world football database (Stride, Thomas, and Wilson 2012).

5. The South Korea-Japan jointly-hosted 2002 FIFA World Cup, which saw the hosts progress to the semi-finals and the last 16 respectively. Both nations have qualified for all subsequent World Cups, and both progressed beyond the group stages again in 2010. Japan have won the Asian Cup tournament four times since 1992; South Korea have failed to reach the semi-finals only once in the last 5 tournaments.

6. In December 2016, Chinese clubs Shanghai SIPG and Shanghai Shenhua were reported to be paying the two highest salaries in world football ('The highest paid footballers' 2016). In January 2017 Shanghai SIPG signed Oscar from Chelsea FC for 60 million pounds, the latest in a series of multi-million pound investments (Bloomfield 2017; Price 2017).

7. Between 2015 and 2017, West Bromwich Albion, Birmingham City, Aston Villa and Wolverhampton Wanderers, four Midlands-based football clubs in the English Premier League and Championship (the top two tiers of English professional football) were purchased by Chinese owners or consortia. In addition, Chinese investors have purchased stakes in European heavyweights such as Manchester City FC, and both Milan clubs (AC and Internazionale).

8. Examples of Chinese football statues that are just one element in an arrangement of different sports sculptures can be found in Olympic Avenue Park, Hebei (see the sporting statues database, http://www.offbeat.group.shef.ac.uk/statues/STFB_Anonymous_20.htm); and Xinghai Square, Dalian (http://www.offbeat.group.shef.ac.uk/statues/STFB_Anonymous_204.htm).

9. Examples of Chinese-sited statues of anonymous footballers tackling, with a variety of different designs include those in Hebei (see the sporting statues database, http://www.offbeat.group.shef.ac.uk/statues/STFB_Anonymous_23.htm); Tianjin (http://www.offbeat.group.shef.ac.uk/statues/STFB_Anonymous_13.htm); Tongzou Olympic Park in Beijing (http://www.offbeat.group.shef.ac.uk/statues/STFB_Anonymous_26.htm); and Dalian North Station Square (http://www.offbeat.group.shef.ac.uk/statues/STFB_Anonymous_23.htm).

10. Examples of Russian-sited statues of anonymous footballers tackling can be found in Krasnodar Krai (see the sporting statues database http://www.offbeat.group.shef.ac.uk/statues/STFB_Anonymous_189.htm); Zarechny (http://www.offbeat.group.shef.ac.uk/statues/STFB_Anonymous_169.htm); the Tretykov Gallery, Moscow (http://www.offbeat.group.shef.ac.uk/statues/STFB_Anonymous_91.htm and O'Mahony 2017); and most notably the St Petersburg Blockade Match Monument (http://www.offbeat.group.shef.ac.uk/statues/STFB_Anonymous_94.htm).

11. The Chinese National Football Museum features statues of members of the Chinese Women's national team, but given their location and material these would be more correctly described as museum models that are semi-permanent exhibits, as opposed to permanent public statues.

12. Further full team statues celebrate the 1964 BSG Chemie Leipzig team (at BSG Chemie Leipzig in Leipzig, Germany: see the sporting statues database. http://www.offbeat.group.shef.ac.uk/statues/STFB_BSGLeipzig_1.htm); the 2002 Turkey World Cup team (in Istanbul: see the sporting statues database http://www.offbeat.group.shef.ac.uk/statues/STFB_TurkeyWC2002.htm), the 2002 South Korea World Cup team (at Gyeonggi: see the sporting statues database http://www.offbeat.group.shef.ac.uk/statues/STFB_SouthKorea_WC2002.htm), and the Ararat Yerevan team (at Hrazdan Stadium, Yerevan: see the sporting statues database http://www.offbeat.group.shef.ac.uk/statues/STFB_AraratYerevan.htm).

13. See http://www.offbeat.group.shef.ac.uk/statues/STFB_Cruyff_Johan_1.htm; http://www.offbeat.group.shef.ac.uk/statues/STFB_VanBasten_Marco.htm; http://www.offbeat.group.shef.ac.uk/statues/STFB_VanDerSar_Edwin.htm.

14. To view the original Moore statue at Wembley Stadium, UK, see the sporting statues database; http://www.offbeat.group.shef.ac.uk/statues/STFB_Moore_Bobby_1.htm. To view the Pelé statue in Três Corações, Brazil, see sporting statues database; http://www.offbeat.group.shef.ac.uk/statues/STFB_Pele_2.htm. A second cast of the Pelé statue was unveiled in 1971 in Salvador, Brazil; http://www.offbeat.group.shef.ac.uk/statues/STFB_Pele_1.htm.

15. Notable examples of this stylistic subgenre of sports statues include that of basketball legend Michael Jordan, sited in Chicago, and most notably those of three Washington baseball

heroes, Walter Johnson, Josh Gibson and Frank Howard, at Nationals Park, Washington DC (see, for example, the sporting statues database http://www.offbeat.group.shef.ac.uk/statues/STUS_Howard_Frank.htm).

Acknowledgements

The authors would like to thank Rowan Simons, William Bi, Cameron Wilson, Christopher Lamb, Nick Catley and Mike O'Mahony for some invaluable discussions and correspondence around Chinese art, football and culture, and/or taking time to read and comment on drafts of this manuscript. We also hugely appreciate the time and effort spent by Mike Farrelly, Ana Chamorro, and all credited photographers in acquiring the images featured – and by Ffion Thomas in helping the first author compile and map China's football statues.

Disclosure statement

No potential conflict of interest was reported by the authors.

ORCID

Christopher B. Stride 🆔 http://orcid.org/0000-0001-9960-2869

References

Alexandrova, Lyudmila. 2014. "USSR's Ready for Labor and Defense Fitness Promotion System Reincarnates." *TASS*, March 25. http://tass.com/opinions/763220http://tass.com/opinions/763220.

Bale, John. 1994. *Landscapes of Modern Sport*. Leicester: Leicester University Press.

Barr, Adam. 2009. "History of Football: Cuju." *Bleacher Report*, August 1. http://bleacherreport.com/articles/228587-history-of-football-cuju.

Beam, Christopher. 2012. "One Billion Fans, One Terrible Team: Why Is China's National Soccer Team So Bad?" *New Republic*, July 3. https://newrepublic.com/article/104640/christopher-beam-one-billion-fans-one-terrible-team-why-chinas-national-soccer-team.

Bloomfield, Claire. 2017. "Oscar Arrives in China after Making £60 m Shanghai Move." *Sky Sports*, January 2. http://www.skysports.com/football/news/12691/10715045/oscar-arrives-in-china-after-making-60 m-shanghai-move.

Bond, Michael H. 1991. *Beyond the Chinese Face*. Hong Kong: Oxford University Press.

Bo Qian. 2017. "Football Sculpture." March 16. http://www.bqdiaosu.com/cases/172.html.

Chen, Peijin. 2007. "Au Revoir to Wulihe Stadium." *Shanghaiist*, February 15. http://shanghaiist.com/2007/02/15/au_revoir_to_wu.php.

"China aims to Become Football Superpower 'by 2050'." 2016. *bbc.co.uk*, April 11. http://www.bbc.co.uk/news/world-asia-china-36015657.

"China Football Ex-chiefs Nan Yong and Xie Yalong Jailed." 2012. *bbc.co.uk*, June 13. http://www.bbc.co.uk/news/world-asia-china-18419829.

"China Sets Goal of Hosting World Cup with Master Plan for Football." 2015. *The Guardian*, March 17. https://www.theguardian.com/world/2015/mar/17/china-sets-goal-of-hosting-world-cup-with-master-plan-for-football.

"Chinese Football Players Unveiled their Bronze Statues." 2002. *Chinanews.com*, May 15.http://www.chinanews.com/2002-05-15/26/185748.html.

"Chinese Sculpture for Rio Olympic Games – Chinese Artist Huang Jian works 'CMB Football Friendship' Rio Inauguration Ceremony." 2016. *Sina*, August 10. http://zj.sina.com.cn/finance/xfgz/2016-08-10/detail_f-ifxutfpc4976289.shtml.

"Chinese Super League: 10 Clubs Say Debts are Cleared after Threat of Ban." 2017. *bbc.co.uk*, July 26. http://www.bbc.co.uk/sport/football/40719730.

Connor, Neil. 2015. "China Opens a Shrine to Mark its Love Affair with Disgraced Former Fifa President Sepp Blatter." *The Telegraph*, December 23. http://www.telegraph.co.uk/sport/football/sepp-blatter/12065899/China-opens-a-shrine-to-mark-its-love-affair-with-disgraced-former-Fifa-president-Sepp-Blatter.html.

Cui, Lequan. 2016. "Research on Competitive Styles of Chinese Ancient Cuju." *First World Football Culture Summit*, October 23. Lecture in Shandong, China.

Faure, Guy O., and Tony Fang. 2008. "Changing Chinese Values: Keeping up with Paradoxes." *International Business Review* 17: 194–207.

"FIFA World Ranking." 2017. *fifa.com*, August 17. http://www.fifa.com/fifa-world-ranking/ranking-table/men/index.html.

"Former Soccer Head Nan Yong Gets 10-1/2 years Sentence." 2012. *Sina*, June 13. http://english.sina.com/sports/2012/0612/476107.html.

Goldblatt, David. 2007. *The Ball is Round: A Global History of Football*. London: Penguin Books.

"Green Island Sculpture Group Only Nan Yong Sitting. Wulihe has Become a Super Real Estate." 2011. *Sohu.com*, September 30. http://sports.sohu.com/20110930/n321068451.shtml.

Griffin, Nicholas. 2015. *Ping-Pong Diplomacy: The Secret History Behind the Game That Changed the World*. New York, NY: Scribner.

Guoqi, Xu. 2008. *Olympic Dreams: China and Sports 1985–2008*. Cambridge, MA: Harvard University Press.

Guoqi, Xu. 2009. "Chinese Puzzle." *Soccer Journal* (official publication of the National Soccer Coaches Association of America) 54 (1): 28–33.

Guoqi, Xu. 2015. *Interview with Second Author*, Peking, December 12.

Guttmann, Allen. 2011. *Sports and American Art from Benjamin West to Andy Warhol*. Amherst: University of Massachusetts Press.

Guy, Peter. 2016. "Mind the Gap." *South China Morning Post*, April 10. http://www.scmp.com/business/article/1934779/china-never-really-stopped-being-copycat-and-thats-why-its-tech-companies.

Hong, Fan, and J. A. Mangan. 2006. "Will the 'Iron Roses' Bloom Forever? Women's Football in China: Changes and Challenges." *Soccer & Society*4 (2–3): 47–66. http://www.tandfonline.com/doi/abs/10.1080/14660970512331390825.

"Humanities Sculpture Series." 2012. *HBS Art*. http://www.hbssart.com/works/rwdsxl/183.html.

Jones, Robin. 1999. "The Emergence of Professional Sport – The Case of Soccer." In *Sport and Physical Education in China*, edited by James Riordan and Robin Jones, 185–201. London: E & F. N. Spon.

Jones, Robin. 2004. "Football in the People Republic of China." In *Football Goes East: Business, Culture and the People's Game in East Asia*, edited by John Horne and Wolfram Manzenreiter, 54–66. New York: Routledge.

Kaufman, Alison A. 2010. "The 'Century of Humiliation,' Then and Now: Chinese Perceptions of the International Order." *Pacific Focus* 25: 1–33. doi:10.1111/pafo.2010.25.issue-1

Li, Ji, and Lianqin Wang. 2010. "The Organization of Chinese Shame Concept." *Cognition and Emotion* 18: 767–797. http://www.tandfonline.com/doi/abs/10.1080/02699930341000202.

Lin, Y. T. 1939. *My Country and My People*. London: William Heinemann.

"Little Red Card." 2011. *The Economist*, December 17. http://www.economist.com/node/21541716.

Ma, William. 2016. "Chinese Art of the Cultural Revolution." *Routledge Encyclopedia of Modernism*. https://www.rem.routledge.com/articles/chinese-art-of-the-cultural-revolution.

Maddison, Angus. 2007. *Contours of the World Economy I-2030AD*. Oxford: Oxford University Press.

Miller, Stephen G. 2004. *Ancient Greek Athletics*. New Haven, CT: Yale University Press.

Mint Museum. 2011. *The Mint the Sport of Life and Death: The Mesoamerican Ballgame*. Charlotte, NC: Museum. http://www.ballgame.org/main.asp?section=5.

Minter, A. 2013. "Why China Hates its Football Team." *The Sydney Morning Herald*, June 20. http://www.smh.com.au/sport/soccer/why-china-hates-its-football-team-20130620-2okfn.html.

Moffett, Sebastian. 2002. *Japanese Rules: Japan and the Beautiful Game*. London: Yellow Jersey Press.

"National Football to Commemorate the World Cup Qualifying 10 years on." 2011. *Sohu.com*, October 7. http://sports.sohu.com/20111007/n321390832.shtml.

O'Mahony, Mike. 2017. "The Art of Goalkeeping: Memorializing Lev Yashin." *Sport in Society* 20 (5–6): 641–659. doi:10.1080/17430437.2016.1158481.

Osmond, G., M. G. Phillips, and M. O'Neill. 2006. "'Putting Up Your Dukes': Statues Social Memory and Duke Paoa Kahanamoku." *The International Journal of the History of Sport* 23: 82–103.

Osnos, Evan. 2013. "Fact-checking a Chinese Hero." *The New Yorker*, March 29. http://www.newyorker.com/news/evan-osnos/fact-checking-a-chinese-hero.

Potts-Harmer, Alfie. 2015. "Lee Wai Tong: 'The King of Football'." *A Halftime Report*, May 23. https://ahalftimereport.com/2015/05/23/lee-wai-tong-the-king-of-football/.

"President Xi's great Chinese Soccer Dream." 2017. *Today*, January 5. http://www.todayonline.com/sports/football/president-xis-great-chinese-soccer-dream.

Price, Steve. 2017. "Why Chinese Clubs are Breaking Transfer Records – And Why Players are Wise to Go." for *These Football Times*, part of the Guardian Sport Network, January 5. https://www.theguardian.com/football/these-football-times/2017/jan/05/china-chinese-super-league-oscar-carlos-tevez.

Sabrié, Gilles. 2016. "Football Dreams." http://www.gsabrie.com. http://www.gsabrie.com/chinafootball/.

Savage, Kirk. 1994. "The Politics of Memory: Black Emancipation and the Civil War Monument." In *Commemorations: The Politics of National Identity*, edited by J. R. Gikllis, 127–149. Princeton, NJ: Princeton University Press.

Schultz, Jaime. 2011. "Contesting the Master Narrative: The Arthur Ashe Statue and Monument Avenue in Richmond, Virginia." *The International Journal of the History of Sport* 28: 8–9. http://www.tandfonline.com/doi/abs/10.1080/09523367.2011.567775?journalCode=fhsp20.

Sevastopulo, Demetri. 2014. "Guangzhou's Chinese Football Factory." *FT World*, January 23. https://www.youtube.com/watch?v=ayzSW7u-pCg.

Simons, Rowan. 2008. *Bamboo Goalposts: One Man's Quest to Teach the People's Republic of China to Love Football*. London: Palgrave-Macmillan.

Simons, Rowan. 2017. "Are China's Football Reforms a Wasted Investment?" *Leaders' Performance Institute*, June 20. https://leadersinsport.com/performance/chinas-football-reforms-wasted-investment-2/.

Smith, Maureen M. 2009. "Frozen Fists in Speed City: The Statue as Twenty-first-century Reparations." *Journal of Sport History* 36 (3): 393–414. http://library.la84.org/SportsLibrary/JSH/JSH2009/JSH3603/jsh3603j.pdf.

Smith, Maureen M. 2012. "Mapping America's Sporting Landscape: A Case Study of Three Statues." *The International Journal of the History of Sport* 28 (8): 1252–1268. http://www.tandfonline.com/doi/abs/10.1080/09523367.2011.567776?src=recsys&journalCode=fhsp20.

Stallard, Katie. 2016. "Chinese Football Academy Has World Cup Goals." *Sky News*, March 24. http://news.sky.com/story/chinese-football-academy-has-world-cup-goals-10216283.

Stayton, Jonathan. 2016. "Guangzhou Evergrande: Inside China's $185 M Football Factory." *CNN*, March 16. http://edition.cnn.com/2016/03/16/football/football-china-guangzhou-evergrande/index.html.

Stevenson-Yang, Anne and Ken DeWoskin. 2005. "China Destroys The IP Paradigm." *Far-eastern Economic Review*. http://www.internationalforum.com/Articles/China%20Destroys%20the%20IP%20Paradigm.pdf.

Stride, Chris B., Ffion E. Thomas, and John P. Wilson. 2012. "The Sporting Statues Project." http://www.sportingstatues.com.

Stride, Chris B., Ffion E. Thomas, John P. Wilson, and Josh Pahigian. 2012. "Modeling Stadium Statue Subject Choice in U.S. Baseball and English Soccer." *Journal of Quantitative Analysis in Sports* 8 (1): 1–36. doi:10.1515/1559-0410.1399.

Stride, Chris B., Ffion E. Thomas, and Ana M. Chamorro. 2017. "Commemorating Tragic Heroes: Statuary of Soccer Players who Died Mid-career." *Soccer and Society*. http://www.tandfonline.com/doi/abs/10.1080/14660970.2017.1331162.

Stride, Chris B., John P. Wilson, and Ffion E. Thomas. 2013. "Honouring Heroes by Branding in Bronze: Theorizing the UK's Football Statuary." *Sport in Society* 16 (6): 749–771. doi:10.1080/17430437.2012.753527.

Sudworth, John. 2014. "Can a School Help China Qualify for the World Cup?" *bbc.co.uk*, July 14. http://www.bbc.co.uk/news/world-asia-28259011.

Tan, Hua. 2004. "Football 'hooligans' and Football Supporters' Culture in China." In *Football Goes East: Business, Culture and the People's Game in East Asia*, edited by John Horne and Wolfram Manzenreiter, 54–66. New York: Routledge.

"Ten Strong Commemorative Sculpture at Wulihe Stadium 5 years Ago was Blown Up." 2012. *21CN*, June 18. http://sports.21cn.com/national/chinateam/gjd/2012/06/18/12169236_1.shtml.

"The Fate of Athlete Sculpture." 2012. *Yangcheng Evening News*, December 12. http://news.qq.com/a/20120812/000663.htm.

"The Highest Paid Footballers in the World: Where does Carlos Tevez's Huge New Deal Put Him?" 2016. *The Telegraph*, 29 December. http://www.telegraph.co.uk/football/2016/12/20/highest-paid-footballers-world/.

Timm, Leo. 2015. "Cuju: 2,000 years of Ancient Chinese Soccer." *Epoch Times*, September 5.

"Top 10 V-shaped sculpture back to 'Wulihe'." 2012. *Liao Shen Evening News*, June 19. http://news.lnd.com.cn/htm/2012-06/19/content_2361582.htm.

Watts, Jonathan. 2009. "China Shows Red Card to Football Match-fixing with Over 20 Arrests." *The Guardian*, December 31. https://www.theguardian.com/world/2009/dec/31/china-football-match-fixing.

Williams, Jean. 2007. *A Beautiful Game: International Perspectives on Women's Football*. Oxford: Berg.

Wilson, Richard. 1981. "Moral Behavior in Chinese Society: A Theoretical Perspective." In *Moral behavior in Chinese society*, edited by R. Wilson, S. Greenblatt, and A. Wilson, 1–20. New York: Praeger.

"Wulihe V-type Monument." [2002] 2013. *Douban*, December 29. https://site.douban.com/126922/widget/notes/4986652/note/323743671.

Yao, Yamen. 2012. "Ten Seasons Memorial Sculpture "Milutinovic" Moved to the Park for Five Years." *China News Network*, June 19. http://sports.sohu.com/20120619/n346047448.shtml.

Young, Percy. 1950. *The Appreciation of Football*. London: Dobson.

Young, John T. 1999. *Contemporary Public Art in China: A Photographic Tour*. Seattle: University of Washington Press.

Zilberman, Victor. 1982. "Physical education in the Soviet Union." *McGill Journal of Education* 17 (1): 65–75.

An exploration of running as metaphor, methodology, material through the RUN! RUN! RUN! Biennale #r3fest 2016

Kai Syng Tan

ABSTRACT
This paper runs through the RUN! RUN! RUN! Biennale's origins, curatorial framework, and its potential future impact. Also known as #r3fest, the Biennale is an interdisciplinary programme exploring running as an arts and humanities discourse. Exploring running as creative material, metaphor and methodology, the 2016 edition threw a spotlight on live art, drawings, films and activities by practitioners in the arts, academia and NGOs which have hitherto been underrepresented in dominant discourses in the emerging field of 'Running Studies'. The paper raises philosophical questions about the synergies between arts and sport. Examples of practice across visual and performance art locate RUN! RUN! RUN! and the paper in the area of curating, suggesting a new way of considering how arts and sports can be organized, considered and presented. My aims include: widening the current discourse, inviting curators, artists and academics to consider and generate yet other experiments that activate running as creative material, metaphor and methodology, and challenging existing assumptions in the arts about sport.

Rundown

Stripped to its barest essentials the act of running is remarkable for its stunning simplicity. The movement of putting one foot in front of the other. And yet such definition betrays its nuanced complexity, multiplicity of meanings and inbuilt contradictions. As John Bale opines, an 'understanding of running cannot be achieved by simply looking at runners'. Of equal consideration is the sociocultural context in which running occurs. Thus, how might one critically interpret running as a political act of defiance in the hands (or rather feet) of women and girls in a conflict-affected region of Afghanistan, alongside privileged (predominantly male) Western fitness tourists testing their resilience, endurance and strength against the exotic extremities of the Saharan landscape in the Marathon des Sables? What can be learned or revealed from mobilising running to comprehend the experiences of refugees fleeing persecution and torture when juxtaposed with aesthetic displays of suffering in endurance sports through documentation in contemporary art? This is the intentionally jarring backdrop to the opening leg of the triptych Run! Run! Run! Biennale 2016, which as curator Kai Syng Tan alludes is the darker 'difficult second album" – David Hindley, on RUN! RUN! RUN! Biennale 2016 Leeds Leg (2016)

Working in collaboration with two other artists Annie Grove-White and Carali McCall, I curated the RUN! RUN! RUN! Biennale #r3fest in 2016. The interdisciplinary programme explored the ways in which running could be activated as a creative material, metaphor and methodology to think through critical issues related to the body, gender, ageing, the city and borders. Featuring 27 colleagues from 16 academic, artistic and charitable institutions, it consisted of three events that took place over three days across three sites. Focusing on running as a tool to consider the limitations and possibilities of the body, the 'Cardiff Leg' was an evening of live art performances at the National Indoor Athletics Centre in Cardiff, Wales. Zooming out, the 'London Leg' investigated how this running body relates with the city, through a film screening and running tour that took place at University College London and the King's Cross vicinity. Zooming out further, the 'Leeds Leg' examined the ways we run – physically and/or metaphorically – across geopolitical and disciplinary borders, through a seminar held at Leeds College of Art (Figure 1).

Following in the footsteps of the inaugural #r3fest, the 2016 run aimed to create a place where the usual norms of disciplinary practice were temporarily suspended, where creative collisions and 'productive antagonisms' occur (Latham and Tan 2016). This collage-like approach of mixing disparate disciplines together to engineer exchanges is itself informed by the exuberance of running (Tan 2014a). As David Hindley, a runner and Sports Education academic at Nottingham Trent University points out, #r3fest provoked 'conversations across different disciplines, in the process stimulating new research directions and creative collaborations to add to our existing understanding of, and fascination with, running' (2016). The 2016 programme had an additional agenda. It was to highlight activities, including those by colleagues from outside the arts and academia, that have hitherto been underrepresented in dominant discourses in the emerging field of 'Running Studies'.

The aim of #r3fest, and this paper, is not to prescribe a magic formula for how the arts and running could collaborate. Instead, its goal is to widen the conversation, call on curators, artists and academics to consider, curate and create yet other innovative entanglements of the arts and running (and, by extrapolation, sport in general), and along the way interrogate and (re-)energise some of the existing conventions and assumptions in the art world.

Points of departure

But before we go into the detail of a few of these innovative experiments, I wish to address: Why running? How can we unpack it to consider its physical and poetic processes and its possibilities as material, metaphor and methodology? Why was #r3fest set up, and why the interdisciplinary, 'running' approach? What is 'Running Studies', and why the need to showcase overlooked examples in the 2016 run?

Running: not run of the mill

An observation by Matti Tainio, of Aalto University's School of Arts Design and Architecture, could be useful to get us started. The artist and runner considers #r3fest an attempt to 'build connections between different running practices' with academic and artistic disciplines (2016). It is an 'important step in a path' that helps us to understand the 'different meanings of running' beyond the concept of sport.

Figure 1. Flyer for RUN! RUN! RUN! Biennale (Tan 2016d).

Running has indeed a rich repertoire of meanings and registers. Since the 1970s, the world has been experiencing what British runner Sir Roger Bannister calls a 'running boom' (cited in Newsholme and Leech 1983; vi). In this 'nation of runners' (Wray 2014), nearly

40,000 runners participate in the annual London Marathon, which has seen 1,003,473 finishers since its inception in 1981 (Virgin Money London Marathon 2017). Worldwide, a marathon is held daily (Marathon Guide 2012), and Palestine held its first, aptly named Right To Movement, in 2013 (Palestine Marathon 2013).

Yet, running is not just about marathons, nor is it a recent development. As toddlers, as soon as we could walk, we ran, and ran about until our parents and teachers reprimanded 'Walk! Don't run!'. In fact, our ancestors have run for 2 million years – which could be an explanation behind why running as a fitness practice appeals to so many people today. In the days before weapons were invented, the *Homo erectus* ran for up to 6 h across 20 miles (Liebenberg 2008), just short of the distance of a full marathon, to hunt for food in a practice known as persistence hunting. After all, human beings are 'born to run' long distances (Bramble and Lieberman 2004), endowed as we are with unique physical attributes 'tailor-made for running' (Bramble and Lieberman, cited in Chen 2006). Nonetheless, as any endurance runner will attest, the physical is only one part of the equation. It was our ancestors' persistence and 'ability to dream far ahead' (Heinrich 2002, 177) that empowered them to take the first steps to chase the antelope in the first place.

The running-dreaming correlation allows us to direct this discussion towards the arts, and this is where we find plenty of evidence about how running has been a resource for writers, artists and thinkers in direct and indirect ways. For American novelist and runner Joyce Carol Oates we possess 'peculiar powers of locomotion' when we dream, which are:

> '[...] atavistic remnants, the hallucinatory memory of a distant ancestor for whom the physical being, charged with adrenaline in emergency situations, was indistinguishable from the spiritual or intellectual. In running, 'spirit' seems to pervade the body; as musicians experience the uncanny phenomenon of tissue memory in their fingertips, so the runner seems to experience in feet, lungs, quickened heartbeat, an extension of the imagining self' (1999).

For Oates, this ineffable energy felt in the toes, lungs and quickened heartbeat of the runner can even be the fuel that is 'nourishing to the imagination'. Her novel *Do With Me What You Will* was composed while she ran at Hyde Park, London. Hyde Park was conducive for Jeremy Bentham too, for that was where he went running before dinner. Fitting his reputation as a neologism-loving eccentric, the philosopher (1748–1832) referred to these as his 'preprandial circumgyrations' (Wheatley 2015, 4). His association with utilitarianism is undisputed, but it is a little-known fact that Bentham was a runner before running was what we call a 'fitness practice' (Latham 2015) today. Perhaps like the novelist Haruki Murakami and the contemporary runner, Bentham could have found running a useful means to declutter his thoughts. For British painter Jo Volley (born 1953), her site of action is Hampstead Heath, where she picks up oak apples during her runs, from which she extracts ink to create her paintings (2014).

Apart from playing an important role in their creative processes, running has also been activated by arts practitioners as material or medium in their work. An example is Turner Prize winner Martin Creed's 2008 *Work No. 850*, in which runners sprinted for 30 s each time within the hallowed halls of the Tate, which are expressions of 'being alive' (2008). Then, there are works in which running is the subject matter. Who can forget the angry young man, Colin, in the short story *The Loneliness of the Long Distance Runner* (Sillitoe 1959), or the feisty Lola who ran and transformed her fate in the cult film *Run Lola Run* (Tykwer 1999)?

Upping the speed and upping the game in art and academia

The list goes on. Clearly, the connections between different running practices with academic and artistic disciplines are multiple, complex and exciting. There are rich possibilities of running as a creative material, metaphor and methodology. Why, then, has the running boom not (yet) been picked up on or reflected in the academic arena? As geographer John Bale states in his book entitled *Running Cultures*, although running is 'one of the world's most widely practised sports and recreations', it has tended to 'elude serious study outside of the natural sciences' (2004). The art world fares no better. Artist-curator Gregg Whelan points out that artists are 'beginning to exploit sport's ability to produce meaningful narratives from physical action' (2017), but why aren't more of them jumping up and down and capitalizing on running in their work? After all, artists have always been opportunistic and co-opted materials from other worlds into their work; think bronze, spray paint, newspaper cuttings, data. A few A-lister artists have 'outed' themselves as exercise and sports enthusiasts. This includes kayaking for Chris Ofili (Searle 2017) and swimming 40 lengths of backstrokes in a purpose-built 16 m underground Victorian-tiled single-lane pool in Shoreditch for Tracey Emin (Godwin 2005; Hind 2014). However, as self-titled 'transvestite potter' and cycling enthusiast Grayson Perry argues, there is a 'popular idea that artists are not supposed to be sporty' (2015). For many, the myth of the 'creative genius' doused in self-destruction and melancholy is more attractive than the one drenched in sweat in a pair of running-shorts. Drugs, alcohol and pills are a sexier fuel than carbs, gels and endocannabinoids, which are cannabis-like hormones manufactured by the brains ('endo' means from within) from vigorous exercise, in particular running (Dietrich and McDaniel 2004). Talk about running in the same breath as art, and the cultural elite run a mile. That may be why Turner Prize winner Keith Tyson, has been alleged to be a closet runner even though he has been spotted running everyday to train for a triathlon. His eye-witness is his neighbour, Jonathan Buckley, himself a novelist and runner (Tan 2014a; 188). Art and architectural departments enshrine the cultural tradition of walking in their curriculum (Glasgow School of Art 2011; Bartlett School of Architecture 2016). If this could be called 'Walking Studies' (think Walter Benjamin, Richard Long, William Wordsworth, Rebecca Solnit), it is not time to up the speed, and up the game, and introduce what Whelan has termed 'Running Studies' (cited in Tan 2015) into the academy, and give the walking canon a good run for its money?

Stepping in to fill the gaps: the inaugural RUN! RUN! RUN!

To help to address the gap, I founded the RUN! RUN! RUN! International Festival of Running in 2014 (Figure 2). Also known as the #r3fest, this was a hybrid programme examining running as an arts and humanities discourse. I approached Alan Latham, a geographer from University College London, to be Co-Director, and artist Jo Volley as co-host. Funded by University College London and the Arts and Humanities Research Council, the one-day event took place at the Slade Research Centre, and was attended by 50 artists, academics and community leaders from 30 institutions and including the Universities of Harvard and Oxford, Goodgym and the Sri Chimnoy Centre (Tan 2014b). Disciplines were jumbled up to generate lively, productive antagonisms, practice was mixed with research, and cultural and academic hierarchies and boundaries irritated. The usual presentations aside, there

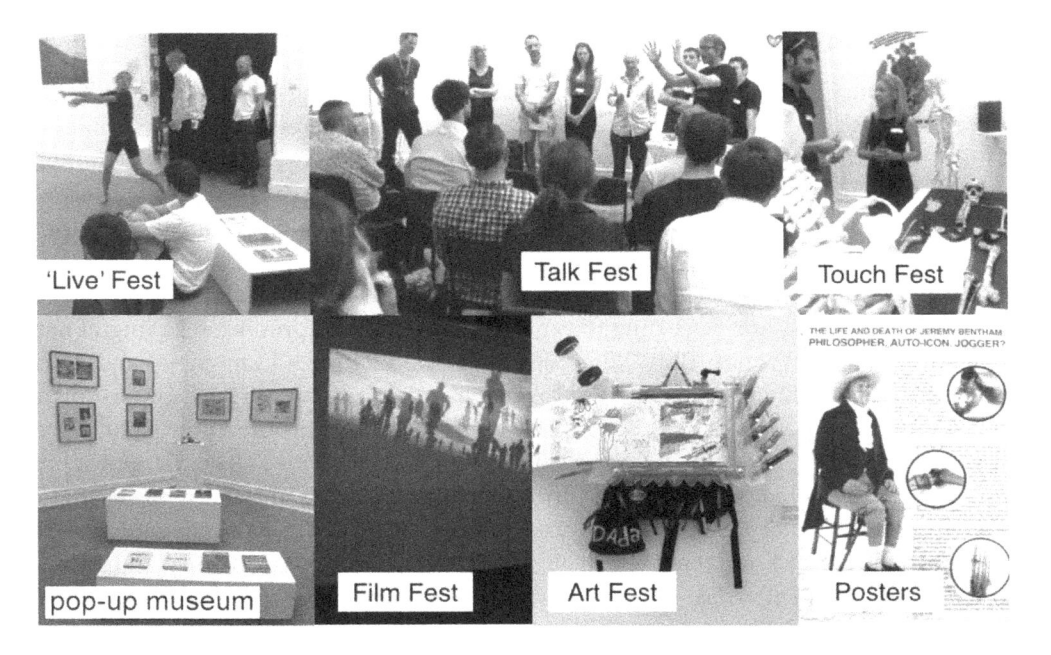

Figure 2. An overview of RUN! RUN! RUN! International Festival of Running (Latham and Tan 2016).

were quick-fire, 8-min speaking slots that we timed with a stopwatch. Object-based learning activities were also programmed in, as paleo-anthropologists brought samples illustrating anatomical parts of the human runner for participants to explore. Academic posters, such as one on the biomechanics of running, were juxtaposed with commissioned artworks, such as Simson&Volley's drawing of a map of her run at Hampstead Heath (Figure 3). A meditation session was deliberately scheduled to take place at the same time as a lecture on running injury by a medic, 'forcing' the festival goers to choose between spiritualism and science. Senior academics intermingled with unknowns (we took a chance with two female performers, including a 23-year-old undergraduate).

While I have investigated the body and mind in motion (and commotion) since 1994, it was only in 2009 that I picked up running as an exercise as part of my effort to grasp first-hand my area of research for my PhD (Tan 2014a). And although as an artist my running experiments have been exhibited in different contexts, including as a participatory performance at Documenta (Tan 2012), I felt that I could also make a meaningful contribution to the field as a curator. In introducing running as a sport to the arts and humanities, Bale has pioneered and advanced 'Running Studies'. Other researchers have taken on the baton to extend and broaden the discussion beyond running as an elite sport, to consider what it means to amateur runners, as a commute, how it relates to landscape, from various frameworks including geography, sociology and theatre (Lorimer 2012; Allen-Collinson and Hockey 2011; Latham 2015; Qviström 2017; Hitchings and Latham 2016; Filmer 2016; Cook, Shaw, and Simpson 2016). But why aren't we allowed to have more fun as a field? Could we not re-enact the childlike pleasures that can come with running? Why can't we scamper about different schools of thoughts from different fields, deliberately mix them up and engineer unexpected outcomes – the same way an artist creates collages and montages of disparate elements? Could we shake and mix things up, and see what happens? Theoretical positionings littered with impressive

Figure 3. Hampstead Heath Oak Apple Run by Simson&Volley (2014). This work is a map of the pathways where oak galls can be found and celebrates the beauty of the material (Tan 2014b).

jargons that cite continental philosophy are fabulous, but where are evidences of walking or rather *running*, the talk? Especially since what we are talking about concerns sport, shouldn't action and practice be at the heart of this discourse? Shouldn't bold practice-led research experiments be a critical part of this inquiry? What about non-western discourses? Could a non-logocentric, 'running' approach open up interesting insights?

These questions led me to the philosophy of 'poetic thinking' which prizes associations, metaphoric correlations, divergence and '10,000 things' over logic, causality and singularity (Hall and Ames 1995; Miller 2003; Graham 1986), which became one of the building blocks of 'productive antagonisms' that Latham and I came up with (Latham and Syng Tan 2016). We wanted a playful, 'ill-disciplined' interdisciplinary approach to counter the negative, tribal or self-serious tendencies of the art and academic worlds; #r3fest was productive antagonisms in action.

The antagonisms were fruitful. The *Guardian* praised it for its 'positive atmosphere', and urged other conferences to 'take a leaf out of #r3fest's book' (Lockwood 2014). The animated curatorial approach of the festival and its expanded definition of running has since caught on. This is evidenced in programmes run by festival alumni, which themselves also feature festival alumni. They include an ESRC-funded event, *Running Dialogues*, in London (Cook 2015), a running-themed performance festival and seminar in Finland co-curated by Gregg Whelan (ANTI Festival of Contemporary Art 2015), a networking programme for artists centering on 'running in its widest contexts', *Running Wild,* at Fermynwoods

Contemporary Art (2015) and a 6-hour run at the Festival of Grenoble in France (Cholat 2016). The Festival was also cited in the popular book *Footnotes* by Vybarr Cregan-Reid (2016 pp246–248), which featured other colleagues he met there too. Two networks with the festival's alumni as members were also set up. The first is called Running Cultures Research Group with a corresponding mailing list (JISCMail 2014). The other is the RUN! RUN! RUN! International body for Research which I founded to run independent and collaborative work. I invited Latham to be Co-Director. Associates hail from Malmo, London, Cardiff and Singapore, including artists Annie Grove-White and Carali McCall (Tan 2014c).

Two years on, in 2016, Grove-White and McCall ran a second Festival, which we called the RUN! RUN! RUN! Biennale.

Widening Running Studies: the RUN! RUN! RUN! Biennale 2016

I wanted to run a second lap because I felt that the conversations had just begun. I wanted to hear and learn more, and to listen to other voices and narratives. Like other 'Studies' (Gender, Media, Walking) I felt that Running Studies should not be an echo chamber of the same old tropes by the same vocal few, but a rich cacophony with new and different expressions. If the first run was a celebratory survey, a proof of concept about running's mileage as an arts and humanities discourse, and how sparks can arise from collaging different disciplines together, the second run is the 'difficult second album' (Tan 2016e). Responding to the shocking turn of events politically, the 2016 run (especially the Leeds Leg) threw a spotlight on running and its entanglement with critical issues of the day that I had found myself affected by as a woman, migrant, artist and human being, and which seemed to be strangely missing from the existing discourses from Running Studies and glossy running magazines alike. In addition, instead of expecting people to congregate in the capital, #r3fest travelled to the regions (including the unusual location of an indoor stadium in Cardiff, Figure 4), and featured the work of regional colleagues (such as BAFTA Cymru-winner, writer Catrin Kean).

Figure 4. Anna Brazier's performance on running as a childlike, defiant act, at #r3fest 2016 Cardiff Leg. Photograph by Gordon Plant (2016).

Then, there was its line-up. The first run had featured the work of newcomers to the game of art, academia and running studies (such as a 23-year old undergraduate who went on to perform at the Oslo International Theatre Festival and a para athlete who responded to the Open Call). The 2016 Biennale continued to showcase emerging artists, including a retired psychotherapist, Anna Brazier, with 30 years of work with the NHS under her belt. Furthermore, #r3fest celebrated the efforts of colleagues who are female (including that of members of A Mile in Her Shoes, a running charity for women affected by homelessness), older (including that of 74-year old runner and founder of Fields of Vision Doug Sandle) and disabled (including that of representatives from Headway East London, a charity for people affected by brain injury). As sociologist Monica Büscher points out,

> Mobilities are embodied, involving fragile, aged, gendered, racialised bodies. Such bodies encounter other bodies, objects and the physical world multisensuously. […] Bodies sense and make sense of the world as they move bodily in and through it, creating discursively mediated sensescapes that signify social taste and distinction, ideology and meaning. (2010, 8)

#r3fest 2016 reminded us that there are different bodies. It spoke loudly of the richness of research, practice, action and activity on the ground that are not just heroic, privileged, territorial, logocentric or white(-washed). It showed us how these efforts follow the well-trodden paths of, as well as depart from, the cultural canon of walking, which is often male (think Richard Long, the Situationists and Will Self) and privileged (a fellow panel member on a running-related programme on BBC Radio 3 waxed lyrical enjoying 'letting my mind go on a holiday' when running and imagining himself as an 'outsider', which is neither a figment of imagination nor choice for those considered outsiders)(2017). It is also sometimes drugged-out (think Samuel Taylor Coleridge's opium or Charles Baudelaire's hashish, against the runners' poison of choice of the runner's high). #r3fest also illustrated how running is 'remarkable for its stunning simplicity', and the diverse demographics of the people are behind the global running boom. #r3fest proved that not all who run and use running in their art or research are what I term MAMIR or middle-aged men in running-shorts, or the MAMIRA, the middle-aged men in running-shorts in academia, both of whom I consider are close cousins of the MAMIL or middle-aged man in lycra.

As a MAWIRA, or middle-aged woman in running-shorts in academia, myself, let me now run through a few examples of the innovative experiments shared at #r3fest.

Cardiff Leg: Live art on running and the body

The Cardiff Leg was subtitled *How does running (dis)connect people with the body?* Through an evening of live art, readings and discussions at the National Indoor Athletics Centre of Cardiff School of Sport, participants discussed the ways in which running draws out the possibilities as well as limitations of the human body.

How running relates to the ageing, female body was foregrounded in three presentations: a performance by Anna Brazier, the retired psychotherapist, a short film *Breath/Mind/Muscle* by co-curator Annie Grove-White, who began running in her 50s to counter the onset of osteoporosis which had affected her mother, as well as a reading by writer Catrin Kean of her new memoir on her marathon-running in different parts of the world. As co-curator Carali McCall dashed back and forth in front of the audience, she held and counted her breath, each time with shorter recovery times that she had imposed for herself. In the ensuing discussions led by Aberystwyth University's Andrew Filmer and myself, the topics of injury, pain and the pleasures of running were covered; all this appropriately taking place inside the massage room within the Centre, overlooked by models of human skeletons and charts about the human anatomy and ways to heal it back to health.

The standout act for the evening was a performance-lecture by award-winning international performance maker Eddie Ladd (Figure 5). This drew on an acclaimed dance-theatre piece that she created in 2010. Entitled *Ras Goffa Bobby Sands/The Bobby Sands Memorial Race,* it was a portrait of the famed hunger striker of the Irish Republican Army through running. For the performance in the theatres, she ran for 50 min on stage on a specially built oversized treadmill (Ladd 2010). While Ladd used an ordinary treadmill in the Health and Exercise Research Centre for her re-enactment, how she manipulated the machine and her body was nothing short of spellbinding. Through the 30-min act, the Welsh artist enacted how Bobby Sands smokes a cigarette, sleeps, and undergoes physical and mental deterioration as the hunger strike progresses, all the while running on the treadmill. At times she seemed unable to catch up with the speeding machine; at others she sedated and tamed it. Requiring and revealing strength and stamina as it did vulnerability and despair, Eddie's piece powerfully used running – and running on a treadmill – as a metaphor for the precarious and paradoxical tensions between life and death, between end (reaching your dream) and the means to the end (pain, sacrifice). In so doing, not only did she pay tribute to a historical figure who was also an amateur runner, but the everyman in their daily grind. The performance also conjured our heritage as persistence hunters, when running was a tool of survival – only that in Sands' case, ironically, he had deliberately rejected food to get his point across. We run and carry on running because we dream far ahead and imagine a better outcome, even if it means pushing our body to its extreme and running it down.

Figure 5. Eddie Ladd and her performance-lecture. Photograph by Phil Martin (Tan 2016c).

London Leg: film screening (and popup tour) on running and the city

Zooming out, the 'London Leg' of #r3fest asked: how does running (dis)connect people with the city?

The evening began with a popup running tour of the changing landscapes of King's Cross with the aim to 'wake up our minds and bodies' ahead of the film screening (Tan and Cole 2016). The tour was conceived and run by personal trainer and alternative tour guide Simon Cole from the acclaimed Hackney Tours. With the slogan of 'alternative, independent, East London', Hackney Tour's unusual repertoire includes Women Run! #Runtivism' (Cole 2017). Cole's proposal of running as a means to understand, feel a sense of ownership of and express one's autonomy in the city, was echoed in my film shown at the film screening, entitled *Hand-In-Hand* (2016a).

Other films explored running as not only subject matter but aesthetic approach. Jenny Baines' *Untitled (Rooftop)* and Joe King's *Mobius Strip* were depictions of the city. Their Structuralist approach to the editing conjured the rhythms and playfulness of running. They also made me think of why 'moving images' are thus called, because they are still images that appear to *move* due to the human eye's ability to 'join up' the images via the phenomenon of the persistence of vision – and are not early persistence hunters or modern-day amateur marathon runners linked by a kind of 'persistence of vision'. Then, there was Musquiqui Chihying's *The Jog*, which parodied the self-seriousness of runners and chore of running, with the Taiwanese artist performing a run on a supermarket's conveyer belt. This created a dialogue with Veronique Chance's rightly clinical tone in her *In the Absence of Running*, which was a documentation of her knee operation for her injury from running, which in turn spoke to Annie Grove-White's *Breath/Mind/Muscle*, screened here again (Figure 6).

Carali McCall's *Extract, from Work No. 4 (Running/Restraint) Back Hill* similarly explored the abilities and limitations of the body, and how this body interacts with the place in which it lives, breathes and moves (2013). In a review of #r3fest, David Hindley reminds us of the words of illustrator Leanne Shapton, who observes that 'artistic discipline and athletic

Figure 6. Still from Breath/Mind/Muscle, Annie Grove-White (2014).

discipline are kissing cousins, they require the same thing, an unspecial practice…' (2016). It is obvious from McCall's film, as it is from Ladd's performance, how work that uses running may require a level of athleticism, endurance and, once again, persistence. These are features that run deep in the tradition of endurance or durational art (think for instance of Chris Burden's *Five-Day Locker Piece* and Teh-Ching Hsieh's *One Year Performances*), and which Gregg Whelan's curated 2015 programme at the ANTI Festival highlighted through its seminar *The Art of Endurance* and Tristram Meecham's *Fun Run*, in which he ran a full marathon (26 miles) in front of a live audience in Kuopio, Finland (2015). For McCall's chosen mise-en-scene in a street in London her body is tethered to an elastic band, one end of which is attached to a bollard. McCall runs back and forth repeatedly in what seems like a 'Sisyphean task' (Tainio 2016), until the elastic band snaps. McCall conceptualizes running as a form of drawing (2014). By extension, when she runs in the city, the city becomes her canvas for her body to draw on, and to wrestle with, literally so.

Wrestling with the ways in which the running body navigates and negotiates the urban space, the discussion that followed was led by artist Jo Volley and geographer Alan Latham, with respondents including writer Simon Freeman (*Like the Wind*) and friends from charities A Mile in her Shoes (Figure 7) and Headway East London. A metropolis like London presents challenges for anyone; those who are homeless or have a neurological difference run into additional barriers in how they are seen and how they see. It is through learning

Figure 7. A Mile In Her Shoes. Photograph by Damian Walker (2016).

about the lived experiences of these colleagues, and how they use running as a means to 'find their feet' (website 2013) and give them a different identity and label. This serves to remind the MAMIRs, MAMIRAs or MAWIRAs among us that there are different bodies, and that they sense and make sense of the world differently, and what they know can enrich what we thought we knew.

Leeds Leg: seminar on running and borders

And gender does come into play in the consideration of how bodies move about, or not. Today, with Trump, Brexit and a rise in protectionist, isolationist policies and behaviours, we are once again inhabiting an era in which walls are being erected, boundaries hardened and our movement as runners, migrants, travellers and women restricted, and minds closed as we fear the other. For those who cannot run away from conflict areas, staying alive can be tough let alone running outdoors, particularly for those who are not male. Running, thus, is not only something that can be positive for your physical and mental well-being, but a demonstration, literally and metaphorically of your agency and autonomy.

These were the territories of the Leeds Leg, held at Leeds College of Art, which was subtitled *How does running (dis)connect people with borders?* Its starting point was Jun Nguyen-Hatsushiba's seminal performance *Breathing is Free: 12,756.3* (ongoing since 2007), which is the artist's attempt to experience world refugee crisis by running the diameter of the earth, 12,756.3 km. Chaired by principal curator Sarah Brown (Leeds Art Gallery), the headline act was a Skype conversation with UN human-rights lawyer Stephanie Case, president of Free to Run, a running group for women in Afghanistan. Her story, as Hindley writes, is 'one of empowerment and transformation, using running, fitness and outdoor adventure programmes as an avenue to freedom, to foster social networks of support, and to help shift the perception of gender roles in war-torn societies where women and girls are disproportionately affected by conflict' (2016). Her narrative was set in an interesting tension with that presented by Debbie Lisle, a Reader in International Relations at Queen's University Belfast. Lisle presented a scathing critique of culture and industries generated by the Marathon Des Sables. This is an iconic race consisting of running for seven days across the Sahara desert that draws hundreds of ultra-marathon runners annually. For Lisle, this represents 'established colonial asymmetries recast in a neoliberal context' as runners 'test their resilience, endurance and strength' against an 'extreme' Saharan landscape'. The 'central conceit' of the marathon, that 'superior Western fitness regimes and technologies will dominate the race', is 'inverted' by the overwhelming success of a handful of Moroccan runners year after year. Set side-by-side with that of Case's, Lisle's argument thus provoked a reflection on the politics of different bodies – white/non-white, saviour/ victim, colonial/ colonized, researcher/'subject'. Also on running and the international stage was *Certainly the Toughest Ultramarathon of Your Life*, a colourful drawing that I created as a response to the (anti-) migrant crisis. The work aimed to tease out the irony between the gruelling journeys that migrants undertake to seek asylum, and the pursuit made by the 'escapees' and 'weekend warriors' of Europe seeking gruelling (and exorbitant) endurance challenges in the name of fitness, adventure and/or self-fulfilment (Tan 2016b).

There are not just geopolitical borders but disciplinary, artistic and personal to consider alongside the role of running in this mix. This is where the efforts of Doug Sandle come in. The founding Chair of Fields of Vision, who is still a runner at the age of 74, provided 'an impassioned defence for marrying the potentially unlikely pairing of the artist and the athlete' through a set of examples from both the arts and sport to illustrate the arts' potential to 'celebrate, encapsulate and express sports practice and culture' (Hindley 2016). Fields of Vision member artist Lisa Stansbie used the work of Dutch artist and triathlete Guido van der Werve, to highlight the common grounds shared by the two disciplines, including physical effort, solitude, repetition and boredom. Carrying on with the theme of the importance of learning from other disciplines, as well as to 'float' more ideas, the Leeds Leg closed not with running but swimming. Drawing on her (auto)ethnographic study, sociologist Karen Throsby uses endurance swimming 'as a conduit for thinking about mind-body boundaries (reflected in the 'mind over matter' rhetoric championed by the marathon swimming community) as well as the freedoms and privileges the sport demands, alluding to the resource-greedy nature of the leisure pursuit, as well the mobility and financial capital necessary to compete' as she swims across borders (Hindley 2016). Amidst this discomforting analysis, Throsby also shares the pleasures of engaging her body in the endurance sport.

What next? Dreaming far ahead

> Where do we go from here? […] amidst the potential to identify aspects of common ground, the assorted line-up (or in Kai's words 'mix-and-mismatch programming') invariably leads to incongruities and divergent paths. By drawing upon and navigating such diverse perspectives, the resultant challenge and blurring of these distinctions will hopefully provide further insights into the ways people understand the pursuit of running in their own lives. (Hindley 2016)

Works of art that have continued to intrigue are not those that provide the answers, but those that problematize, interrogate and provoke. Covering the RUN! RUN! RUN! Biennale's origins and curatorial framework, the paper has raised philosophical questions about synergies between arts and sport, as well as suggested a new way of considering how arts and sports can be organized, considered and presented. For Matti Tainio, for all its 'disconnectedness', #r3fest presented

> […] a path the participants were willing to travel together, but there wasn't an established way to do it – *yet*. The various interests and agendas still need time to grow closer to each other. We need to develop this discourse further in order to be able to really understand and articulate the change that is taking place. For this, we should arrange more meetings and take time to talk about our art and our research. (Tainio 2016)

It is not my intention of to spell out an optimal path for the arts and running. While it was created with the goal of filling in what I have perceived as gaps in the field, the #r3fest is itself deliberately incomplete, sketchy, filled with ellipsis and its own gaps that it invites you to fill and dig further. By running through the curatorial framework of the #r3fest, which creates spaces of interdisciplinary productive antagonisms, and by shining a spotlight at 2016 run on the innovative efforts by colleagues that are hitherto underrepresented in dominant discourses in so-called 'Running Studies', my aim has been to help to widen the discourse, invite curators, artists and academics to consider, curate and create yet other experiments that activate running as creative material, metaphor and methodology, and challenge our existing assumptions in the arts. Particularly amidst an increasingly unstable and unwell reality marked by fear, division, anxiety and funding cuts today, I argue that the roles of the arts, sport and their hybrids as spaces of distraction, reflection, connection and collaboration are more important than ever. This is the challenge, and opportunity, for academics and artists next.

Acknowledgements

I would like to thank colleagues David Hindley, Matti Tainio, Carali McCall, Annie Grove-White, Alan Latham, Andrew Filmer, and all the participants and audiences of the RUN! RUN! RUN! Biennale 2016 for their inspiration and support for #r3fest, which has given me much food for thought, some of which I have attempted to reflect in this paper. #r3fest 2016 was sponsored by Leeds College of Art, and the site sponsors were University College London's Department of Geography and Cardiff School of Sport. In addition, I would like to thank A Mile In Her Shoes and Jo Volley for permission to use their images here.

Disclosure statement

No potential conflict of interest was reported by the author.

References

A Mile in Her Shoes. 2016. *A-Mile-in-Her-Shoes*. http://www.amileinhershoes.org.uk.

Allen-Collinson, Jacquelyn, and John Hockey. 2011. "Feeling the Way: Notes toward a Haptic Phenomenology of Distance Running and Scuba Diving." *International Review for the Sociology of Sport* 46 (3): 330–345. doi:10.1177/1012690210380577

ANTI Festival of Contemporary Art. 2015. *International Seminar – Art of Endurance Seminar*. https://vimeo.com/145036633.

Bale, John. 2004. *Running Cultures: Racing in Time and Space*. London: Psychology Press.

Bartlett School of Architecture. 2016. "MAAH_Course Information Sheet_Template'. Bartlett School of Architecture." https://webcache.googleusercontent.com/search?q=cache:bos7LNIcNnkJ:https://www.bartlett.ucl.ac.uk/architecture/programmes/postgraduate/ma-architectural-history/documents/MAAH_Course_Information_Sheet_2016_16112.pdf+&cd=3&hl=en&ct=clnk&gl=uk&client=safari.

Bramble, Dennis M., and Daniel E. Lieberman. 2004. "Endurance Running and the Evolution of Homo." *Nature* 432 (7015): 345–352. doi:10.1038/nature03052.

BBC Radio 3. 2017. "The Arts of Running." Free Thinking. http://www.bbc.co.uk/programmes/b087yrll.

Büscher, Monika, ed. 2010. *Mobile Methods*. 1st ed. New York: Routledge.

Chen, Ingfei. 2006. "Human Evolution: Born to Run." *DISCOVER Magazine*, May 2006. http://discovermagazine.com/2006/may/tramps-like-us.

Cholat, Florent. 2016. *Les 6 Heures De Grenoble*. http://kaisyngtan.com/portfolio/handinhand/.

Cole, Simon. 2017. "Hackney Tours – Alternative Experience Walks, Radical Running Tours & Brilliant Bike Rides in the Most Exciting Part of London." https://hackneytours.com/.

Cook, Simon. 2015. "Running Dialogues Summary." http://www.freestak.com/wp-content/uploads/2015/04/Running-Dialogues-Seminars-Summary.pdf.

Cook, Simon, Jon Shaw, and Paul Simpson. 2016. "Running Order: Urban Public Space, Everyday Citizenship and Sporting Subjectivities." In *Critical Geographies of Sport: Space, Power and Sport in Global Perspective*, edited by Natalie Koch, 157–172. Routledge.

Creed, Martin. 2008. *Work No. 850*. http://www.martincreed.com/site/works/work-no-850.

Cregan-Reid, Vybarr. 2016. Footnotes: How Running Makes Us Human. London: Ebury Press.

Dietrich, A., and W. McDaniel. 2004. "Endocannabinoids and Exercise." *British Journal of Sports Medicine* 38 (5): 536–541. doi:10.1136/bjsm.2004.011718.

Fermynwoods Contemporary Art. 2015. "Wild Projects #5." http://www.fermynwoods.co.uk/archive/workshopstalksevents/wild-projects/wild-projects-5/.

Filmer, Andrew. 2016. "Motion Capture." https://www.academia.edu/27066641/Motion_Capture.

Free To Run. 2016. *Our Mission*. http://www.freetorun.org/our-mission/.

Glasgow School of Art. 2011. "Sculpture Year 3 Studio Course Specification." http://webcache.googleusercontent.com/search?q=cache:RE_-ui_vE5UJ:www.gsa.ac.uk/media/218366/Sculp%2520Yr%25203,%2520term%25203,%2520Studio%2520-%2520BA%2520(Hons)%2520Fine%2520Art.pdf+&cd=5&hl=en&ct=clnk&gl=uk&client=firefox-b-ab.

Godwin, Mike. 2005. "Neal Stephenson's past, Present, and Future – Reason Magazine." Reason.com. http://reason.com/archives/2005/02/01/neal-stephensons-pastpresent-a/print.

Graham, A. C. 1986. *Yin-Yang and the Nature of Correlative Thinking*. Singapore: Institute of East Asian Studies.

Hall, David L., and Roger T. Ames. 1995. *Anticipating China: Thinking through the Narratives of Chinese and Western Culture*. New York: State University of New York Press.

Grove-White, Annie. 2014. Breath/Mind/Muscle. Video.

Heinrich, Bernd. 2002. *Why We Run: A Natural History*. Harper Perennial: Reprint.

Hind, John. 2014. "Lager, Red Bull and Swimming 40 Lengths: A Tracey Emin Weekend." *The Guardian*, August 17, sec. Art and design. http://www.theguardian.com/artanddesign/2014/aug/17/tracey-emin-weekend-lager-red-bull-swimming.

Hindley, David. 2016. "#R3fest Leeds Leg Review." *RUN RUN RUN Biennale* (blog). December 3. http://kaisyngtan.com/r3fest/leeds-leg-review/.

Hitchings, Russell, and Alan Latham. 2016. "How "Social" is Recreational Running? Findings from a Qualitative Study in London and Implications for Public Health Promotion." *Health & Place*. Accessed January 8, 2017. https://doi.org/10.1016/j.healthplace.2016.10.003.

JISCMail. 2014. 'JISCMail – RUNNING-CULTURESList at WWW.JISCMAIL.AC.UK'. Accessed August 20, 2017. https://www.jiscmail.ac.uk/cgi-bin/webadmin?A0=RUNNING-CULTURES.

Ladd, Eddie. 2010. *Ras Goffa Bobby Sands/the Bobby Sands Memorial Race*. Accessed May 13, 2017. http://www.eddieladd.com/the-Bobby-Sands-memorial-race.html.

Latham, Alan. 2015. "The History of a Habit: Jogging as a Palliative to Sedentariness in 1960s America." *Cultural Geographies* 22 (1):103–126. doi:10.1177/1474474013491927

Latham, Alan, and Kai Syng Tan. 2016. "Running into Each Other: Run! Run! Run! a Festival and a Collaboration." *Cultural Geographies*. http://cgj.sagepub.com/.

Liebenberg, Louis. 2008. "The Relevance of Persistence Hunting to Human Evolution." *Journal of Human Evolution* 55 (6): 1156–1159. doi:10.1016/j.jhevol.2008.07.004.

Lockwood, Alex. 2014. "Running and Academia: The Intellectual Aspect of Pounding the Pavements." June 30, 2014. https://www.theguardian.com/lifeandstyle/the-running-blog/2014/jun/30/running-academia-intellectual-aspect-pounding-pavements.

Lorimer, Hayden. 2012. "Surfaces and Slopes." *Performance Research* 17 (2): 83–86. doi:10.1080/13528165.2012.671080.

Marathon Guide. 2012. "MarathonGuide.Com – International Marathons Races Directory and Schedule." http://www.marathonguide.com/races/races.cfm?place=intl.

McCall, Carali. 2013. "Work No. 4 (Restraint Running) Back Hill, 2013 – Edited Version on Vimeo." https://vimeo.com/115101499.

McCall, Carali. 2014. "A Line is a Brea(D)Thless Length: Introducing the Physical Act of Running as a Form of Drawing." PhD, University of the Arts London. http://ualresearchonline.arts.ac.uk/6511/.

Miller, James. 2003. *Daoism: A Short Introduction*. London: Oneworld Publications.

Newsholme, Eric, and Tony Leech. 1983. *Runner: Energy and Endurance*. California: Walter L. Meagher.

Oates, Carol Joyce. 1999. "Writers on Writing." *The New York Times*. http://www.scribd.com/doc/7391268/Writers-on-Writing.

Palestine Marathon. 2013. "Palestine Marathon – Right to Movement." http://righttomovement.com/.

Perry, Grayson. 2015. "'Cycling is the Perfect Sport for Transvestites'". *The Guardian*, May 2, sec. Life and style. http://www.theguardian.com/lifeandstyle/2015/may/02/cycling-is-the-perfect-sport-for-transvestites.

Plant, Gordon. 2016. "RUN! RUN! RUN!". http://www.gordons.photos/runrunrun.

Qvistrōm, Mattias. 2017. "Competing Geographies of Recreational Running: The Case of the "Jogging Wave" in Sweden in the Late 1970s." *Health & Place* 46 (July): 351–357. doi:10.1016/j. healthplace.2016.12.002.

Searle, Adrian. 2017. "Chris Ofili: Weaving Magic Review – A Totally Tropical Tapestry." *The Guardian*, April 25, sec. Art and design. http://www.theguardian.com/artanddesign/2017/apr/25/chris-ofili-weaving-magic-review-a-totally-tropical-tapestry.

Sillitoe, Alan. 1959. "Loneliness of the Long Distance Runner". New York: Signet First Edition.

Tainio, Matti. 2016. "#R3fest London Leg Review." *RUN RUN RUN Biennale* (Blog), December 13. http://kaisyngtan.com/r3fest/london-leg-review/.

Tan, Kai Syng. 2012. "Kaidie Passes on (Some of) Her Final Messages in an Interactive Performance of a "Running Discourse" at DOCUMENTA (13), Kassel, Germany." *Kaidie's 1000-Day Trans-Run: 12.12.2009–09.09.2012* (Blog), September 8. http://3rdlifekaidie.com/2012/09/kaidie-documenta-kaisyngtan/.

Tan, Kai Syng. 2014a. "THE PHYSICAL AND POETIC PROCESSES OF RUNNING: A Practice-Related Fine Art Discourse about a Playful Way to Transform Your World Today." University College London. http://discovery.ucl.ac.uk/1420270/1/Tan_Kai_Syng_Thesis_Redacted.pdf.

Tan, Kai Syng 2014b. "A FAB FIRST RUN 2014." *RUN RUN RUN Biennale* (Blog), June 28. http://kaisyngtan.com/r3fest/our-first-run/.

Tan, Kai Syng. 2014c. "RUN BY." *RUN!RUN!RUN! International Body for Research* (Blog). October 1. http://kaisyngtan.com/portfolio/run-by/.

Tan, Kai Syng. 2015. "PechaKucha 20x20 – RUN! RUN! RUN!" PechaKucha 20x20. http://www. pechakucha.org/cities/kuopio/presentations/run-run-run.

Tan, Kai Syng. 2016a. "Run Run Run. Hand in Hand. Run into and Run with One Another. on Vimeo." https://vimeo.com/172991771.

Tan, Kai Syng. 2016b. "Tough Ultramarathons and Life on the Run." *Berghahn Journals Transfers Transfers*. http://journals.berghahnbooks.com/transfers.

Tan, Kai Syng. 2016c. "RUN! RUN! RUN! BIennale 2016 CURATORIAL FRAMEWORK." *RUN RUN RUN Biennale* (blog), October 19. http://kaisyngtan.com/r3fest/2016-curatorial-statement/.

Tan, Kai Syng. 2016d. *RUN RUN RUN Biennale Flyer (Overview)*. http://kaisyngtan.com/r3fest/.

Tan, Kai Syng. 2016e. "What Has Running Got to Do with Our Divided World? – RSA." *Royal Society of the Arts Blog* (Blog). November 16. https://www.thersa.org/discover/publications-and-articles/rsa-blogs/2016/11/what-has-running–got-to-do-with-the-migrant-crisis.

Tan, Kai Syng, and Simon Cole. 2016. *LONDON Leg: Pop-up Warm-up Event*. http://kaisyngtan.com/r3fest/2016-london/.

Tykwer, Tom. 1999. *Run Lola Run*. Germany: Sony Pictures.

Virgin Money London Marathon. 2017. "06 the Mass Event." http://london-marathon.s3.amazonaws.com/vmlm2014/live/uploads/cms_page_media/206/6.%20The%20Mass%20Event.pdf.

Volley, Jo, and Henrietta Simson. 2014. Running Map. Iron gall ink, silver and gold pigment bound in gum arabic on BFK Rives paper. http://kaisyngtan.com/r3fest/our-first-run/.

Wheatley, George. 2015. *A Visit (in 1831) to Jeremy Bentham*. University College London. http://discovery.ucl.ac.uk/1462164/1/wheatley.pdf.

Whelan, Gregg. 2017. "Run It by Me", March 3. https://www.pressreader.com/uk/runners-world-uk/20170303/281642484901246.

Wray, Katie. 2014. "Are We Becoming a Nation of Runners?" *BBC*, November 30, sec. England. http://www.bbc.co.uk/news/uk-england-30036800.

Contemporary physical activities: the aesthetic justification

Matti Tainio 🔟

ABSTRACT

The customary view of today's recreational physical activities turns the human movement into a rational practice that is pursued for practical reasons only: for health, vitality, stamina and longevity. This prevalent point of view affects the understanding of the ends, content and quality of physical activities and it creates a bias where the biological, physiological and medical characteristics of physical activities are emphasized while the sensuous, experiential and creative aspects are suppressed. This results in a partial understanding about the significance of human movement in contemporary culture. The article analyses the reasons for this distorted view of physical activity and formulates a rationale for the aesthetic justification for the contemporary way of being active. In addition, the article explores on the role of the (aesthetic) experience in contemporary physical activities as well as examines the possibilities of change the aesthetic justification can provide the physical activity.

Introduction

My everyday physical activity is distance running. When I am running through a landscape, be it urban or rural, I feel that I am engaged in an aesthetic activity. I can enjoy the environment visually as well as hearing and smelling it. I can feel the warmth of the sun or the sting of the freezing wind. I feel my feet working rhythmically and I can feel the structure of the ground through the thin soles of my shoes. I feel my heart pounding and my lungs gasping in air. I can feel my clothes moving against my sweating skin. I do not think much, but my senses are open, and I often have a good time.

When I read popular articles about sport or discuss doing recreational physical activity with other hobbyist participants, I notice mentions of the aesthetic qualities of the activity, but they are mainly just passing remarks of feelings, experiences and environment. Even though people actively participating in physical activities seem to enjoy exertion in an aesthetic manner, they do not express it directly, but in a hidden, indirect way. Instead, the emphasis is on other aspects of the activity; there is plenty of talk about distances, heart rates, speed, calories, health benefits, results, rankings and progress. Most of them are things you can quantify or reduce to statistics. It seems that the enjoyment is treated as just a side-effect of physical activity, while its work-like and health-related qualities are appreciated as a reason for movement. There must be some reason why the sensuous and aesthetic in sport and other physical activities are not valued as a justification for being active or expressed as a reason for activity.

The promotion and justification of today's mainstream recreational physical activity is done in a manner that turns human movement into a rational practice that is pursued for practical reasons only: to become or stay healthy, for vitality, stamina and longevity. These are also the arguments the national authorities both in my native Finland and elsewhere in affluent countries use to persuade inactive people to exercise. For instance, a statement by the National Sport Council in Finland before municipal elections in 2017 emphasized the rational health-related and economic justifications for being active (Valtion liikuntaneuvosto 3. Mar 2017). Using this type of rhetoric affects the understanding of the ends, content and quality of physical activities. My argument is that it has created a bias where the biological, physiological and medical characteristics of physical activities are emphasized, and the sensuous, experiential and creative aspects present in them are suppressed. Focusing on physical well-being and social utility in physical activity has beneficial effects, but it obscures other advantageous aspects of it. The result is partial understanding about the significance of human movement in contemporary culture.

However, embracing the subjective experiences and taking into account their aesthetic quality expands the meaning of the physical activities. Recognising the importance of experience is assisted by taking into account some recent developments in aesthetics: firstly, the scope of contemporary aesthetics has expanded beyond art and artistic (Welsch 1997); and secondly, the recent development of pragmatist aesthetics has introduced individual experience as the origin of aesthetic analysis (Shusterman 1997). Acknowledging the aesthetic aspects of physical activity produces new connotations for it (e.g. Martin 2008) and can consequently make it meaningful and attractive in a novel way both for those who are already active and those who are passive because they find the current ideals of physical activity discouraging.

The distorted understanding of physical activity can be traced to various origins. One, and perhaps the most important source, can be linked back to the emergence of modern physical practices in the late eighteenth and early nineteenth centuries. The ideals that were present during the development of German gymnastics and modern sport in England still influence understanding of physical activity in the twenty-first century (Pfister 2003). The second significant reason for the biased conception of physical activity is the hegemony of modern achievement-oriented and competitive sport over other physical practices during the twentieth century. The quantified objectives of sport assisted the development of scientific coaching and sport sciences that employ methods borrowed from natural sciences for improving measurable sporting results. The resulting conception of humans as machine-like beings is still apparent in contemporary physical activities.

In order to illustrate the consequences of the described biased conception, this article examines the field of contemporary physical activities by analysing the historical origin of various justifications for physical activity and the relations between contemporary aesthetics and physical activity. The analysis of those justifications shows the impact of early conceptions on the understanding of physical activity today as well as how the justifications affect actual practices. The exploration of relations between physical activities and aesthetics provides a new perspective on the condition of physical activity in contemporary culture.

The resulting presentation of the current situation reveals how the field of physical activity is detaching from its legacy and how various physical traditions have recently been intertwined, forming a new concept of human movement.

Current landscape of physical activities

In affluent western societies, participation in physical activities has become enormously popular and at the same time more personally adjustable than ever before. There are more activities to choose from and more individual flexibility to determine the content of activities. When current physical activity is observed from a distance, achievement-oriented sport seems to define the field. Closer analysis shows that contemporary physical activities have largely departed from this tradition. The shift has been hard to see because of the dominance of sport: the variety of physical activities have been interpreted through the concept sport. Assessing activities through sport-related concepts – achievement and (personal) records, constantly measuring the performance and the use of terminology inherited from sporting tradition – tends to obscure other relevant approaches to physical activity. In addition, the organizational structure established to support sport has an impact on understanding aspects of contemporary physical activities.

However, if competitive, elite and professional sport practices are left aside, the landscape of contemporary physical activities changes: instead of unity, there is a plurality. Instead of one culture of sport, there are various approaches to human movement. Moreover, the boundaries between practices have become fluid, allowing movement between different physical traditions as well as the emergence of different objectives and inclinations within existing practices (Kreft 2008; Tainio 2015). Even though sport is still the dominant format for various hobbyist activities and exercise, it is not leading their development. Diverse practices descending from other modern physical activities as well as practices adopted from outside western culture play an important part in the development of everyday physical activities. In addition, recent lifestyle activities with *post-sport* orientation have brought new ideas to the contemporary landscape of physical activity. Parkour and skateboarding are typical examples of these activities, but similar post-sport orientation can be found in more traditional sports (Atkinson 2010a). Together, these various approaches shape the current concept of physical activity and give new meanings to it (Tainio 2015).

Transformation of physical activities: the shift away from the hegemony of sport

Today, physical activity is a significant part of the contemporary lifestyle, but only a few decades ago the situation was rather different: even though the emergence of sport made physical activity a culturally and socially important part of life in western cultures during the early twentieth century, for most of the century a physically active lifestyle was not a widespread phenomenon in affluent western societies. The emergence of a different, more active lifestyle began during the 1960s and the real turning point took place in the seventies along with the development of jogging and the first running boom.

The development of jogging exemplifies the subtle change. The basic physical practice did not transform, but the shift in the concept of physical activity was significant. (Latham 2013) Although jogging was developed to improve health, it had unpredictable effects on contemporary physical activities: jogging formed a model for later self-directed exercise practices as well as a model of the free social organization of individuals engaged in the same physical practice: the joggers formed a tribe. In addition to this, jogging provided stimulation for the idea of using creativity in the context of a physical practice by encouraging joggers to employ public space, streets and parks for their exercise. Physical activity does not have to be confined to special spaces, but can make use of urban space and be visible to others. Furthermore, this transformation made it possible to see physical activity as a personal expressive act: exercise that was not confined by rigid rules could be used for physically exploring personal potentials and inclinations. The free-form organization of jogging can be seen as a forerunner of today's physical practices with a rhizomatic structure, lacking an obvious centre or leader, an official organization or structure (Daskalaki and Mould 2013).

Contemporary standardization of movement: aerobics and the development of commercial physical activities

Another significant trend in the field of contemporary physical activities is the industrialized development of fitness programmes. The modern fitness industry has existed since the early twentieth century (Featherstone 1995), but it did not become mainstream until the 1980s, when aerobics experienced a boom after Jane Fonda started to promote her exercise system by selling the instructions on video tapes (Markula 1995). Since aerobics, similar supervised exercise programs have evolved under various trademarks (Parviainen 2011).

Despite the commercial priorities, heavy standardization (Parviainen 2011) and the limited conception of an ideal body, these fitness programs have induced a significant transformation in women's physical activity. Aerobics classes became a site where being sweaty and out of breath is approved. Even though the body image promoted in contemporary fitness classes is limited, they have expanded the standards for female bodies: being thin is not the only approved option; one can be also 'toned' or even muscular (Markula 1995).

Focus on experiences: post-sport practices

The emergence of post-sport practices into the mainstream forms the third major shift that has contributed to the transformation from modern sport toward the current field of physical activity (Wheaton 2004). While giving less importance to quantifying the activity, post-sport practices emphasize creativity, a playful attitude and exploration of the environment through physical activity. The concept of achievement and the quest for excellence are present in post-sport activities, but instead of quantified figures they are seen as personal improvement that cannot be compared with the development of others. In addition, achieving excellence requires a creative contribution. In order to combine creativity and achievement, the attitude toward standardization and rules differs from that of sport. Practising post-sports involves an imperative of creativity; it is not possible to excel by copying others, one has to develop something original to reach excellence (Beal 1995).

The substance of physical activities

Unlike art, modern physical activities are not valued for themselves. Since the emergence of modern physical activities in the early nineteenth century, they have been connected to various aims external to the practice itself, in order to justify the time and energy spent.

The most common justifications employed morally based arguments that connected physical activity with health, character-building (e.g. manliness), becoming a proper citizen, nationalism and later preparation for the demands of working life. In addition, physical activities have been seen as a form of education and thus able to improve resilience and operate as a means of personal transformation. These arguments were common in both nineteenth century German gymnastics and English sport, and traces of them can still be found in contemporary sporting and exercise practices (Pfister 2003).

Today, the dominant justification of regular exercise is health benefits (Eichberg and Loland 2009). This is used to validate the majority of activities, exercise programmes and dietary choices. Although health was a significant paradigm in all modern physical activities, it has become a more important validation of physical activity since the late twentieth century (O'Donovan et al. 2010), as the other justifications associated with physical activity (manliness, discipline, morality and nationalism) have lost their value as a consequence of social changes during the last decades of the twentieth century. Furthermore, the rise of contemporary recreational exercise practices has eroded the values previously connected with organized physical activities (Atkinson 2010b).

The justifications used in the promotion and validation of physical activity influence its content as well as build its meanings; while the conventional justifications promote the beneficial effects of exercise, they also suggest a narrow model for understanding human movement leaving little margin for individual variation. Emphasizing some aspects and benefits of an activity obscure others that promote other kinds of consequences. Both the emphasized and concealed aspects of sport can be beneficial, but advocate different values.

During recent decades, experience has developed into an important objective and content of physical activity. The idea of an experience as a yardstick for an activity arose first in connection with post-sport activities, which took a more adventurous and risk-taking attitude toward physical activity than previous practices. Moreover, these activities were not guided by detailed rules and thus were more open to personal expression.

The approach emphasizing experiences forms a distinct departure from the old ideals and is today transforming the landscape of physical activities as a whole. This approach that originated within post-sports is adopted by participants of other, more traditional activities, thus contributing to separation of the ideals of modern sport (Atkinson 2010b; Wheaton 2010; Tainio 2015). The actual shift is hard to detect by observing the activities themselves; however, the phenomenon becomes visible in the social media presentations, where the exercises are shared in the form of photographs and written reports. These reports constantly focus on the experience and give less consideration to the results, fitness and health effects. Despite the interest in experiences, their content is mostly left unexplained; when the experiences and the excitement gained through an activity are reported, their quality usually remains unexplored. The reports can be detailed and accurate, but the analysis of experience seldom goes beyond the descriptive. Furthermore, the experiences and enjoyment are regularly explained as physio-biological phenomena (e.g. Boecker and Dishman 2015), where the activity is seen as a catalyst that triggers a biological event that produces certain bodily feelings and consequently enjoyment.

The existing justifications and promotional goals of physical activity do not explain why human movement is interesting and worth pursuing. Knowledge about the benefits of a physical activity for health or the development of personal qualities cannot be the only reason to engage in it. Certainly, activities are undertaken because of expectations of becoming healthier, losing weight or gaining muscle, but are these reasons to pursue the activity in the long term? My view is that the activity must produce some other benefits that are not directly linked to the initial goals. The old justifications do not answer this. Here, the recent justification of activity through experiences and their aesthetic qualities gives a more promising starting point. Exploring the character of the experiences and the source of excitement through physical activity can reveal more complex reasons for being active: reasons that have an aesthetic character.

Aesthetics and physical activity

The historical legacy and prevalent understanding about the meaning of physical activities explain the absence of the aesthetic in human movement. Even though experiences in physical activity have recently been emphasized, their connection with the aesthetic has not been elaborated. My question here is: how would the conception of physical activities change if its aesthetic aspects were deliberately given more emphasis? My view is that emphasizing the sensuous and aesthetic features in human movement would enhance the meaning of contemporary physical activities by expanding their framework outside the tradition of sport and fitness practices. The importance of physical, health and social benefits will not suffer from the wider perspective on physical activity; however, their meaning will gain new dimensions from the expanded view.

When aesthetics is understood in its contemporary sense as sensuous knowing instead of connecting it with the perceivable qualities of art and beauty, the discipline becomes an important vehicle for understanding the content of physical activity. Consequently, aesthetics can be connected with all the aspects that make physical activity attractive, interesting and worthwhile. From the aesthetic perspective, health is just a positive by-product of the activity, not the ultimate goal. The other established justifications for physical activity have even less importance. Aesthetics opens a view onto physical activity as part of a good life where the path travelled is more important than the goals promised and achieved.

Aesthetic experience and physical activity

In most cases, the aesthetic experience in contemporary physical activity is neglected – the experiences are presented as if a connection between the experience and the aesthetic would not exist. This can be seen in the manner physical activity is presented in social media. I follow various groups on Facebook connecting hobbyist athletes in Finland. The typical activity is sharing images and short reports about exercise, particularly when the experience has been a special one. These images can be landscapes picturing the site, anything between the great views or the wet snow, or they can be selfies showing exhaustion or the frosty gear after outdoor exercise in the Nordic winter. The verbalization of these Facebook postings do not describe the experience in depth, but express the feeling in the moment: 'First jog this year! Finally, the weather wasn't too freezing and even I could survive outside. However, the snowy landscape made my run' (post in Facebook group Kestävyyttä pintakaasulla 24/7 January 17 2016).

Even though the messages reveal little about the quality and content of the experience, they reveal the importance of the aesthetic enjoyment as part of the activity. However, employing rational reasons makes engaging in an activity more substantial than referring to plain enjoyment. The descriptions often show signs of the traditional sport ethos by reporting the measured statistics of the exercise. People seem to enjoy the experiences for their aesthetic aspects, but still justify them through achievement and health.

As early as 1934, John Dewey advocated the connection between aesthetics and understanding the surrounding world, where the bodily connection with the world formed the basis for the aesthetic experience. For Dewey, the apex of aesthetic experience was art as an experience, not as a separate category ([1934] 2005). Contemporary studies see the connection between the aesthetic and the understanding of the surrounding world as even more solid and inescapable: the only way of perceiving the world is through our senses, thus the experiences always have an aesthetic nature.

For instance, German philosopher Wolfgang Welsch sees that our understanding of the world is constructed through aesthetics: our senses operate as the only means of obtaining information about the world, and primary judgments about it are made by employing aesthetic means. The fundamental understanding of reality is based on aesthetic thinking, not immaterial processes of thought. Since all the solid foundations for absolute knowledge and moral choices that were previously provided by religion have been exhausted alongside the development of modern European culture, the aesthetic judgement of singular events is the only way to decide the correct action: the world as a whole is changeable, suspended and produced. It cannot be confined by a solid set of rules (1997).

The cognitive sciences support a similar view: George Lakoff and Mark Johnson have explored the bodily basis of our thinking and connected it with our sensorimotor experiences of the environment. According to them, even the most abstract ideas and subjective experiences are based on our physiology and the way it connects to the surrounding environment. 'Our concepts cannot be a direct reflection external, objective, mind-free reality because our sensorimotor system plays a crucial role in shaping them.' (1999, 44); our body and its senses inevitably define our conception of the world (ibid).

These views provide a new basis for the aesthetics of physical activity. It does not need to be related to the surface level, to beauty or artistic qualities, but to general awareness of the activity in all its dimensions: How is the activity felt? What kind of experiences does it produce? How does it change the way one experiences the world? What is the effect of the environment and company while physically active? Is it important what the activity looks like and how it matters? The sensuous connection between the moving body and its surrounding environment can be seen as the central subject matter when linking physical activities and aesthetics. Yet, this is not visible in the discourse about contemporary physical activities.

In the context of contemporary physical activities, employing the aesthetic experience opens the first person view onto a specific practice. Concentrating on personal aesthetic experiences makes it possible to recognize and analyse the multiple perspectives that are present and constantly changing in physical activity. The basic level of contact with the world is through the sensing body that feels the ground under the feet, the pounding heart, the air flowing into the lungs as well as the wind cooling the skin. This somatic level forms the foundation that affects all other levels of experience. It is also the level that is recognized when the bodily feelings in and after active movement are detected. Unlike the current manner of superficial commenting on experiences in movement and their mistaken recognition as just physiological reactions, this *somaesthetic* approach gives tools for the more refined analysis and practical study of physical activity in the context of applied aesthetics.

Awareness of the experience can be expanded from the direct corporeal experience in various directions. Firstly, there is the environmental experience that is constantly present in physical activity. Despite its presence, its role can vary from indifferent to crucial, depending on the practice. Engaging in a competitive activity does not shut off the environmental relation, even though it can dilute it. In a recreational activity, one can approach the environment consciously and observe it in a more detailed manner. There is no real reason why one could not stop to enjoy the scenery or smell the forest. However, many of the habits present in contemporary physical activity contribute to a muted connection with the experienced environment: wearing headphones during activity and exercising in a gym constructs a private environment that cannot be shared. On the other hand, there are activities that highlight the environmental context. Many outdoor activities search for novel ways to experience the urban environment: skateboarders look for new spots to explore the environment through the board; snowboarders build ridable features in parks and industrial areas in order to experience their activity in an environment; and running events are organized in the night in order to experience urban nightscapes (Tainio 2015).

When other people are involved in the activity, the aesthetic experience has a social dimension (Berleant 2005). The human companion or the human opponent affect the experience. When pursuing an activity with someone, the experience becomes shared, which can amplify highlights or smooth negative encounters (Kupfer 1983). An experience becomes better articulated through the process of sharing. On the other hand, a living opponent turns an activity in a more unpredictable direction, it becomes a drama. The outcome is uncertain even when the contest is a friendly one. The unpredictable nature of this kind of activity makes the aesthetic experience more complex (Kreft 2012).

The perspective of everyday aesthetics is also relevant when analysing the aesthetics in physical activities, especially in the context of recreational practices. Being physically active regularly forms a diversion from everyday tasks, but it is still part of everyday life. Involvement in physical activity adds to the everyday experiences. Kupfer (1983) links the benefit of physical activity to those everyday moments when one suddenly finds a connection to the best moments of physical activity when casually jumping over a puddle or gracefully slipping into an overcoat. These do not present the finest examples of human motion, but their connection to the experiences gained during physical activity enhances our appreciation of them.

The connection between the experiences of physical activity and everyday life also has other consequences. Anderson (2001) sees physical activity as a site of creativity that can reveal our human agency and shift the manner in which we act in our everyday life. This shift can take place even though one does not approach physical activity from an aesthetic perspective, but a conscious awareness of the sensuous aspects of activity makes it more probable. For both Kupfer and Anderson, the variation between everyday tasks and freedom in physical activity is key to the positive changes movement can generate.

Play and good life

Friedrich Schiller's ideas about the significance of aesthetics in human life can be used as a starting point for elaborating the positive consequences of an aesthetic view on physical activity.

Schiller ([1794] 1982) saw that the problem in his time was the dominance of *utility*: disproportionate interest in practical and measurable values leads to a partial life, which can be cured through aesthetic education. His remedy for the imbalance is *play*, which he suggests to be at the heart of humanity: 'he is only fully a human being when he plays' (107).

According to Schiller ([1794] 1982), two opposite forces, *drives*, affect human life. First, there is the *sensuous drive*, an inclination to focus on unique cases and their materiality and the change in the very moment. Second, there is the rational *formal drive*, visible in the concentration on utility and truth. Undue concentration on either makes the man incomplete. However, in the space expanding between the sensuous and formal drives resides the *play drive* that combines the best of sensuous and formal drives and limits their extremities. The play drive extends the qualities of the person further than concentration only on the formal or sensuous drive alone can. However, it is hard to find an equilibrium and maintain the play drive. The balance is always transient; there is tension that draws the person toward the extremities. The importance of play lies in its ability to connect the two other drives, make the person complete and open him/her up to the beauty of life: supporting the art of living and forming a foundation for the good life.

Contemporary scholars exploring aesthetics in sport and other physical activities have ended-up with similar conclusions, although in a narrower field: physical activity can form a significant part of a good life if it is understood as an aesthetic activity. Being physically active and free from everyday duties is regularly justified by its utilities, but the benefits can be more extensive when play element is included in the activity. To achieve this aim, undue seriousness and concentration on benefits external to the activity itself should be constrained. When an activity is found interesting and worthwhile, the enjoyment should be found in the activity itself, not through its external ends. Successfully balancing the utilitarian ends and free bodily enjoyment allows the play element to be manifested in an activity.

Richard Shusterman brings the body to the centre of aesthetics with the concept of somaesthetics that focuses on the aesthetics of bodily existence: 'Somaesthetics can be provisionally defined as the critical, meliorative study of the experience and use of one's body as a locus of sensory-aesthetic appreciation (aisthesis) and creative self-fashioning' (1999, 302). Somaesthetics combines the analysis of bodily consciousness with practical somaesthetic exercises that provide tools for exploring one's own connection with the world (Shusterman 2008). When viewed through somaesthetics, physical activity can be seen as ameliorative and creative self-expression. Shusterman does not discuss the field of sport-related physical activities, but his philosophy of the living body and the way it conveys information about itself and the bodily connection with the outside physical world provides foundations for the analysis of the aesthetics of contemporary physical activities.

Kupfer (1983) says that physical activity creates time and space which everyday duties do not reach. The importance of aesthetics in physical activity is linked to the nature of our everyday lives. It is a place where we are free 'to act for the sake of enjoyment of the activity' (114). According to Kupfer, there is an implicit aesthetic deprivation in our everyday life, causing a feeling of dissatisfaction. Openness to the aesthetic and concentration on felt experiences brings us into better contact with our bodies and expels the 'disembodiment of modern life' (118). Engaging in a physical activity with an aesthetic approach can relieve the tensions of modern life by providing new bodily perspectives for confronting reality. Competitive sport can generate similar results: the intensity of effort in a contest may bring out the best in the participants – creating new and unforeseen aesthetic experiences.

Anderson (2001) regards participation in physical activity as humanizing, since it creates a margin where one can take risks and act spontaneously and connect with ourselves in a self-defining manner that is not possible elsewhere. Being active creates room for physical creativity and, furthermore, allows us to express 'controlled wildness' (144). However, these aspects are more likely to emerge if the participants are open to the aesthetic potential of the activity. Any activity can be dull and mechanical if the external goals, the utility of it, become more important than being receptive to the experiences it offers. Moving an activity away from the mechanical and quantitative model requires adopting habits that connect the activity back to our ordinary experiences.

According to Kreft (2012), at the centre of the aesthetics of being physically active is the participants' aesthetic experience – 'the sensitive openness and receptiveness' – where they can feel the fullness of life (223). The appeal of the activity is important for its aesthetics values: the participation is voluntary, because the activity is 'existentially challenging and aesthetically attractive' (232). The key to the unique aesthetic experiences in physical activity is the variation between playfulness and seriousness. Being active and trying one's best is serious activity, but at the same time the participants are aware that serious activity exists within play.

Instead of associating physical activity firstly with health or achievement, the views just discussed connect it with corporeal openness, enjoyment and creativity. Moreover, they see participating in an activity as a source of aesthetic experiences that produce positive effects on the quality of everyday life. Emphasizing the aesthetic aspects does not eliminate the health effects or the idea of achievement in physical activity. Health effects exist, even though the objectives of physical activity changes, however they cease to be the central reason for being active. Also, achievement, the key concept of modern sport, is implicitly present in all the texts referred to above, but not as the intrinsic objective of the activity, but as a means for aesthetic experiences: trying one's best can bring one to an area where new experiences become possible.

Reconstruction of the substance of physical activities

The experiences pursued in physical activity do not need to be extreme. Ryynänen (2015) makes a theoretical exploration of a similar phenomenon in contemporary art, where the extreme uses of body are emphasized and moderate bodily acts disregarded. According to his critical analysis of various works of art, concentration on extremes causes a bias in the use of the body. In order to adjust and balance the situation, Ryynänen points out how ordinary acts are employed in an artistic setting and how they can be more valuable than breaking boundaries by extreme actions. Instead of shocking the audience, an artist can show examples and use their body in a way achievable for everyone and contribute to positive changes in society.

In a similar manner, the extreme physical acts in sport that stretch our conception of human capability have very little to do with mundane physical activity. The concept of achievement calls for a new mode of operation that values moderate acts instead of extremes. Building a connection between achievement and experiences is the key element in shifting physical activity in this direction, and therefore the concept of achievement requires reorientation: it should be seen as a wider evaluation of the quality of physical experiences, thus emphasizing the experiences of the masses rather than the talented.

The quality of experience should be the main objective for recreational activity, but in an expanded view. Increasing the magnitude of experience is not the only way to enhance the quality of experiences. The same goal can be reached by the expansion of one's skills and abilities, for instance exploring new running routes and enjoying the new views, or trying out orienteering instead of a regular run. For an older athlete, whose performance is declining, it can be a change of perspective, learning to appreciate more subtle experiences and the finesses of the ordinary instead of the extreme. No measurable results are needed, but a shift in the viewpoint that revitalizes the activity and gives it new kind of substance.

The concept of achievement has already changed within recreational sports and exercise: the results are still quantified, but the position in a competition is less important. Most recreational athletes compete against themselves and their previous results instead of the other participants in the race. In team sports, the nature of activity is different, but especially in recreational contests, a good game can be more meaningful than the result (Naukkarinen 2011). A dramatic and even struggle has a greater aesthetic density and it produces more varied experiences than an overwhelming victory. Moreover, here the aesthetic experience has an obvious social dimension, where the purpose emerges from meeting other enthusiasts and struggling together with them (Kupfer 1983).

Post-sport practices have developed their own standards concerning performance and achievement even further. These activities emphasize skill, but with creative input. Skateboarders' achievements will not reach perfection if they are not showing signs of creativity. People can enjoy their practice without creative input, but the standard that requires originality creates pressure to try new approaches and explore the limits of the practice. This kind of achievement cannot be measured: it is recognized by comparing one's creativity with known tricks, locations and styles, and finally it is proved through the respect of others involved in the activity. (Beal 1995; Rannikko and Liikanen 2015)

Besides achievement, the substance of physical activity requires a wider perspective. In the first place, contemporary physical activity should be understood as being in connection with practices that reside outside the traditional frame of sport and exercise. Acknowledging these connections will add diversity to the meanings physical activity carries. Some activities are already connected to various dissonant practices and can exemplify the transformation that results from a wider perspective. For instance, walking is a sport, but much more often something else. The meanings walking carries, vary when it is connected to pilgrimages, wars and expeditions, city-life or demonstrations. Furthermore, a walk can be a social stroll in the city or a pilgrimage of hundreds of kilometres, which again carry different connotations. As a result, walking has served as inspiration for philosophy, poems, essays, travelogues and manifestos (Solnit 2001). All these aspects formulate the conceptual content of walking and subsequently affect the practice itself.

When the impact of the remodelled concept of achievement and the wider perception of the meaning of physical activity is used to place physical activities in a relation with contemporary culture, a variety of new perspectives on physical activity will be opened up. The new concept of achievement is already visible in various activities and the innovative uses of physical activity outside the concept of sport are emerging both autonomously and through active development. For instance, today's running practice has inspired various innovative applications: participants in the *GoodGym* organization (GoodGym: https://www.goodgym.org/) combine their running exercises with doing errands for older people and people with disabilities, while barefoot running forms counter-movement to today's high-tech filled running culture (Bajič 2014). Changes of this kind in the concept of physical activity broaden its field and create original meanings for it.

Creative acts in physical activity

Creativity in physical activity involves exploring the possibilities of physical activity determined by the limits of personal potentials and inclinations. Playful and creative experimentation can bring new ingredients into an established practice. This involves looking for new perspectives on the practice, perspectives that abandon the paradigmatic idea of the activity and still retain the essence of it. Stretching the limits of a practice change it, but still keep it recognizable. It is also possible to use creativity in ways that are not predefined or in conflict with the established idea of the practice. This kind of stretching the limits of the practice can lead to the development of a new practice. Some contemporary art projects have employed and emphasized the possibilities of creative acts in physical activity. However, the objective of these intentionally artistic endeavours (for instance *Great North Run Culture*: www.greatnorthrunculture.org and *Run! Run! Run! Biennale*: http://kaisyngtan.com/r3fest/) reaches further into the field of the art proper than the creative experimentation in ordinary physical activity (Tainio 2017).

In some physical activities, creativity exists as an inherent part of the practice, but there is no reason to refrain from creative actions within the traditional activities. Actually, their seeds are present even in the traditional sports that are practised outside official sport organizations. Eichberg has identified several variants of football that somehow, often in creative ways, differ from the official version of the sport (association football), but are still recognizable as football (Eichberg 2010). In a similar manner, many recreational physical activities have departed from the official sport and developed parallel practices that resemble the sport, but do not conform with the official version. The boundaries between the official activities and their variants are fluctuating; an individual engaged in an activity can participate in competitions that follow the official rules of the practice, but in her exercises adapt the practice according to personal liking. Even though individual athletes can play in both fields, institutions have difficulty in dealing with the new situation (Kreft 2008; Atkinson 2010a).

I started running in my early thirties, because I wanted to keep fit. Today, about fifteen years later, I keep running, because I want my running to guide me to new experiences. My goals have never been precise. However, after a few years of running I aimed at a marathon and today I am thinking about trail running events and plan even longer distances. Nowadays, time has less importance than the overall experience or surviving the route. At the outset I carefully chose the right type of footwear for my feet and gait, but during the past five years I have been adopting a minimalist style, using shoes without suspension and I am planning to give up shoes completely. I have even used my running practice as a tool for making art (Tainio 2015, 220–227, 245–246). All the choices I have made are guided by curiosity and personal inclination, not any rules and regulations. According to traditional thinking, my running is declining, but adapting the practice uncovers new possibilities.

The consequences of the aesthetic attitude toward physical activity

There is a value laden understanding of the meaning of physical activity where the excessive concentration on the utilitarian aspects and emphasis on the external ends of being active produces a narrow concept of physical activity. The narrow concept is visible in the common justifications of physical activity that originate from the nineteenth century and are still used frequently. They affect the perception of the contemporary physical practices by focusing on the benefits external to the activity: health, character building, preparation for the demands of working life and means of personal transformation. This dated understanding hides the wider cultural connections, which participating in physical activity has today and it disconnects human movement from those aesthetic aspects that make being physically active interesting and worthwhile.

Elaborating the potential of aesthetics and emphasizing the possibilities of creativity in physical activities widens the understanding about the field of physical activity in contemporary society and deepens its meanings. Paying attention to the aesthetic qualities present in current physical activities gives people more understanding about the reasons why they are engaged in some practice as well as encouraging them to try activities in order to gain new aesthetic experiences. Sometimes this quest can be seen as an artistic approach.

Including aesthetic aspects as a significant part of physical activity emphasizes experiences different in kind from the current conception of sport and exercise. The result would be a more inclusive physical culture that encompasses a wider range of activities and a wider range of possible experiences. There are serious reasons to connect aesthetics and physical activity – especially in contemporary culture where various forms of human movement are an immovable part of it.

Disclosure statement

No potential conflict of interest was reported by the author.

Funding

This work was supported by the Kone Foundation.

ORCID

Matti Tainio 🆔 http://orcid.org/0000-0001-7105-1460

References

Anderson, Doug. 2001. "Recovering Humanity: Movement, Sport, and Nature." *Journal of the Philosophy of Sport* 28 (2): 140–150. doi:10.1080/00948705.2001.9714609

Atkinson, Michael. 2010a. "Fell Running in Post-sport Territories." *Qualitative Research in Sport and Exercise* 2 (2): 109–132. doi:10.1080/19398441.2010.488020.

Atkinson, Michael. 2010b. "Entering Scapeland: Yoga, Fell and Post-sport Physical Cultures." *Sport in Society* 13 (7–8): 1249–1267. doi:10.1080/17430431003780260.

Bajič, Blaž. 2014. "Running as Nature Intended: Barefoot Running as Enskillment and a Way of Becoming." *Anthropological Notebooks* XX (2): 5–26.

Beal, Becky. 1995. "Disqualifying the Official: An Exploration of Social Resistance through the Subculture of Skateboarding." *Sociology of Sport Journal* 12: 252–267. doi:10.1123/ssj.12.3.252.

Berleant, Arnold. 2005. "Ideas for a Social Aesthetic." In *Aesthetics of Everyday Life*, edited by Andrew Light and Jonathan Smith, 23–38. New York: Columbia University Press.

Boecker, Henning, and Rod K. Dishman. 2015. "Physical Activity and Reward. the Role of Endogenous Opioids." In *Routledge Handbook of Physical Activity and Mental Health*, edited by Panteleimon Ekkekakis, 57–70. Oxford: Routledge.

Daskalaki, Maria, and Oli Mould. 2013. "Beyond Urban Subcultures: Urban Subversions as Rhizomatic Social Formations." *International Journal of Urban and Regional Research* 37 (1): 1–18. doi: 10.1111/ijur.2013.37.issue-1.

Dewey, John. [1934] 2005. *Art as Experience*. New York: Perigee.

Eichberg, Henning. 2010. "Bodily Democracy and Development through Sport – Towards Intercultural Recognition." *Physical Culture and Sport Studies and Research* XLIX: 53–64. doi:10.2478/v10141-010-0016-y

Eichberg, Henning and Sigmund Loland. 2009. "Sport and Popular Movements: Towards a Philosophy of Moving People." *Sport, Ethics and Philosophy* 3 (2): 121–138. doi:10.1080/17511320902981990

Featherstone, Mike. 1995. "The Body in Consumer Culture." In *The Body: Social Process and Cultural Theory*, edited by Mike Featherstone, Mike Hepworth and Bryan S. Turner, 170–196. London: Sage Publications.

GoodGym. 2016. GoodGym Website. Accessed September 16, 2016. https://www.goodgym.org/

Kreft, Lev. 2008. "Martin in the Field." *Sport, Ethics and Philosophy* 2 (1): 71–83. doi:10.1080/17511320801896166.

Kreft, Lev. 2012. "Sport as a Drama." *Journal of the Philosophy of Sport* 39 (2): 219–234. doi:10.1080/00948705.2012.725898.

Kupfer, Joseph H. 1983. "Sport – The Body Electric." Chap. 5 in *Experience as Art, Aesthetics in Everyday Life*, 111–140. Albany: State University of New York Press.

Lakoff, George, and Mark Johnson. 1999. *Philosophy in the Flesh: The Embodied Mind and Its Challenge to Western Thought*. New York: Basic Books.

Latham, Alan. 2013. "The History of a Habit: Jogging as a Palliative to Sedentariness in 1960s America." *Cultural Geographies* 22 (1): 1–24. doi:10.1177/1474474013491927.

Markula, Pirkko. 1995. "Firm but Shapely, Fit but Sexy, Strong but Thin: The Postmodern Aerobizing Female Bodies." *Sociology of Sport Journal* 12: 424–453. doi:10.1123/ssj.12.4.424.

Martin, Christopher. 2008. "John Dewey and the Beautiful Stride: Running as Aesthetic Experience." In *Running & Philosophy: A Marathon for the Mind*, edited by Michael W. Austin, 171–179. Malden, MA: Blackwell Publishing.

Naukkarinen, Ossi. 2011. *Arjen estetiikka* [Aesthetics of Everyday]. Helsinki: Aalto University.

O'Donovan, Gary, Anthony J. Blazevich, Colin Boreham, Ashley R. Cooper, Helen Crank, Ulf Ekelund, Kenneth R. Fox, et al. 2010. "The ABC of Physical Activity for Health: A Consensus Statement from the British Association of Sport and Exercise Sciences." *Journal of Sports Sciences* 28 (6): 573–591. doi:10.1080/02640411003671212.

Parviainen, Jaana. 2011. "The Standardization Process of Movement in the Fitness Industry: The Experience Design of Les Mills Choreographies." *European Journal of Cultural Studies* 14 (5): 526–541. doi:10.1177/1367549411412202.

Pfister, Gertrud. 2003. "Cultural Confrontations: German Turnen , Swedish Gymnastics and English Sport – European Diversity in Physical Activities from a Historical Perspective." *Culture, Sport, Society* 6 (1): 61–91. doi:10.1080/14610980312331271489.

Rannikko, Anni, and Veli Liikanen. 2015. "Taitavuuden hierarkiat vaihtoehtolajien ohjaussuhteissa." [Hierarchies of Skill and the Guiding Relationsships in the Alternative Sports.] In *Liikutukseen asti. Vaihtoehtoliikunta, nuoruus ja erottautumisen mieli* [To the Movement: Alternative Sport, the Youth and the Will to Stand out.], edited by Päivi Harinen, Veli Liikanen, Anni Rannikko, and Pasi Torvinen, 81–87. Jyväskylä: LIKES-tutkimuskeskus.

Ryynänen, Max. 2015. "Throwing the Body into the Fight: The Body as an Instrument in Political Art." *The Journal of Somaesthetics* 1: 108–121.

Schiller, Friedrich. [1794] 1982. *On the Aesthetic Education of Man in a Series of Letters*. Translated and edited by Elizabeth M. Wilkinson, and L. A. Willoughby. Oxford: Clarendon Press.

Shusterman, Richard. 1997. *Practicing Philosophy: Pragmatism and the Philosophical Life*. New York: Routledge.

Shusterman, Richard. 1999. "Somaesthetics: A Disciplinary Proposal." *The Journal of Aesthetics and Art Criticism* 57 (3): 299–313. doi:10.2307/432196.

Shusterman, Richard. 2008. *Body Consciousness*. A Philosophy of Mindfulness and Somaesthetics. New York: Cambridge University Press.

Solnit, Rebecca. 2001. *Wanderlust: A History of Walking*. New York: Penguin.

Tainio, Matti. 2015. *Parallel Worlds: Art and Sport in Contemporary Culture*. Helsinki: Aalto Art Books.

Tainio, Matti. 2017. "Possibilities in Combining Contemporary Art and Sport: An Introduction." In *Proceedings of ICA 2016 'Aesthetics and Mass Culture'*, 70–73. Seoul: Korean Society of Aesthetics.

Valtion liikuntaneuvosto. 2017. "Liikunnalla ja urheilulla terveyttä, hyvinvointia ja elinvoimaisuutta kuntaan." [National Sport Council: Physical Activity Brings Health, Wellfare and Vitaly to Finnish Municipalities.] Published March 3, 2017. http://www.liikuntaneuvosto.fi/files/450/Lausunto_kuntavaalit.pdf

Welsch, Wolfgang. 1997. "Aesthetics beyond Aesthetics: For a New Form to the Discipline." Chap. 4 in *Undoing Aesthetics*, 78–102. London: Sage.

Wheaton, Belinda. 2004. "Introduction: Mapping the Lifestyle Sport-scape." In *Understanding Lifestyle Sports: Consumption, Identity and Difference*, edited by Belinda Wheaton, 1–28. London: Routledge.

Wheaton, Belinda. 2010. "Introducing the Consumption and Representation of Lifestyle Sports." *Sport in Society* 13 (7-8): 1057–1081.doi:10.1080/17430431003779965.

The crusade against 'Foreigners': the Romanian national football team through the eyes of a modernist writer

Cătălin Parfene

ABSTRACT

Established in 1922, the Romanian national football team was composed throughout the interwar period mainly of representatives of ethnic minorities, primarily Hungarians and Germans coming from Transylvanian clubs. The team's status as a national symbol prompted an ardent debate around the squad's Romanianization, which I followed in the discourse of one of the most modernist interwar Romanian writers, the novelist and philosopher Camil Petrescu (1894–1957), present in the country's literary canon as founder of the modern novel. Petrescu's interwar press articles target the Romanianization of the Romanian national football team by removing the representatives of ethnic minorities. Despite the political framework characterized by nationalism, Romanianization and centralization, football's Romanianization eventually failed in the interwar period.

My attempt in this article is to analyze a lesser-known dimension of the intellectual work of Camil Petrescu (1894–1957), the modernist Romanian writer par excellence, present in the Romanian canon as founder of the modern novel: his obsessive plea for the Romanianization of the national football team during the 1930s.

In the introductory part, I will explain the motives behind the bizarre ethnic composition of the Romanian team, connecting it with the political changes after the First World War and also referring to sport as an integral part of culture, to the sport journalism of the period and to the historiography of the problem. In the second part, I will present a sketch of Camil Petrescu's intellectual biography, in the context of the various political ideologies and regimes at the time, and I will follow Petrescu's radical anti-modernist discourse in his activity as football journalist, where his plea for Romanianization was accompanied by attitudes opposed to ethnic minorities and also by presenting Nazi Germany as the model for international football.

What kind of *national* team? A symbol of the nation composed of 'Foreigners'

When our national team entered the arena,
the following recommendation was heard
from all the corners of the stadium:
Hungarian team from the territories stolen by Romania. (Daily *Comedia*, 1927)

Adalbert Ritter, Alois Szilágy, Elemér Hirsch, Dezsö Jakobi, Nicolae Hönigsberg, Francisc Zimmermann, Aurel Guga, Carol Frech, Paul Schiller, Ferenc Rónay and János Auer. One look at this first ever Romanian national football team in history poses a legitimate question for anyone familiar at least with the anthroponyms in central and eastern Europe: 'Was this the *Romanian* national team?' This question is indeed legitimate, since only one of the above-mentioned 11 players present on the football pitch on 8 June 1922, the date of Romania's debut in international football (2–1 in the match with Yugoslavia), had a Romanian name and was an ethnic Romanian, the captain Aurel Guga. When looking further at the football clubs of these 11 players – Chinezul Timişoara (with three players), CA Oradea (with two players), MTK Târgu Mureş, CA Cluj, Haggibor Cluj, CA Timişoara, Universitatea Cluj and AMEFA Arad (each of them with one player) – another question naturally arises: 'Was this perhaps a Transylvanian representation?'. Hoping that a look at the second international match of Romania (1–1 with Poland, on 3 September 1922) might help us in answering the two questions, the picture only becomes more complicated: the new names (Alexandru Szatmári, József Bartha, Sándor Kozovits, Emil Rigolo Koch, Stanislas Micinski, Adalbert Ströck and Zoltán Drescher) and clubs (Stăruinţa Oradea, Unirea Timişoara and Polonia Chernivtsi) that appeared in fact pose a new question if we pretend to forget what had happened four years before, that is the demise of the Austro-Hungarian state: 'Was this perhaps an Austro-Hungarian team?'.

Why did the Romanian national team emerge in 1922 as a team composed mainly of minority players, especially from Transylvania? After Greater Romania was formed in 1918, the incorporation of former Habsburg provinces of Transylvania (Banat and Bukovina) and of the former Russian province of Bessarabia, meant that the percentage of the ethnic minorities rose dramatically. According to the official demographic data, while in the Old Kingdom (before 1918) ethnic minorities comprised 8 per cent of the population, in Greater Romania (after 1918) the percentage rose to 30; even more in some big cities. An urban phenomenon par excellence, football was practised mainly by Hungarians, Germans and Jews, the latter being already Magyarized in Transylvania, that is the specific population of multicultural Transylvanian cities, in which the Romanians were a small minority. The representatives of these communities became Romanian citizens after 1918, hence it was precisely from the above-mentioned province that the international players of Romania were to be drafted in the national team. Another factor that contributed to this Transylvanian monopoly was the weak presence of ethnic Romanians in football in the Old Kingdom, where the players were mostly British, working as industrial or financial functionaries.

Moreover, after 1921 when the national championship of Greater Romania included the teams of the new provinces, the Old Kingdom clubs had little chance of winning the title or playing in finals, which became virtually monopolized by Transylvanian clubs like Chinezul Timişoara (champions in 1922, 1923, 1924, 1925, 1926 and 1927), Victoria Cluj, CA Oradea and Colţea Braşov, that is, 'the distinguished teams which imitated the Hungarians and especially the Austrians' (Economu 1935, 133). During the 1920s, only twice did the Old Kingdom clubs manage to play in the finals: Juventus Bucharest lost in 1926, while Venus Bucharest won the title in 1929, both teams having Hungarian and Austrian players and coaches, and also footballers belonging to the ethnic minorities.

Football became not only a social and urban, but also a mass phenomenon in comparison with other sports:

> By the early 1920s, football had become a popular form of mass culture. Not only had football firmly ensconced itself in the politics of the day, it had gone beyond the realm of sport and politics and become a mass phenomenon of its own. (…) As an integral part of popular culture, football in the 1930s was largely politically and economically driven. (…) [A]lliances were often made that were entirely politically motivated, such as the exclusion of the Central European clubs and national teams from Allied competition. (Marschik 2001, 11, 18)

Prince Carol himself, the future king Carol II, who closely oversaw the establishment of the Romanian national football team in the crucial year of 1922, when his father, Ferdinand I, was officially crowned King of Greater Romania in the Transylvanian town of Alba Iulia, emphasized the superior development of Transylvanian football when compared to the Old Kingdom:

> The sport which became the most popular in our country is football. I was pleased with the occasion of the football match [in Belgrade] (…). Transylvania brought us a considerable contribution in sport. There are sport societies [in Transylvania] whose teams successfully fought with teams from the Occident that have world fame. (…) My dream is to have a stadium. We have cities in Greater Romania that have a stadium, while Bucharest does not. (*Universul*, June 14, 1922)

Moreover, sport was already perceived as an integral part of the very culture itself. Starting from the early 1930s, several titles on sport and arts were published in Romania: *Sport și cultură* (Sport and Culture) (Kirițescu 1932), *Sportul și artele* (Sport and Arts) (Ionescu 1934), *Sportul și teatrul* (Sport and Theatre) (Petrescu 1936b, 378–381). Starting from the premise that art becomes accesible through the human senses, the French philosopher Maurice Nédoncelle later proposed in his *Introduction à l'esthétique* four categories of arts: visual (picture, sculpture, architecture), auditive (music, arts of language), synthetic (cinema, theatre) and tactile-muscular (sport, dance) (Nédoncelle 1953). Among the sports in Romania, football clearly had pre-eminence: for example, in 1927, from the 160 sports associations registered, 140 were football clubs, while in 1934 the 403 football clubs surpassed by far the second-placed tennis and winter sports, each of them with only 52 associations (Manușaride 1986).

Football in Romania was a modern, imported phenomenon, which found a regular place in the anti-modernist discourse of the extreme right newspapers of Octavian Goga, Nichifor Crainic and Nae Ionescu. Given the fact that from its establishment in 1922 the Romanian national football team was composed mainly of players belonging to the ethnic minorities (between eight and ten of the eleven on the pitch), most of them being ethnic Hungarians and coming from Transylvanian clubs, the main issue for those papers was the Romanianization of the team. Basically, it was about the so-called principle of 'numerus valachicus', that is, majority quota for ethnic Romanians in every business and institution, being transposed into the team's composition. The call for this ethnic criterion in establishing the line-up of the national team came mostly from the nationalist segment of the press: *Țara Noastră* ('Our Country') of Octavian Goga, poet, member of the Academy, virulent anti-Semite and extreme right politician, and future prime minister; *Cuvântul* ('The Word') of Nae Ionescu, philosopher and influential figure of the nationalist and far right movement; or *Calendarul* ('The Calendar') of Nichifor Crainic, one of the most influential ideologists of the Romanian extreme right. Soon, even the leftist press and the newspapers disapproving extreme nationalism had to obey the Romanianization trend of the 1930s. 'We have to bow in front of this popular trend', *Rampa* ('The Footlights'), a cultural and democratic newspaper founded by socialist writer N. D. Cocea, noted (*Rampa*, 14 October 1932).

...........Camil Petrescu, whose activity I will detail in the following pages, wrote in both *Ţara Noastră* and *Rampa*. Petrescu's already well-established position as writer and philosopher made him a charismatic figure in the football press of the interwar years (*Gazeta Sporturilor*, 29 December 1933). Nevertheless, other views on sport and football especially were very critical. Nichifor Crainic, writer and philosopher, criticized in a leading article in his newspaper, *Calendarul* ('The Calendar'), not only the ethnic composition of the national team, but also the 'decadence' of sport itself. He gave the negative example of Imre (Emeric) Vogl, an ethnic Hungarian who was Romania's captain at the time, and placed sport in the same category as pornography:

> Romania's team is composed of eight minority players and four Romanians. (…) The soul of the youth is obsessed with sports stars, cinema stars and pornographic readings. (…) Nobody can convince us that the horrible cinema buffoons Laurel and Hardy, or (…) Emeric Vogl are agents of mental cultivation or spiritual education. (*Calendarul*, June 15, 1933)

'The imagined community of millions seems more real as a team of eleven named people', as Eric Hobsbawm put it (Hobsbawm 1992, 143). With the Romanian football national team symbolizing the nation itself and closely overseen in the 1920s by the Royal Family through Prince Carol, the future King Carol II, Romanianization would have been the logical consequence of the constant policy of the post-1918 governments, that is, the replacement of 'foreign' elites with ethnic Romanians (Livezeanu 1995, 14, 18–19). In this respect, I used the position of historians who argued on how the words 'foreign' and 'foreigner' were applied in the Balkans to national minorities (Jelavich 1983, 135–136). However, despite the general view of the nation not as a civic reality, no matter the constitutional stipulations, but as an ethnic project in practice, Romanianization in football remained an issue throughout the interwar period, only to be achieved in the 1950s during the Communist regime.

The academic literature on the topic of Romanianization in football is almost non-existent. The fact is that, like Romanianization itself, this topic is still germane even in today's Romania, and only recently has a young scholar, Bogdan Popa, begun to address the subject, but only tangentially within his broader interest in sports culture in interwar Romania (Popa 2013). Ironically, although written by two representatives of minorities, Chiriac Manuşaride and Chevorc Ghemigean, a book published in the late Communist years about Romanian football and entitled *Aproape totul despre fotbal* (Almost Everything about Football), did not mention a single word about the particular situation of the interwar national football team (Manuşaride 1986)! Also, a book by Mihai Ionescu, pompously entitled *Fotbal de la A la Z* (Football from A to Z), took no notice of it either and used Romanianizing 'tricks' when presenting the representatives of minorities who played for the national team (Ionescu 1984). This is not surprising at all, since the books were published in the 1980s, a period when national(ist) Communism, the ideological viewpoint in Nicolae Ceauşescu's Romania, reached demential dimensions even in football: Romanian players of Hungarian origin had their names Romanianized in the official documents and in the press: Musznay became Mujnai, Kulcsár became Culcear, László Nagy was even translated as Vasile Mare, Székely became Dan Daniel, and so on.

Camil Petrescu and his obsessive plea for Romanianization in football

> Let us hope, as they [the Romanian Football Federation's officials]
> promised, that they will give us a Romanian team. (Camil Petrescu, *Foot-ball*, 1937)

Born in 1894, in Bucharest as a posthumous child, Camil Petrescu fought in the First World War, was wounded twice, taken prisoner by the Hungarians and became half deaf. Afterwards, he studied philosophy in Bucharest and became a renowned novelist, playwright and journalist. After falling in love with several actresses, at the age of 53 he finally married an actress, Eugenia Marian, having two boys with her but divorcing although they kept living together as a family. One of his sons, Camil Petrescu junior, was among the 'rebels' during the Communist regime, introducing West European and American rock music to Romania in the 1960s. When Camil Petrescu died in 1957 in Bucharest, there were rumours saying that he was killed by his ex-wife or that he commited suicide on the hospital bed.

As a young writer, he made his debut in 1914, in *Facla* (The Flame), a leftist publication founded by socialist N. D. Cocea. He continued his literary and journalistic activity in the early 1920s at modernist *Sburătorul* (literally translated as 'The Flying Man', but representing the equivalent of the *Incubus* in Romanian mythology), being intellectually influenced by Europeanists like Eugen Lovinescu and socialists like the above-mentioned N. D. Cocea. However, during the early 1930s he wrote for the daily *Ţara Noastră* (Our Country), an extreme right-wing newspaper founded by the virulent anti-Semite Octavian Goga. It was in the 1930s that he wrote most of his important novels and considered himself the best novelist of the twentieth century, according to his friend Mihail Sebastian, also a writer. With the establishment of King Carol II's dictatorship, Camil Petrescu was appointed to the traditionally political office of Director of the National Theatre in 1939. Nevertheless, following the Communist takeover of the country, he was elected member of the Romanian Academy in 1947 and received several Communist decorations, while his last novel, unfinished because of the author's death, was considered a classical piece of Socialist Realism.

Thus, even this short look at Camil Petrescu's intellectual trajectory shows us a sinuous course from the left to the right and then again to the left, as well as a balance between modernist and anti-modernist postures, all of these making of Camil Petrescu's case one of an ambiguous intellectual. Camil Petrescu's philosophy of nation and political thinking can be traced in his texts published in 1936 under the title *Teze şi antiteze* (Theses and Antitheses), mainly in *Suflet naţional. Analiza descriptivă a termenului* (National Soul. Descriptive Analysis of the Term) and *Despre noocraţia necesară* (About the Necessary Noocracy). His main ideas were elitist, offering an alternative project to 'horrible' liberal democracy and totalitarianism (either Communist or Fascist) alike. The starting point was Plato's idea of noocracy ('power of the wise'), but the main influences came from the so-called French Non-Conformists in the 1930s, who were advocating a 'Third Way' between liberal democracy and Communist or Fascist totalitarianism, where the key word was 'esprit': 'ni droite ni gauche, ni communisme ni capitalisme, ni etatisme ni anarchisme, ni individualisme ni collectivisme, ni idealisme ni materialisme' or 'le "ninisme"', as it was ironically named (Loubet 1998, 228). Emphasizing, however, that this primacy of 'spirit' was characteristic of Nazism and Fascism alike, and even to Liberalism, Camil Petrescu added a 'new coordinate' for 'an original action': the intellect, thus advocating that 'the destiny of the world is to surpass itself through intellectualization' (Petrescu 1936a, 231).

However, the intellectual Camil Petrescu observed with a certain sadness the transition from the theatre culture of the nineteenth century to a sports culture in the twentieth century, the former losing its dimension as a social phenomenon to the advantage of the latter (Petrescu 1936b, 378–381). But at the same time, he encouraged sport, and especially football, by writing articles on this topic and even publishing two magazines, *Football naţional*

(National Football) (1933) and *Foot-ball* (1937). His main idea as a sport journalist was the Romanianization of the football national team, Camil Petrescu being in fact the most prominent name among the initiators of this campaign.

Thus, in 1932 Petrescu was writing under the pseudonym 'Grămătic' (the Romanian term for a medieval scribe) for the daily *Țara Noastră* (Our Country), a newspaper founded by Octavian Goga, poet, member of the Academy, extreme right politician and future prime minister. Here, Petrescu was writing about 'the Romanian representative (not national) team' (*Țara Noastră*, 6 May, 1932a), on how 'it is exaggerated when a team like this is saluted with the Romanian national anthem' (*Țara Noastră*, 12 June, 1932b) or on how 'shameful' it was to shout 'Go Romania!' during the team's matches (*Țara Noastră*, 15 June, 1932c). His solution was a more 'fair' ethnic distribution within the team:

> Poor *Ștefan cel Mare* [Stephen the Great, Prince of medieval Moldavia, 1457–1504] would feel so bad winning with 'Kotormany' [Rudolf Kotormány, Romanian international player of Hungarian origin]. Even more so since we can form a Romanian team, where the minorities should also be well-represented, (Vogl, Glanzmann, Dobay, Steinbach, etc.) and which should have great chances of victory. We believe that Lăpușneanu, Albu, Robe, Ciolac, Sepi, eventually Chiroiu, if not Ghermelie and Baciu also should not be missing from our national team. It is more honourable to lose with them [the ethnic Romanian players] than to win with the others [the minority players]. (*Țara Noastră*, June 15, 1932c)

While this kind of opinion might suggest a compromise by Petrescu in order to satisfy the well-known anti-Hungarian stance of the patron Octavian Goga, the later texts in *Foot-ball* magazine published in 1937 by Petrescu himself, leave no doubt about the sincere embrace of the Romanianization cause by the writer. *Foot-ball. Revistă săptămânală pentru deprinderea 'jocului curat' în sport, artă, literatură, viața socială* (Football. Weekly Magazine for Familiarization with 'Fair-Play' in Sport, Art, Literature, Social Life), as the name shows, dealt only half with football, while the other half comprised pages of 'pure' culture. From the eight pages, the first two contained Petrescu's comments on the national team and the national championship, the next two were composed of international football news and relevant quotes from the Romanian press, while the last four dealt mainly with theatre, literature and literary critique, as well as with Petrescu's harsh polemics against his adversaries, who called him 'Cămilă' (meaning Camel) and whom he in turn called 'greasy', 'viscous', 'stupid', 'imbecile', 'louse', 'ox', and so on.

In pursuit of his goal of Romanianization in football, Petrescu often made a clear distinction between the ethnic Hungarians and the ethnic Romanians, as in the next example:

> In the international matches (...), Baratki (as well as Bodola, another great expert) [Gyula Barátky and Gyula Bodola, Romanian international players of Hungarian origin] IS CHEATING... (...) Instead, Bogdan the bulldog [Ionică Bogdan, Romanian international player of Romanian origin] (...) played honestly as usual and won the match. (*Foot-ball*, October 14, 1937a)

Furthermore, the relevant quotes from the other newspapers were carefully selected and published to sustain the same goal of Romanianization. They were full of praise for the Romanian players of different club teams, and many quotes came from the right and extreme right press: the Iron Guard newspaper *Buna Vestire* (The Annunciation), where Petrescu himself was writing at the time, Pamfil Șeicaru's *Curentul* (The Stream), Stelian Popescu's *Universul* (The Universe), and so on. When an experimental team, entitled Romania B and composed only of ethnic Romanians, was formed for a match against the youth team of Hungary, Petrescu wrote that 'this squad has one great merit, that is, it is Romanian'

(*Foot-ball*, 21 October, 1937b). And with Romania B losing 0–3 against the Hungarian youth team, the writer explained:

> How can one explain the fact that the Romanians of the B team, and the Romanian debutants in the national team in general, always play badly? The answer can only be that they are terrorized by a responsibility which is never imposed upon the minority elements... The men enter the field paralysed by emotion... (*Foot-ball*, November 4, 1937d)

Under different pseudonyms (N. Grămătic, Ion Răscoală), Camil Petrescu was writing almost the whole magazine by himself, being helped by an avant-garde poet in the vein of Saşa Pană, Teodor Scarlat. In this young follower's case, Romanianization acquired delusional dimensions. Scarlat ardently advocated the replacement of the German lithographs represented on the boxes of matches with Romanian paintings:

> [T]he Romanian (?) Anonymous Society which is manufacturing the matches is simply mocking us all. (...) Why are the small boxes of matches illustrated with pictures that do not have anything in common with the past or present life of this people? Why? (*Foot-ball*, November 11, 1937)

If the targets of the Romanianization campaign were mainly the ethnic Hungarian players of the Transylvanian clubs, the addressees were the officials of the Romanian Football Federation, mainly its presidents. In 1932, when its president was Aurel Leucuţia, nephew of Prime Minister Iuliu Maniu and future National-Peasantist minister, later imprisoned by Communists, Camil Petrescu was disavowing Leucuţia's policy:

> Still we cannot accept what the Football Federation's commission is preparing for us. We cannot, under no circumstances, oppose our former allies [France's national team] a team composed of Csincser, Hocksari, Burger, Beke, Rafinsky, Hrechus, Kotormany, Kocsis, Schwarz, Dobay. (*Ţara Noastră*, June 12, 1932b)

The article continued with Petrescu's suggestions for the Federation's officials.

In 1937, the situation was quite similar: the president of the Federation was another National-Peasantist politician, also nephew of Prime Minister Iuliu Maniu, Viorel Tilea. Tilea, future ambassador in London, was very close to King Carol II, being the 'new man' meant to replace 'the old' Maniu in the monarch's political vision, as shown in the memoirs of the politicians Grigore Gafencu (1991, 172–173) and Mihail Manoilescu (1993, 311). Camil Petrescu was again critical towards the new management of Romanian football:

> The Federation once announced, somehow semi-officially, that it would prefer in the future Bucharest players in the national team, because they give more satisfaction at least in Bucharest. (…) Sunday, this Federation introduced in the [national] team two players from Cluj (…). Both of them were catastrophic, they were the direct cause of the defeat. 'Relatively' de-magyarized, the Federation remained fiercely regionalist. Sometimes it exaggerates, like on this Sunday. (*Foot-ball*, October 28, 1937c)

Even when the Federation's experimental team, Romania B, was composed of ethnic Romanians, Petrescu's discourse remained critical, embracing now an anti-regionalist, centralist view by advocating the exclusive presence of Bucharest players in the national team. Some other official regulations made in 1935, like the so-called '8 + 3 formula' (a rule compelling an ethnic quota of eight ethnic Romanians in the line-up of the national team) had disastrous consequences, as Romania did not win any game in the 1935 Balkan Cup. Although officially maintained, in practice the rule fell into disuse. Before the 1938 World Cup qualifying match against Egypt, the writer bitterly noted that '[t]he selected team is composed – with the exception of Dragomirescu and Brandabura [players from Bucharest clubs] – of the same players from the Federation's "old guard" [players from Transylvanian clubs, mainly minorities]' (*Foot-ball*, 18 November, 1937).

Moreover, from the beginining of the 1930s Camil Petrescu had been an ardent supporter of Venus Bucharest (*Foot-ball*, 27 November, 1937e), seen at the time as the Romanian team par excellence and the main rival of the powerful 'irredentist' Transylvanian clubs in the national championship. The same conflicts – ethnic minorities vs. Romanians and regionalism vs. centralization – were transposed into the competition between club teams Ripensia Timişoara and Venus Bucharest, the only two clubs to win the national championship between 1931 and 1940. In fact, Venus was one of the few Old Kingdom clubs which managed to win the title in the interwar period, and it did so by hiring Hungarian players and coaches like Ferenc Platkó (former and future coach of FC Barcelona), József Pozsár, Béla Jánosy (former coach of Újpest Budapest) or Károly Weszter, and by bringing in foreign players who were eventually naturalized as Romanians for the national team, like the Greeks Konstandinos 'Kostas' Humis or Beffa, not to mention the ethnic Hungarian players born in Transylvania. However, it was exactly this distorted 'Romanian' image that made Venus not only the most popular team in the country, but also the club that primarily benefited from the centralization policy, especially with its protector and President Gabriel Marinescu (general prefect of the Bucharest Police and Minister of the Interior, nicknamed 'The Emperor') becoming president of the Romanian Football Federation in 1940.

With the majority of the proponents of Romanianization praising the Fascist Italian model and Mussolini's successful use of sport in general and football in particular in order to construct an imagined national community (Martin 2004, 1–3), Camil Petrescu's football model seemed to be Nazi Germany, where football was developing 'in the general note' of the Nazi state's development, as he wrote in the international football pages of his magazine (*Foot-ball*, 27 November, 1937e). However, Petrescu's dream of having the Romanian national football team composed mainly of ethnic Romanians would become reality only around the time of his death, during the first decade of the Communist regime, when the writer seemed no longer preoccupied with football topics.

Conclusion

First promoted by the Romanian press in the early 1930s, with Camil Petrescu among the fiercest voices, Romanianization in football became institutionalized at the end of the 1930s, in a political framework characterized by the replacement of 'foreign' elites with ethnic Romanians, as part of the big issue of unifying the nation. However, the regulations were hardly respected and, in fact, they were abandoned because of the negative results of the national team. Usually, neither the victories nor the defeats of the national team were Romanian due to the squad's ethnic composition, and as Camil Petrescu decreed, a Romanian loss was more 'honourable' than a victory by the minorities. On the few occasions when the team was 'Romanian', the discourse shifted to anti-regionalism and Bucharest centralism and maintained its critical stance.

On the one hand, the case study of the Romanian national football team is representative of Romanian interwar understanding of nation-building. On the other hand, this case study is a peculiar one due to the failure of Romanianization and centralization, which were the official policies in Romania after the 1918 Great Union. Connected with nation-building were the issues of national representation, modernization, homogenization and ethnic cleansing. Ideally, national representation had to have ethnicity as the main criterion. However, the special conditions in Romanian football led to certain strategies for achieving a more 'equitable' formula of ethnic Romanians' representation in the national team. Transylvania was more urban and industrialized, and had a solid sports culture when compared to the Old Kingdom. Hence, under the direct surveillance of the Romanian Dynasty, the Romanian national team was built mainly on a Transylvanian base in terms of football clubs and players, while the shift to Old Kingdom (Bucharest) and Romanian ethnicity representation was a permanent struggle. Romanianization and a set of restrictive laws and regulations were meant to homogenize the ethnic diversity of the national team and to attenuate the transnational image of the squad. However, compromise and ambiguity were the key words in Romanian interwar football, irrespective of the criticism in the press, where Camil Petrescu, himself a symbol of intellectual compromise and ambiguity, was the key figure.

Disclosure statement

No potential conflict of interest was reported by the author.

References

Crainic, Nichifor. 1933. "Diversiunea sportivă [The Sports Diversion]." *Calendarul*, June 15.

Economu, Virgil. 1935. *Football*. Bucureşti.

Gafencu, Grigore. 1991. *Însemnări politice 1929-1939* [Political Notes 1929-1939]. Bucureşti: Ed. Humanitas.

Grămătic, N. [Petrescu, Camil]. 1932a. "Cronica sportivă. Bocskay-Venus 2-1; Bocskay – Unirea-Tricolor 1-0 [The Sports Chronicle]." *Ţara Noastră* [Our Country], May 6.

Grămătic, N.. 1932b. "Formarea echipei naţionale pentru matchul cu Franţa [The Making of the National Team for the Match against France]." *Ţara Noastră*, June 12.

Grămătic, N.. 1932c. "Echipa românească bate echipa Franţei cu 6-3 [The Romanian Team Wins 6-3 to the French Team]." *Ţara Noastră*, June 15.

Grămătic, N. [Petrescu, Camil]. 1937a. "Comentarii [Comments]." *Foot-ball*, October 14.

Grămătic, N. 1937b. "Comentarii". *Foot-ball*, October 21.

Grămătic, N. 1937c. "Comentarii". *Foot-ball*, October 28.

Grămătic, N. 1937d. "Comentarii". *Foot-ball*, November 4.

Grămătic, N. 1937e. "Comentarii". *Foot-ball*, November 27.

Hobsbawm, Eric. 1992. *Nations and Nationalism since 1780: Programme, Myth, Reality*. Cambridge: Cambridge University Press.

Ionescu, Adrian. 1934. *Sportul şi artele* [Sport and Arts]. Bucureşti: Ed. ONEF.

Ionescu, Mihai. 1984. *Fotbal de la A la Z. Fotbalul românesc de-a lungul anilor* [Football from A to Z. Romanian Football Along the Years]. Bucureşti: Ed Sport-Turism.

Jelavich, Barbara. 1983. *History of the Balkans: Twentieth Century*. vol. 2. Cambridge: Cambridge University Press.

Kiriţescu, Constantin. 1932. "Sport şi cultură [Sport and Culture]" *Educaţie fizică*, 4--5.

Livezeanu, Irina. 1995. *Cultural Politics in Greater Romania. Regionalism, Nation Building, and Ethnic Struggle, 1918–1930*. Ithaca, NY: Cornell University Press.

Loubet del Bayle, Jean-Louis. 1998. "Le mouvement personnaliste français des années 1930 et sa postérité." *Politique et Sociétés* 17 (1-2): 219–237.

Manoilescu, Mihail. 1993. *Memorii* [Memoirs], Vol. II. Bucureşti: Ed. Enciclopedică.

Manuşaride, Chiriac, and Chevor Ghemigean. 1986. *Aproape totul despre fotbal* [Almost Everything about Football]. Bucureşti: Ed. Sport-Turism.

Marschik, Matthias. 2001. "Mitropa. Representations of 'Central Europe' in Football." *International Review for the Sociology of Sport* 36 (1): 7–23.

Martin, Simon. 2004. *Football and Fascism: the National Game under Mussolini*. Oxford, New York: Berg Berg Berg .

Nédoncelle, Maurice. 1953. *Introduction à l'esthétique* [Introduction to Aesthetics]. Paris: Presses Universitaires de France.

Petrescu, Camil, ed. 1936a. "Despre noocrația necesară [About the Necessary Noocracy]." In *Teze și antiteze* [Theses and Antitheses], 215–241. București: Ed. Cultura Națională.

Petrescu, Camil, ed. 1936b. "Sportul și teatrul [Sport and Theatre]." In *Teze și antiteze* [Theses and Antitheses], 378–381. București: Ed. Cultura Națională.

Petrescu, Camil. 1937. "Venus – România". *Foot-ball*, November 18.

Popa, Bogdan. 2013. *Educație fizică, sport și societate în România interbelică* [Physical Education, Sport and Society in Interwar Romania]. București: Ed. Eikon.

Scarlat, Teodor. 1937. "Puncte bune, puncte rele [Good Points, Bad Points]." *Foot-ball*, November 11.

UrbanDig Project: sport practices and artistic interventions for co-creating urban space

D. Chatziefstathiou, E. Iliopoulou and M. Magkou

ABSTRACT

The paper argues that sports and art can compose a common cultural language that operates as a tool for communities to co-create urban space. In particular, we present the research/artistic/community platform 'UrbanDig Project', based in Athens, Greece. The platform employs artistic and sport practices as a means to activate and bridge local communities, collect stories, call for participation and action and finally narrate, re-imagine and even re-construct urban space. We choose to discuss certain moments of the platform's projects, as fruitful examples of its social impact. Within the conceptual framework of the production of space and the sports-art representations, we discuss how sport and artistic practices can intervene in the urban space, map the communities' aspirations and lead to collective decision-making as an alternative grassroots participatory-planning method.

Introduction

The 'UrbanDig Project' (hereafter UDP) is an artistic/research/community platform, developed by the not-for-profit organization 'Ohi Pezoume Performing Arts Company', based in Athens, Greece. Behind the project lies the motivation to compose and present a site-specific performance as a final festive finale of a rigorous period of research and community engagement based on the cultural wealth of certain neighbourhoods. The selected neighbourhoods thus become the setting for the deployment of a systematic and elaborated methodology that allows genuine interaction and involvement of the community and the urban space (both public and private). In this way, the performing arts of theatre and dance exit their typical setting, the theatrical scene and the pre-constructed plot, in order to meet urban space, local communities and physical activity in a real life/material environment. Although primarily an arts-based platform, the UDP's work unfolds through the use of a methodology in which sport is among the key tools used during the projects' development as well as in the final site-specific performances.

The aim of the paper is to demonstrate that sports and the arts can sharply complement each other, intervene and contribute to co-producing urban space. The UDP exemplifies this hypothesis as, through the combination of artistic and sport practice, a common language is created that operates as a tool for communities to co-create urban space.

Sport and the arts

The worlds of sport and the arts are usually separated in approaches of academic inquiry, professional practice or policy development. As a result, the number of sources existing in this field is rather scarce and limited. The most common discussion on sport and the arts is actually whether sport *is* art.

Is sport an art?

As both are characterized from fluidity in their definition and encapsulate multiple dimensions and meanings, some have argued that sport can legitimately be regarded as art. However, as Platchias (2010) has emphasized, this should by no means lead to assumptions that everything could be art or everything could be sport. The conceptual link between the two is mostly drawn on the pronounced parallels they both share such as institutionalization, or the fact that sport and the arts can be performed on stages, or arenas, presented for a public. At a theoretical level, common characteristics between these two concepts mostly refer to the aesthetic and to the artistic (Reid 1970, 1980; Wright 2003; Lacerda 2012; Edgar 2013), as for example in the analysis of Elcombe (2012) who sees in sport the aesthetic experience and in the arts the ideal embodied metaphor. Some theorists argue that sport can be legitimized as art (Wertz 1985; Platchias 2010); others strongly disagree (Best 1985); while others offer a flexible interpretation that in some ways sport is art and in some other ways it is not (Cordner 1988).

Although the debates around the question 'is sport an art?' raises interesting philosophical debates and merits investigation, they are rather abstract and theoretical with little information about the kind of relations that sport/arts allow, (re)produce or constrain. The following non-philosophical discussions found in the literature demonstrate more how these two worlds can intersect and influence each other's spaces.

Sport representation in the arts/arts representation in sport

The edited collection 'Fields of Vision: the Arts in Sport' (Sandle et al. 2013) is one of the limited resources that depict sport-arts representations. Within this publication, Morpeth (2013) expresses his sporting experiences as a fan into artwork such as 'Kick it Out' in order to raise awareness about racial issues in sport. Stansbie (2013) also brings her open-air swimming experiences and narratives into her art (sculpture, photography, drawing and film). Thomas and Stride (2013) analyze the role statues of club heroes play in stadiums for the symbolic identity of the club, the fans' beliefs, culture, etc. O'Mahony (2013) examines how the sporting moment of the Black Power salute in the 1968 Mexico Olympic Games has become a transgressive piece of art featured in the statue erected in their university, the San José State University in California. Long (2013) introduces us to John Innes, 'the Opera Man', who has become part of the match-day entertainment for the British rugby league team Leeds Rhinos. Another intersection of sport and the arts is their use in pedagogy. Adams and Palmer (2013) explore how artistic assessments have helped their sports studies students to think more creatively, while Digby and Stirling (2013) consider the connection between sport and the arts as a unique opportunity for educational interventions that use both the arts and physical movement.

In the Olympic context, Baron Pierre de Coubertin, the founder of the modern Olympics, had seen a deep educational value in the 'marriage between sport and the arts'. Today the Olympic Games constitute one of the most recognizable terrains of both sport and engineered cultural industries (e.g. global iconic stadia, urban regeneration projects; the Cultural Olympiad; cultural opening and closing ceremonies). Chatziefstathiou and Henry (2012) have identified the Olympics as a fluid environment of athletic embodiments which relate to the physical/material moment of perceived space; of ideals and dispositions combining sport, culture and education such as the philosophy of Olympism and the Olympic values, relating to the ideational moment of conceived space; and of spectatorship and community programmes at local, regional, national and international levels, which refer to the moment of lived space. Such a community programme was 'imove' in the lived spaces of Yorkshire as part of the Cultural Olympiad activities in London 2012, aiming to transform peoples' lives through their moving bodies (Gordziejko 2013).

Beyond the Olympics, any event is a terrain of social action and collective behaviour that finds expression in rituals and staged performances (Turner 1969, 1974). Schechner (2003) considers performance as a key process of transformation and that theatre and rituals are influencing social interactions. A community event with its festivities and collective interventions becomes a social space that (re)creates the audience's relations and multiple identities. Although the role of performance and dramaturgy has been explored well from a cultural perspective (Turner 1969; Handelman 1990; Azara and Crouch 2006), it is largely unexplored in the sport events literature. Among the few studies in this field the work by Ziakas and Costa (2010) analyzed how theatre and sport harmoniously co-exist in an event called *Water Carnival*[1] at the rural community of Fort Stockton in north-west Texas.

In this context, we introduce another key factor in the existing debate regarding the art-sports intersection: urban space. As already stated, we argue that sport and the arts can compose a common cultural language that can operate as a tool for communities to co-create urban space. To be more specific, we elaborate on the example of the UDP where the arts and sport create synergies in public discourse with a positive impact on the social capital and community development of the participants. Arts and sport practices are deployed as means to imagine and re-construct urban space. Before entering into the case study itself, we dedicate the next section to our perception of the production of urban space, in order to complete our twofold conceptual framework.

The production of urban space

Space is much more than a concrete three-dimensional model composed by axes, distances and points. On the contrary, it is a system that combines multiple spatial moments: firstly, there is material space, referring to the physical environment that can be quantifiably measurable, which Edward Soja (1996) calls the *Firstspace* linked to Lefebvre's ([1974] 1991) *perceived space*; secondly, there is *Secondspace* or Lefebvre's *conceived space*, referring to the imaginary space of mental constructions 'entirely ideational, made up of projections into the empirical world from conceived or imagined geographies' (Soja 1996, 79); thirdly, there is *Thirdspace*, 'a space of extraordinary openness, a place of critical exchange' (Soja

1996, 5). Lefebvre calls it *lived space*, which is the significant spatial moment of action, lived experience and the 'spatialization' (Shields 1999) of social life.

Introducing this conceptual triad, we underline the need to define a broad umbrella, under which all real and imaginary perspectives of space are dialectically united, producing what Henri Lefebvre would define as a social space:

> [S]ocial space is not a thing among other things, nor a product among other products: rather, it subsumes things produced, and encompasses their interrelationships in their coexistence and simultaneity – their (relative) order and/or (relative) disorder. (Lefebvre [1974] 1991, 73)

Within the urban context, we suggest a *space*, in which social relations are being produced and reproduced, while producing space, in a process, where the production and the product cannot be separated: '[t]he social relations of production have a social existence to the extent that they have a spatial existence' (Lefebvre [1974] 1991, 129).

Verifying the spatial existence of social relations of production, our proposed conceptual approach introduces the *spatiality* of actions, concepts and practices. Spatiality becomes actually an approach to both emerging notions and certain case studies. It is the *spatial approach* that brings to the surface new, yet interesting, aspects of social life, dissociating them from 'the realm of verbalism, verbiage and empty words' (Lefebvre [1974] 1991, 129), in order to give the *image* of what Fredric Jameson (1990) calls the 'unrepresentable' world. On the other hand, spatiality offers critical hints of the production of space itself; space is not produced in a social vacuum by any means. Christian Schmid (2008, 28) puts it precisely: 'space "in itself" can never serve as an epistemological starting position. Space does not exist "in itself"; it is produced'.

Within this understanding, we aim to elaborate on how sport and the arts can sharply intervene and contribute to co-producing urban space. To make our statement clear, we argue that both sport and the arts carry our proposed conceptual triad, as:

(i) they both operate in material space, requiring materiality, or else *physical presence and activity*. The *body* constitutes the vehicle that lets 'appearance manifest reality' (Arendt [1958] 1998, 50), since bodily conditions (labour, pain, etc.) let the individual exit his/her private space towards the public realm;

(ii) they both develop within the realm of imagination, ideals and mental constructions. They both carry the seed of utopia;

(iii) they can both be unique vehicles for community engagement and participatory action, contributing to alternative experiences of urban space and life.

Case study: 'UrbanDig Project'

The methodology

The central philosophy of the UDP is that art can be the sparkle to start improbable encounters and cooperations among stakeholders of a particular area and beyond. Locals (either native or migrants), researchers, academics, artists, shop-owners, public administration representatives, etc. sit round the same table, having a common aim: to unearth bottom-up narratives of the area's past, present and future. Using qualitative research, artistic interventions and community actions, the platform manages to create a large pool of data, open to the community for the creation of multiple outcomes. With respect to qualitative research, different processes include oral history, semi/unstructured interviews, focus groups and mapping processes[2] (historical mapping, aspirations mapping, sensory mapping, skills mapping). Regarding artistic interventions, the platform's artistic team employs quick performances, workshops and especially one-to-one live art in order to collect material in an alternative, entertaining and stimulating way.

Finally, referring to community actions, each project employs neighbourhood festivals, assemblies and collective decision-making processes[3] in order to cultivate a sense of community that shares its stories, aspirations, myths, agonies and desires. The synthesis of these three methodological pillars and their various methodological tools, create different working groups and a rich programme of actions for each project. During the different processes, a large pool of data is being created that leads to three main outcomes: (i) a site-specific performance that operates as a festive finale, (ii) raw and curated material in the hands of the research community, the neighbourhood and broader audience, (iii) material for broader knowledge-sharing, with respect to UDP's cooperation with external partners (e.g. the Municipality, private foundations, etc.). Thus, we have to note that, for UDP, sport is perceived as a palette of activities that require physical labour and embodied expressions and allow interaction.

> Our performances are based on the archive and especially the relations we build in each place we go. These relations are created through collaborations among inhabitants, researchers, students, artists, etc. and activities for all ages and nationalities. We publish all gathered material, we use it for our performances and we support any further initiatives as much as we can. We are mostly interested in the newborn relations during our projects. (Sachinis Giorgos, director and co-founder of UDP)

Embodied expressions

Sport practices and physical exercise are critical in most UDP performances. For example, in *Mockob Celim*,[4] a performance based on the novel of the Greek author Georgios Vizyinos about the life of a Turkish soldier who feels rejected from his father, the critical and theoretical resonances between physical rigour, sport and theatre intersect and exemplify the actor's presence on stage to convince his father that he is a 'manly man' despite the fact that his mother is forcing him to wear skirts. Mockob employs intense physical drills to prove his masculinity. The stage features a circus arena that highlights the extreme theatricality that the actor demands of his own body as a means of proving to the audience (i.e. his father) his male gender.

The *Marathon Dam*[5] performance was organized as part of the festivities for World Environment Day (2010, 2012). The dam was created between 1926 and 1929 for the primary purpose of the municipal water supply for Attica, the wider area around Athens. The tall wall (54 m) of the dam becomes the main theatrical stage. A fighter from the future is climbing down the wall (Figure 1) in an effort to find any water resources as everything had dried-up. The fighter has a strong muscular body and engages in physically demanding battles, endeavours and actions in his despair to survive the environmental calamity. The aim is to make the individual and collective conscience of the audience aware of the environmental threats through sharp images of embodied metaphors.

Figure 1. The climber is climbing down the Marathon Dam.

In addition, social and political issues close to drama and theatre are also embodied in sport-related themes in other UDP performances, such as, for instance, Caligula, where swimmers appearing in changing rooms embody the decline of the Roman Empire.[6]

On another level, during 2014–2015, the UDP platform developed a community project in a former refugee neighbourhood in Athens, called Dourgouti. The community project *Dourgouti Island Hotel*,[7] combined all three aspects of UDP's conceptual and methodological framework, i.e. qualitative research, artistic interventions and community actions. Among other processes, Dourgouti Island Hotel introduced embodied expressions and narrations of local stories. For instance, Capoeira martial art, performed by the local capoeira school

(Figure 2), was employed in order to narrate Dourgouti's history during the period of Nazi occupation.

Additionally, yoga practices had taken place in the neighbourhood's public space (Figure 3) in order to provide alternative and sport-related experience of Dourgouti's squares and openly engage with locals and visitors in an activity that was performed jointly and allowed interaction, besides being a silent, 'individual' and 'esoteric' physical activity.

Regarding the final site-specific performance, theatre and dance intertwined with sport practices re-introducing the neighbourhood's history and spaces to its inhabitants and the wider audience. For instance, during the 'immigrant's escape adventure', the performer practices parkour in the streets of Dourgouti in order to escape from those who chase him (Figure 4).

Xouthou Street @Omonia square

This section demonstrates a different deployment of the arts and sport, not only as *performances* but also as playful instruments for community building and grassroots participatory-planning in urban space. To be more specific, it refers to a part of the UDP at Omonia Square in the heart of Athens. Omonia square, the main square of Athens, was the focus of activity for UDP from October 2015 to June 2017. Throughout this period, a programme of research, artistic and placemaking activities open to all was organized focusing on the square and the surrounding area's diminishing public space, while involving a community of artists, researchers, visitors and local users.

Figure 2. The local capoeira school performs the neighbourhood's history.

Figure 3. Yoga in the public space.

Figure 4. Parkour in the streets of Dourgouti.

The specific intervention in Xouthou Street was organized in summer 2016 in the frame-work of the Omonia UDP's activity 'Hotel Transit – homes on the move'[8] that explored com-munities in transit and their relation to local urban space. It was conceived and organized in the framework of the TANDEM Europe[9] cultural exchange programme between the organization Ohi Paizoume/UrbanDig Project from Athens and Ideas Factory from Sofia (February 2016–January 2017). 'Hotel Transit' built on UDP methodologies and explored the socio-spatial versus the individual stories focusing on urban spaces through multiple notions of 'transit' and 'home' in times where perceptions of migration and transition redefine societies. For 15 months, the two organizations worked together on a project building on the resilience of urban communities on the move in both Sofia and Athens, while trying to serve as a tool to influence advocacy by 'humanizing' and 'empathizing' policies and decision-making processes involving migrants and people in transit.

Xouthou Street is a small pedestrian street a few metres from Omonia square. The reason why it was chosen as a space of intervention is that it served as an ideal 'metaphor' for the co-existence of different communities in contemporary cities. On one side of the street there was a hotel used as a temporary home for families from Afghanistan and Syria and managed by a humanitarian organization. On the other side, there was an empty plot that the municipality was planning to use for a major building. The area had been the focus of activity of another civil society organization, Alternative Tours of Athens, that had undertaken research and had interacted with the local residents in order to gather their opinions about the future of this empty plot, in a participatory decision-making exercise. UrbanDig as a project and as a platform proposed an activity that would link the work of the two starting points of Xouthou Street and bring together the organizations and people that work on the different realities of the same material space to create a bridge between the two different worlds that are located at the different sides of the streets: the temporary residents and the local residents.

Perceived space

The first step towards this goal consisted in an exploration and understanding of the physical/material space through wandering around the area, involving different teams from the organizations' members, but also visitors and other people interested through open calls. Sensory mapping, taking notes on how the space makes us feel, what kinds of interactions are encouraged and discovering the usual 'users' of the space were the elements that sparked the activity. This step also included the organization of a number of workshops with children of refugee and immigrant families hosted in the hotel (Figure 5). Although workshops were thoroughly planned, the limitations of language in the communication exchange caused the facilitators/trainers to seek refuge in the most easily accessed and understood tools: the arts and physical activity. This step was necessary in order to build trust. The real material space though is experienced through the actual contact of the body with the space. Sensory mapping, thematic tours and oral history are a few of the methodological tools that the UDP deploys when working in a specific neighbourhood. They all require the physical presence of the 'errant' body that opens up and uses its senses to explore, 'dig' and experience the material space, a sine qua non exploration which becomes the starting point for any intervention.

The conceived/imaginary space

The second step consisted in organizing a public activity where the local residents and the refugee communities would interact and spend a day together. Despite their physical proximity in the material space, these communities rarely interact. But on this occasion they were asked to share their aspirations on the possible uses of the empty public space

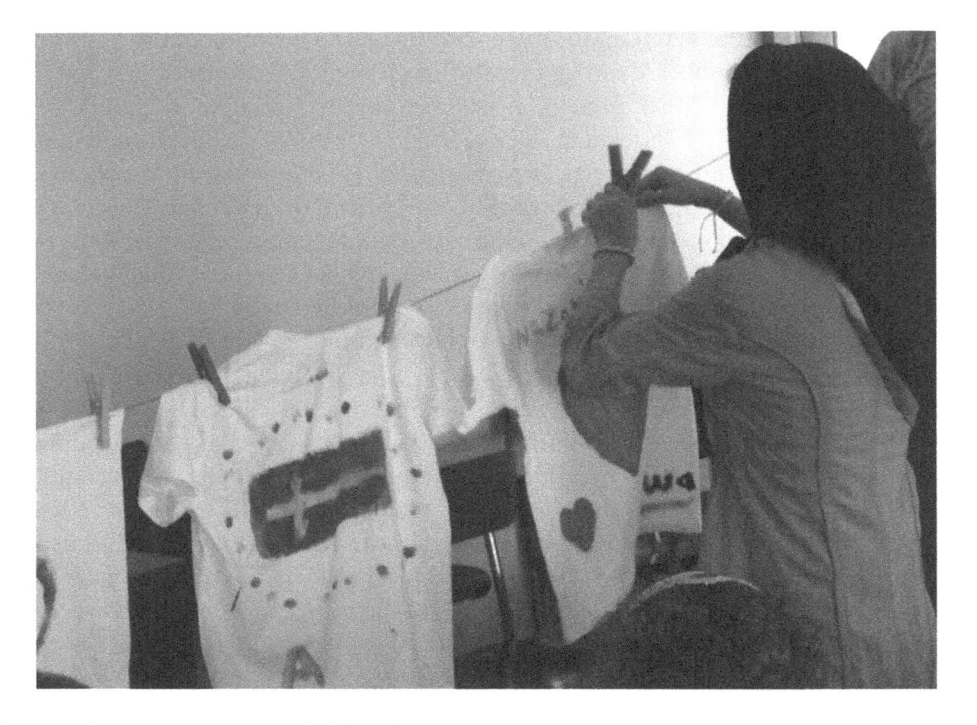

Figure 5. 'Laundry', together with child refugees.

Figure 6. Giorgos Sachinis, director and founder of the UDP performs pantomime in Xouthou Street.

through a physical game. Using pantomime and their body (Figure 6) as the only tool, they had to transfer a sense of utopia and to bring 'life' to the empty space by imagining how it would look if it were a playground, a basketball field or garden. Migrant families mingled with locals and used the imaginary space accordingly. The collective activation of the mental construction of a conceived space was achieved through the use of the body, regardless of whether this can be seen either through the lenses of an artistic method (pantomime/arts) or a physical activity (game/sports). It is also interesting to note that among the potential uses of the space, the ones linked to physical activity (basketball field or playground) were the ones mostly appreciated in this collective imaginary of the ideal use of this empty space, since physical activity made them easily portrayed.

At the end of the activity, participants were asked to vote and collectively/democratically decide on what would be the best use of this space. Activating conceived interpretations of the material space through a collective exercise is not a self-evident process. Nonetheless, the actual interaction, the artistic approach and the physical activity and presence of the body, especially through the use of pantomime activated the realm of imagination and the social construction of a conceived space that is worth articulating collectively.

The lived/community activated space

The aim of the project proved quite ambitious. It did however mark a step towards drawing a meta-map of a 'temporary home' collectively co-created and helped explore the way different communities in transit experience home, neighbourhood, togetherness and interaction with local communities. Furthermore, a year later the municipality decided to withdraw initial plans for a major construction in the area and to transform the public space into a garden as a result of an enhanced coordinated effort in cooperation with other stakeholders.[10] This was also the winning result of the pantomime game.

By giving a voice to migrants and refugees through using their body and artistic and physical expression, the activity allowed them to be treated as equal citizens and translate their motivations and aspirations beyond their 'temporary' situation. Most importantly, language is not a barrier any more. The activity involved them in participative decision-making processes and connected individual aspirations to city policies. The process and outcome of such processes gain importance as they suggest a bottom-up alternative to urban cultural capital management, and most significantly they create improbable/innovative bridges between the arts, sport, science, research and between residents and 'temporary' residents and users of the public space of all ages and backgrounds. The arts and sport through the deployment of the human body become the facilitators of trust for this bridge-building and introduce a unique vehicle when working with diverse communities since they facilitate genuine human interaction and authentic connection. Such activities are important and urgent because understanding, documenting and giving voice to the issue of vulnerable communities can help educate consciousness and reverse prejudices. It also gives food for thought to policy-makers regarding the contribution of these people to the identity of different city spaces.

Conclusions

As a conclusion, UDP is a multidisciplinary platform that suggests and tests methods inspired by the art-sports cultural intersection in order to engage individuals and communities in certain processes as well as in order to narrate gathered material in performative ways. It explores a site-specific artistic expression as well as a community-led co-creation of urban space. Therefore, the production of urban space is critical for both its conceptual framework and the way it approaches certain case studies.

Urban space *receives* everyday actions. History and contemporary transformations within the physical space leave their mark, linking the past to the present referring to both socio-spatial co-existence and segregation. Additionally, urban space *represents* and is being *represented*. It interacts with the individual and collective imaginary becoming a space of stereotypes, habits, encounters, avoidances and crossings, continuities and discontinuities. While being represented by the everyday actors through their perceptual systems, it concomitantly represents their memories, traumas and emotional involvement. Finally, urban space *reproduces*. Being a social product, produced by social relations, its restructuring is linked to the broader restructuring of social life, turning the *right to the city* into a clear demand to reclaim a common space for all.

Sport and the arts can be the key to unlocking forms of this common space for all. For instance, the deployment of both the arts and sport during the Xouthou activity was a demonstration of the powerful connection of these two human expressions. The notion of playfulness embedded in them gave a festive element to this community engagement activity. Finally, especially interesting is the potential sport and the arts have when working with communities from diverse backgrounds since they rely heavily on the use of the body and its connection to the space rather than verbal language that requires de-coding interpretation efforts.

Notes

1. *Water Carnival* is a community celebration that presents a staged show surrounded by many festivities, wherein sport is featured as a core activity.
2. For more, see https://www.urbandigproject.org/single-post/2016/10/25/UrbanDig-Project-Trailer-1-1.
3. For instance, World Café and Open Space Technology.
4. For more, see https://www.urbandigproject.org/copy-of-mockob-selim-mid.
5. For more, see https://www.urbandigproject.org/marathon-dam.
6. For more, see https://vimeo.com/52018251.
7. For more, see https://www.urbandigproject.org/dourgouti-island-hotel-project.
8. For more, see http://www.tandemforculture.org/collaborations/hotel-transit-homes-on-the-move/.
9. Tandem is a cultural collaboration programme that strengthens civil society in Europe and neighbouring regions co-created by the European Cultural Foundation and MitOst. More information at http://www.tandemforculture.org/.
10. The organization Alternative Tours of Athens (ATA) took the lead for this.

Disclosure statement

No potential conflict of interest was reported by the authors.

References

Adams, Iain, and Clive Palmer. 2013. "The Sporting Image: Engaging Students and Staff in Creativity." In *Fields of Vision: The Arts in Sport*, edited by Doug Sandle, Jonathan Long, Jim Parry and Karl Spracklen, 85–98, LSA Publication No. 125. Eastbourne: LSA.

Arendt, Hannah. [1958] 1998. *The Human Condition*. Chicago, IL: The University of Chicago Press.

Azara, Iride, and David Crouch. 2006. "La Calvacata Sarda: Performing Identities in a Contemporary Sardinian Festival." In *Festivals, Tourism and Social Change*, edited by David Picard and Mike Robinson, 32–45. Clevedon: Channel View Publications.

Best, David. 1985. "Sport is Not Art." *Journal of the Philosophy of Sport* 12 (1): 25–40. doi:10.1080/00948705.1985.9714426.

Chatziefstathiou, Dikaia, and Ian Henry. 2012. *Discourses of Olympism: From the Sorbonne 1894 to London 2012*. Basingstoke: Palgrave Macmillan.

Cordner, Christopher. 1988. "Differences between Sport and Art." *Journal of the Philosophy of Sport* 15 (1): 31–47. doi:10.1080/00948705.1988.9714459.

Digby, Paul, and Liz Stirling. 2013. "Using Art and Sport to Create a Third Space of Learning in Primary School Education." In *Fields of Vision: The Arts in Sport*, edited by Doug Sandle, Jonathan Long, Jim Parry, and Karl Spracklen, 147–162, LSA Publication No. 125. Eastbourne: LSA.

Edgar, Andrew. 2013. "Sport and Art: An Essay in the Hermeneutics of Sport." *Sport, Ethics and Philosophy* 7 (1): 1–9. doi:10.1080/17511321.2013.761879.

Elcombe, Tim. 2012. "Sport, Aesthetic Experience, and Art as the Ideal Embodied Metaphor." *Journal of the Philosophy of Sport* 39 (2): 201–217. doi:10.1080/00948705.2012.725901.

Gordziejko, Tessa. 2013. "Create the Physical: Imove and the Art of Human Movement." In *Fields of Vision: The Arts in Sport*, edited by Doug Sandle, Jonathan Long, Jim Parry, and Karl Spracklen, 163–174, LSA Publication No. 125. Eastbourne: LSA.

Handelman, Don. 1990. *Models and Mirrors: Towards an Anthropology of Public Events*. Cambridge: Cambridge University Press.

Jameson, Fredric. 1990. "Cognitive Mapping." In Marxism and the Interpretation of Culture, edited by Cary Nelson C and Lawrence Grossberg, 347–360. USA: University of Illinois Press.

Lacerda, Teresa Oliveira. 2012. "Education for the Aesthetics of Sport in Higher Education in the Sports Sciences: The Particular Case of the Portuguese-Speaking Countries." *Journal of the Philosophy of Sport* 39 (2): 235–250. doi:10.1080/00948705.2012.725905.

Lefebvre, Henri. [1974] 1991. *The Production of Space*. Oxford: Blackwell.

Long, Jonathan. 2013. "Opera Man and the Meeting of 'Tastes." In *Fields of Vision: The Arts in Sport*, edited by Doug Sandle, Jonathan Long, Jim Parry, and Karl Spracklen, 73–84, LSA Publication No. 125. Eastbourne: LSA.

Morpeth, Nigel. 2013. "Kick It out: Art, Sport and Pedagogy." In *Fields of Vision: The Arts in Sport*, edited by Doug Sandle, Jonathan Long, Jim Parry, and Karl Spracklen, 119–130, LSA Publication No. 125. Eastbourne: LSA.

O'Mahony, Mike. 2013. "Performing Victory in Mexico City, San José and Martinique." In *Fields of Vision: The Arts in Sport*, edited by Doug Sandle, Jonathan Long, Jim Parry, and Karl Spracklen, 23–32, LSA Publication No. 125. Eastbourne: LSA.

Platchias, Dimitris. 2010. "Sport is Art." *European Journal of Sport Science* 3 (4): 1–18. doi:10.1080/17461390300073403.

Reid, Louis Arnaud. 1970. "Sport, the Aesthetic and Art." *British Journal of Educational Studies* 18 (3): 245–258. doi:10.1080/00071005.1970.9973287.

Reid, Louis Arnaud. 1980. "Human Movement, the Aesthetic and Art." *British Journal of Aesthetics* 20 (2): 165–170. doi:10.1093/bjaesthetics/20.2.165.

Sandle, Doug, Jonathan Long, Jim Parry, and Karl Spracklen, eds. 2013. *Fields of Vision: The Arts in Sport*. LSA Publication No. 125. Eastbourne: LSA.

Schechner, Richard. 2003. *Performance Theory*. London: Routledge.

Schmid, Christian. 2008. "Henri Lefebvre's Theory of the Production of Space: Towards a Three-Dimensional Dialectic." In *Space, Difference, Everyday Life. Reading Henri Lefebvre*, edited by Kanishka Goonewardena, Stefan Kipfer, Richard Milgrom, and Christian Schmid, 27–45. New York: Routledge.

Shields, Rob. 1999. *Love and Struggle: Spatial Dialectics*. London: Routledge.

Soja, Edward W. 1996. *Thirdspace. Journeys to Los Angeles and Other Real-and-Imagined Places*. Cambridge, MA: Blackwell .

Stansbie, Lisa. 2013. "Extreme Exposures: The Practice and Narratives of Channel Swimming as a Methodology for the Creation of Contemporary Art." In *Fields of Vision: The Arts in Sport*, edited by Doug Sandle, Jonathan Long, Jim Parry, and Karl Spracklen, 131–146, LSA Publication No. 125. Eastbourne: LSA.

Thomas, Ffion, and Chris Stride. 2013. "The Thierry Henry Statue: A Hollow Icon?" In *Fields of Vision: The Arts in Sport*, edited by Doug Sandle, Jonathan Long, Jim Parry, and Karl Spracklen, 33–52, LSA Publication No. 125. Eastbourne: LSA.

Turner, Victor. 1969. *The Ritual Process*. Chicago, IL: Aldine.

Turner, Victor. 1974. *Dramas, Fields, and Metaphors*. New York: Cornell University Press.

Wertz, Spencer. 1985. "Representation and Expression in Sport and Art." *Journal of the Philosophy of Sport* 12 (1): 8–24. doi:10.1080/00948705.1985.9714425.

Wright, Leslie. 2003. "Aesthetic Implicitness in Sport and the Role of Aesthetic Concepts." *Journal of the Philosophy of Sport* 30 (1): 83–92. doi:10.1080/00948705.2003.9714562.

Ziakas, Vassilios, and Carla Costa. 2010. "Between Theatre and Sport in a Rural Event: Evolving Unity and Community Development from the Inside-Out." *Journal of Sport & Tourism* 15 (1): 7–26. doi:10.1080/14775081003770892.

Index

Page numbers in **bold** refer to tables and those in *italic* refer to figures.